The First Punic War

The First Punic War
A military history

J. F. Lazenby

Stanford University Press
Stanford, California
1996

Stanford University Press
Stanford, California
© 1996 J. F. Lazenby
Originating publisher: UCL Press Limited, London
The name of University College London (UCL) is a registered
trade mark used by UCL Press with the consent of the owner.
First published in the U.S.A by
Stanford University Press, 1996
Printed in Great Britain.
Cloth ISBN: 0-8047-2673-6
Paper ISBN: 0-8047-2674-4
LC 95-78817

Cover illustration: *Regulus* by J. M. W. Turner, 1828
(courtesy of the Turner Collection, Tate Gallery, London).
Regulus, taken prisoner by the Carthagians, is said to have been
sent to Rome to negotiate a peace, but refused to do so, and
returned to Carthage to face torture and death.

To Jerry Paterson — my strong right arm for so many years

Contents

Preface

It is odd, though understandable, that there is no modern book in English on the First Punic War, and this is an attempt to fill that gap. The war is, of course, covered in the standard histories of Rome and Carthage, and in books on the Punic Wars as a whole. But the accounts in the former are necessarily concise, and the three latter known to me all have serious faults. Thus the war takes up only 28 pages in Dorey and Dudley's *Rome against Carthage*, and the authors ignore many of the controversies. Brian Caven's account in *The Punic Wars* is over twice as long, and is lively and full of insight. But it still lacks detail and unaccountably gives no references to the ancient evidence. Finally, Field-Marshal Bagnall's version, again in a book called *The Punic Wars*, is occasionally interesting on strategy, but is marred by irritating inaccuracies of detail. The most comprehensive account of the war in English is by Thiel in his *History of Roman sea-power before the Second Punic War*, but, as its title suggests, this book is mainly concerned with the naval side of the conflict, and the fighting on land is only sketched.

It may, indeed, be thought that there is no point in studying the First Punic War in isolation. But whereas it is clearly not possible to understand the Second and Third wars without knowing something about the First, the converse is not true, and to study the First as just the opening round in a three-round contest may actually distort one's view of it. It is true that Polybios, our earliest surviving source, himself saw this war as but the prelude to what he regarded as the crucial period in Rome's rise to "world" dominion, but it is only in this limited sense that we have to take what happened later into consideration. Thus he may mislead us in thinking that the war began as a conflict between Rome and Carthage rather than Rome and Hiero of Syracuse, or that the Roman naval building programme in 261/0 was motivated by the intention to conquer Sicily.

Despite this, however, the war clearly deserves a book on its own. It was the longest continuous war in Graeco-Roman history, one of the greatest naval wars ever fought, and the war which finally set Rome on the path to Empire. Given the lack of significant new evidence, it is not possible to give a radical reappraisal of it, and I make no pretence to do so, though I hope I may have clarified some points of detail, and perhaps shown more clearly why Rome won. Basically what I have attempted to do is to present a narrative of the war, with discussion of strategic and tactical issues where possible, based on the ancient evidence, and on such recent research as seemed to me significant. In the case of the latter, as anyone is bound to do, I have drawn heavily on my predecessors, and in particular Walbank, whose comprehensive *Historical commentary on Polybius* is indispensable.

The sources for this war are not as good as for the Second, largely through the loss of the relevant books of Livy, and we must reconcile ourselves to the fact that we shall never know the answers to many questions. Even the facts are difficult enough to establish, and it is rarely possible to discuss tactics and strategy at anything but a superficial level. The same is true of the armed forces of the two sides, both naval and military. For example, we do not even know exactly what a quinquereme was, and this was the principal battleship of both fleets, and there is little evidence for how the Roman army was raised, equipped and organized, unless we assume that Polybios' account of the army of his day applies to the army of a century earlier, which in some details it clearly does not. Again, we can only guess the answers to demographic and logistical questions, since even the accuracy of the Roman census figures for the period is doubtful. In view of all this, it goes without saying that with the possible exception of Regulus and Claudius Pulcher, on the Roman side, and Hamilcar Barca on the Carthaginian, the personalities of the protagonists are irrecoverable, and this war is not enlivened by the presence of a Hannibal or a Scipio.

But the sources are fascinating, nonetheless, since they appear to reflect a pro-Roman tradition, originating with the near-contemporary, Fabius Pictor, and reflected in the Livian derivatives, Eutropius and Orosius, a pro-Carthaginian tradition going back to the contemporary, Philinos, and reflected in Diodoros, and a third, apparently separate strand of tradition, reflected in the fragments of Cassius Dio and his epitomator, the Byzantine Zonaras. Foursquare in the middle of all this stands the sketch of the war in the first book of Polybios, who although probably more pro-Roman than pro-Carthaginian, was certainly not slavishly so, and at least provides a framework around which one can attempt to weave a narrative using the other, later sources, at least as padding.

My thanks are due, as usual, to my colleagues at Newcastle for their invariable help and support, and to my wife who, in the midst of completing a PhD thesis, drew the maps and plans. I would also like to thank Steven Gerrard of UCL Press, who initially welcomed my proposal, and who, with Sheila Knight, helped to see the project through to – I hope – a successful conclusion.

J. F. Lazenby
Newcastle upon Tyne

Maps and plans

Chronology

NB: for the years 264–247 and 242–241 I have given the names of the consuls who were principally in command each year.

289–285 Mamertines seize Messana.

280–275 Rome's war with Pyrrhus.

280/79 treaty between Rome and Carthage against Pyrrhus.

278–276 Pyrrhus in Sicily.

275 Battle of Beneventum; Pyrrhus leaves Italy.

272 Tarentum falls to Rome.

270 Rhegium recaptured by Rome.

270/69(?) Hiero seizes power in Syracuse.

265/4 Hiero's victory over the Mamertines at the Longanus; Mamertine appeal to Carthage and then to Rome; alliance between Hiero and Carthage.

264 (Ap. Claudius Caudex, M. Fulvius Flaccus, consuls): outbreak of war; Claudius Caudex crosses to Sicily, and lifts siege of Messana.

263 (M'. Valerius Maximus, M'. Otacilius Crassus, consuls): both consuls campaign in Sicily; Hiero makes peace with Rome.

262 (L. Postumius Megellus, Q. Mamilius Vitulus, consuls): both consuls lay siege to Agrigentum..

261 (L. Valerius Flaccus, T. Otacilius Crassus, consuls): fall of Agrigentum; Carthaginian navy raids Italy; Romans decide to build fleet.

260 (Cn. Cornelius Scipio, C. Duilius, consuls): Scipio captured at Lipara; Duilius wins battle of Mylae.

259   (L. Cornelius Scipio, C. Aquillius Florus, consuls):
Scipio attacks Corsica and Sardinia; Aquillius campaigns in
Sicily.

258   (A. Atilius Caiatinus, C. Sulpicius Paterculus, consuls):
Caiatinus campaigns in Sicily; Paterculus attacks Sardinia and
wins battle off Sulci.

257   (C. Atilius Regulus, Cn. Cornelius Blasio, consuls): Atilius
Regulus wins battle off Tyndaris and raids Malta; Blasio
commands in Sicily.

256   (L. Manlius Vulso, M. Atilius Regulus, consuls): both consuls
defeat Carthaginian navy off Ecnomus and proceed to
Africa, where Regulus remains, winning battle at Adys and
capturing Tunis; abortive negotiations with Carthage.

255   (Ser. Fulvius Paetinus Nobilior, M. Aemilius Paullus,
consuls): Regulus defeated and captured near Tunis; consuls
bring fleet to rescue survivors, winning victory off Cape
Hermaia and raiding Cossyra, but are caught in storm off
Camarina on return.

254   (Cn. Cornelius Scipio, A. Atilius Caiatinus, re-elected
consuls): both consuls campaign in Sicily, capturing
Panormus and other towns.

253   (Cn. Servilius Caepio, C. Sempronius Blaesus, consuls):
while Caepio commands in Sicily, Blaesus raids Africa,
nearly losing his fleet on the Syrtis, and losing half of it in
storm off Cape Palinurus.

252   (C. Aurelius Cotta, P. Servilius Geminus, consuls):
Roman fleet reduced to 60 ships; both consuls command in
Sicily, capturing Thermae and Lipara.

251   (L. Caecilius Metellus, C. Furius Pacilus, consuls): both
consuls serve in Sicily; Carthaginians reinforce army there.

250   (C. Atilius Regulus, L. Manlius Vulso, re-elected consuls):
Metellus wins victory at Panormus; consuls commence siege
of Lilybaeum.

249   (P. Claudius Pulcher, L. Iunius Pullus, consuls): Claudius
loses battle off Drepana, and Iunius loses fleet in storm near
Camarina.

248   (C. Aurelius Cotta, P. Servilius Geminus, re-elected consuls):
both consuls continue to besiege Lilybaeum and Drepana.
Carthalo raids Italy.

247   (L. Caecilius Metellus, N. Fabius Buteo, consuls – Metellus for second time): Metellus continues with siege of Lilybaeum, Buteo with that of Drepana, where he captures island of Pelias. Hamilcar Barca arrives in Sicily and raids Bruttium.

246–244   skirmishing around Heirkte.

244–243   Hamilcar moves to Eryx; continued skirmishing.

242   (C. Lutatius Catulus, A. Postumius Albinus, consuls): Catulus sent to Sicily in command of new fleet; wounded at Drepana.

241   (A. Manlius Torquatus Atticus, Q. Lutatius Cerco, consuls – Torquatus for second time): Lutatius Catulus wins decisive battle off Aegates Island on 10 March, and with brother, Lutatius Cerco, negotiates peace.

240–237   Mercenary War in Africa.

238   Rome decides to annex Sardinia.

237   Hamilcar Barca arrives in Spain.

229   death of Hamilcar Barca in Spain; Hasdrubal takes command.

227   C. Flaminius appointed first praetorian governor of western Sicily, and M. Valerius (Laevinus?) of Sardinia.

221   assassination of Hasdrubal in Spain; Hannibal takes over.

219   Hannibal captures Saguntum.

218   beginning of Second Punic War.

CHAPTER 1

The evidence

The conflict that is the subject of this book, the First Punic War, lasted from 264 to 241.[1] It was the longest continuous war in Greek and Roman history, and one of the most important. It marked the point at which Rome ceased to be a purely Italian power and became committed to the path that was to lead to empire. Before the war no Roman troops had ever set foot outside the mainland of Italy, and Roman sea power was negligible. During it Roman troops found themselves fighting in Sicily, Corsica, Sardinia and even, briefly, in north Africa, and, as a result of it Rome acquired her first "provinces" overseas, in Sardinia and western Sicily.

The war was also, in terms of the numbers of men involved, the greatest naval war in Greek and Roman history – indeed, one of the greatest ever fought. If the figures given by our main source for the battle of Ecnomus, in 256, are correct, more men probably took part there than in any other naval battle in history.[2] Moreover, as a result of the naval "arms race" on which Rome embarked in 260 and subsequent years, she became the most powerful naval state in the Mediterranean world – something that is often forgotten when people consider how she eventually came to dominate that world.

Apart from the brief Roman forays to Corsica, Sardinia and Africa, and one or two Carthaginian raids on Italy, the war was fought out in and around the coasts of Sicily, and domination of that island was the primary objective of both sides. An interesting modern parallel, in some ways, is "Operation Husky", the allied landings in Sicily in the Second World War. It is worth remembering that the Allies came from Tunisia, which was the Carthaginian homeland, and that their landing in Sicily was intended to be and became the prelude to landings in Italy. The United States 2nd

Armoured Division actually disembarked at Licata, on the south coast of Sicily, off which Ecnomus was fought.

But whereas Operation Husky can be studied down to the last detail in contemporary records, including photographs and newsreels, the First Punic War is poorly documented, even for an ancient war. Apart from some archaeological evidence (see below), and copies of a few inscriptions, the nearest thing to contemporary evidence that has survived are a few fragments of the Roman poet Naevius, who was born between 274 and 264 and lived until about 204. Unfortunately, although some of these can be seen to refer to specific episodes in the war, others are too vague. In any case, they tell us very little.

Undoubtedly, the most important evidence consists of some 60 chapters of the first book of the *Histories* of the Greek historian, Polybios. But Polybios was not even born until at least 30 years after the war had ended,[3] and since he was a Greek, who did not come to Italy until 167, it is most unlikely that he ever met anyone who had taken part in it; he certainly never claims to have done so, in contrast to his claim to have questioned men who took part in the second war (e.g. 3.48.12).

For him the questioning of participants was the most important part of historical study (12.4c. 2–5), and this was one of the reasons why he chose to make 220 the opening date for the main part of his work (4.2.2). He was, indeed, dubious about the value of non-contemporary history, since most of the evidence would be mere "hearsay from hearsay" (4.2.3). Thus although it is important to be clear about his own methods and attitudes, the first thing to do is to try to discover what kind of evidence he used.[4]

For our war it was probably almost wholly literary, and consisted mainly of the writings of two earlier historians – Philinos and Fabius Pictor – whom he describes (14.1) as "those who have the reputation of writing most authoritatively about it", but neither of whose works has survived. Philinos was a Greek from Agrigentum (Akragas, Agrigento) in Sicily, and probably contemporary with the war. Indeed, Polybios' account of the siege of Lilybaeum in 250/49 is so vivid (41.4 ff) that it is often thought to be based on an eyewitness account by Philinos.

The latter's work seems to have been a monograph devoted exclusively to the war, rather than a more general history,[5] and possibly because of the Roman treatment of his native city in 261 (19.5), he was hostile to Rome and therefore enables us to see something of the Carthaginian viewpoint. Polybios, indeed, thought he was too pro-Carthaginian (14.3), and was scornful, for example, of his belief that the Roman intervention in Sicily

2

contravened a treaty explicitly precluding them from the island (3.26). Since Philinos' work survives only in fragments (cf. FGH 174), consisting of references in later works, it is difficult to see how good a historian he really was, though there is reason to believe that he wrote in a somewhat sensational style. Polybios possibly used him more for the later years of the war, though he certainly did not neglect his account of the earlier years.[6]

Polybios' other principal source, Quintus Fabius Pictor, was born into the famous patrician gens ("clan") of the Fabii, and became a member of the Senate (3.9.4). He is said to have fought in the war against the Gauls that culminated in the battle of Telamon in 225 (Eutr. 3.5; Oros. 4.13.6), and to have gone to Delphi as an envoy of the Senate in 216 (Livy 22.57.5, 23.11.1–6). He was thus a contemporary of the Second Punic War, rather than the First, but certainly in a position to have met people who had taken part in the First. Unlike that of Philinos, his work appears to have consisted of a general history of Rome from its foundation to his own time, but, like Philinos', it, too, only survives in fragments (HRR i.5 ff). Fabius Pictor was the earliest Roman historian, but wrote in Greek (DH 1.6.2; Cic., de div. 1.43), apparently with the intention of justifying Roman policy to the Greeks. Since there were no Roman precedents for the writing of history, it was inevitable that he, too, was influenced by the contemporary Greek fondness for sensational and paradoxical episodes, and he may well have made use of Philinos' work. But he was also Roman enough to use evidence that lay nearer to hand, for example in lists of Roman magistrates and their deeds, the records of Roman priests, and family traditions, including monuments bearing laudatory inscriptions.[7]

Polybios himself may also sometimes have made direct use of this kind of material. This is suggested by his account of the treaties between Rome and Carthage (3.26.1), which, he says, "are preserved to this day, inscribed on bronze in the treasury of the Aediles in the temple of Jupiter Capitolinus", though he may never have actually seen the originals.[8] Although a Greek, he was one of the prominent citizens of the Achaian League summoned to Rome after the final defeat of Macedonia in 167, on suspicion of "anti-Roman activities", and subsequently kept there for the next 17 years. But he was lucky enough to become intimate with one of the most eminent of Roman nobles, Scipio Aemilianus, the son of the conqueror of Macedonia, who had been adopted into the Scipionic family. As a result, he did not return home to Greece when the survivors amongst his fellow-exiles were finally allowed to go in 151, but spent something like the last 50 years of his life either in Italy or in the company of Romans. He thus had a unique opportunity for getting at the kind of material of which only Romans would normally have been aware.

Polybios' justification for his digression on the treaties is typical of his attitude to the study of history.[9] It will be useful, he claims (3.21.9–10), both to the practical statesman and to students. This partly repeats what is said right at the beginning of the work, though there the study of history is also said to have an additional value – to teach people to endure the vicissitudes of fortune (*tychê* – τύχη: 1.2). It is notoriously difficult to define what Polybios meant by this – his use of the word and other similar expressions runs the whole gamut from mere synonyms for "as it happened" to something like a notion of "divine providence". But clearly he did believe that a knowledge of history would enable people to bear whatever might happen to them, whether as a result of inexplicable "acts of God" or of some inexorable destiny, and the very fact that his own views on the subject seem muddled and incoherent at least suggests that he did not try to bend the facts to suit some preconceived pattern.

But though Polybios conceived of history as essentially a teaching tool, he did not entirely reject the pleasurable element in it, and was not above indulging in the odd rhetorical flourish: an example in the part of his work that concerns us is his description of the amazement of the Romans and the anxiety of the people of Lilybaeum as they watch the Carthaginians trying to run the Roman blockade in 250 (44.4 ff); as was said above, this may be based on an eyewitness account by Philinos. But Polybios strongly believed that usefulness was the principal value of history, and continually criticizes writers who aimed only to please their readers – for example Phylarchos, the third-century historian, who, he believed, confused history with tragedy (2.56.10 ff).

But if history was to teach, it had to be true, and for Polybios, "truth is to history, what eyesight is to a living creature" (14.6, 12.12.3) – without truth, history just becomes a useless story. To arrive at the truth, he believed, it was necessary for the historian to study memoirs and other documentary evidence, acquire personal knowledge of the relevant geography, and have personal experience of both political and military affairs (12.25e) – not for him the endless poring over "sources" of the modern, academic, "armchair" historian. Nor would he have approved of the narrow specialism of many modern historians, since for him the specialist monograph was in danger of distorting the truth (cf. 4.10).

Needless to say, he was probably unable to live up to these impossibly high ideals. Indeed, he was himself prepared to allow departures from the absolute search for truth – for example, the reporting of obviously false miracles was permissible if it sustained piety among common people (16.12.3–11), and, worse still, a certain bias in favour of one's own country was not only allowable, but desirable, provided that no actually false statement of fact was made (16.14.6). But, as it happens, the miraculous plays little part in his own writing, and although his bias against, for example, the enemies of his own state, the Achaian League, is notorious, it is usually fairly obvious and detectable.

For our purposes the important question is whether he was biased in favour of Rome, and at least we can say that this was not permitted according to his own rules, unless he came to regard Rome, as it were, as his country by adoption. However, although he obviously admired the Romans, he was by no means uncritical of them. For example, he denounces their behaviour over Sardinia, soon after the end of the First war (3.28.1 ff, cf. 30.4). There is thus no particular reason to think that he distorted the truth because of any pro-Roman attitude, and in particular that his account of the outbreak of our war is so tainted (see below, pp. 37 ff). It is also noticeable that he condemns the behaviour of Cn. Cornelius Scipio, the consul of 260, though he was an ancestor by adoption of his chief patron when he came to Italy (21.4–7). With one other feature of his work where he allowed himself a certain latitude – the speeches – we need not concern ourselves, since there are no speeches in the part of his work that we are studying.

Whether or not he elsewhere went beyond what his evidence strictly allowed is an almost impossible question to answer. He probably could not really have known, for example, what the participants in the First Punic War actually felt and thought, since it is hardly likely that they left any account of their thoughts and feelings. But when, for example, he says that the Romans "agonized" (ἠγωνίων: 10.6) over the prospect of the Carthaginians' winning control of the whole of Sicily, we can surely accept that this is likely to have been the case, even if at best he derived it from one of his sources, and it is not totally impossible that it goes back to the account of someone who shared the "agonizing".

Whether the facts he presents are in general true we, of course, have no means of telling, since there is so very little other evidence, and none that we can be sure is likely to be more accurate. All one can say is that if we reject his evidence, it is virtually impossible to give any account of the war beyond the baldest summary, and that there is rarely any absolutely compelling reason to doubt the truth of what he says. He may, for example, give wrong figures for the number of ships that took part at Ecnomus (see below, pp. 82 ff), but his figures are not of the same order as, for instance, those Herodotos gives for Xerxes' forces. On the whole, Polybios is a remarkably sober historian – some would say too sober – and this inclines one to trust him. It will be a principle of this book to do so, unless there is a very good reason to take the contrary view.

Apart from Polybios, the only continuous ancient accounts of the war to have survived are very sketchy, and it is particularly unfortunate that Livy's is almost wholly lost. All that survives are the *periochae* ("Tables of contents") of the four relevant books, included in the medieval manuscripts of his works, and the epitome made by Florus in the first century AD, running to a single chapter (18) in his first book, and in general so silly that one rather hopes he does not accurately reproduce what Livy said. But probably also going back to Livy as their main source, we have 11 chapters (18–28) in the second book of the *Breviarium* ("Summary") of Roman history addressed to the emperor Valens (AD 364–78) by Eutropius, and just over five chapters (7–11.3) in the fourth book of the *Historiae adversum paganos* ("Histories against the pagans") by the fifth-century AD Christian writer Orosius. Thus although we do not have Livy himself, and can therefore never hope to give as detailed account of this war as of the Second, where Livy's narrative survives complete, the Livian tradition is well represented.

More important, perhaps, is the epitome of the eleventh and twelfth books of Cassius Dio's history of Rome by the early twelfth-century AD Byzantine monk, Zonaras, supplemented by the fragments of Dio's work to be found in various other Byzantine compilations. Although he came from Nicaea in Bithynia and wrote in Greek, Dio belonged to a Roman senatorial family, his father having been governor of Cilicia and Dalmatia. He himself was twice consul, the first time about AD 222, the second in AD 229. Soon after this he retired to his native city, ostensibly for reasons of ill health. His work, in 80 books, covered the whole history of Rome from the landing of Aeneas down to the year of his own second consulship, and he tells us (72.23.5) that he spent ten years in gathering material for it. Unfortunately, it is not certain what sources he used for the part of his work that concerns us, but if Zonaras accurately summarizes what he had to say, as he seems to do, we have here a version that appears to be independent of both Polybios and Livy.

Apart from these works, perhaps the most important source is the fragments of Books 23 and 24 of the *Library of history* (Βιβλιοθήκη ἰστορική) of the Sicilian historian, Diodoros, who was a contemporary of Julius Caesar and Augustus. Diodoros himself was often a careless and over-imaginative historian, and the value of the fragments is frequently depreciated by the haphazard way in which the excerptors worked. But his account of this war appears to have been more pro-Carthaginian than those of our other sources, and may thus preserve rather more of Philinos' version of events than Polybios does. Philinos is referred to as an authority at least twice in the surviving fragments (23.8.1 and 24.11.2), and possibly also in 23.17, where the manuscript actually has the name "Philistos".

In addition, there are a number of passages referring to the war in the second-century AD Appian's history of Rome, and one or two relevant passages in Dionysios of Halikarnassos' *Roman antiquities*, a history of Rome written towards the end of the first century BC, though it only actually went down to the outbreak of our war. Then there are the nine books of "Memorable deeds and sayings" of Valerius Maximus, who lived at the time of Tiberius Caesar, and anecdotes in the *Stratagems* of Frontinus (consul AD 73 or 74, 98 and 100), and of Polyainos, the latter dedicated to the Roman emperors Marcus Aurelius (AD 161–80) and Lucius Verus (AD 161–9).

Mention should also be made of the book *On famous men* (*De viris illustribus*) found in many manuscripts of the younger Pliny's works, but certainly not by him. Guesses about its author would put him anywhere from the first century BC to the fourth century AD, with modern scholarship tending towards a later date, but although his work is now often included with those of Aurelius Victor, the latter, too, was almost certainly not responsible, and it is better to leave the author anonymous – hence the common use of the term *Auctor* (i.e. "Author"). Finally, we should, perhaps, also note the "*Commonplace Book*" (*Liber memorialis*) of Lucius Ampelius, apparently of the fourth or fifth century AD, which contains some references to our war, and there are also, of course, many incidental references elsewhere in Latin literature, including, for example, the ode of Horace (3.5), immortalized by Kipling in his story "Regulus".[10]

Evaluating this evidence is often very difficult, and there are no hard-and-fast principles to adopt. If something Polybios says is directly contradicted by another, later source, it usually seems best to accept what Polybios says. But even this is certainly not always the case, and it is very much more difficult to know what to think about the many things mentioned in the other sources that are not mentioned by him. Here an *argumentum e silentio* is particularly dangerous, since his account of this war is obviously less detailed than that of later episodes. All one can really do is to weigh up the other evidence and decide for oneself whether or not to believe it, for even what seems absurd to one person may seem perfectly reasonable to the next.

One method of evaluating the evidence adopted by some scholars is to try to see what sources were being used in their turn by the sources that are extant. But even attempts to disentangle "Philinos" from "Fabius Pictor" or that bogeyman of some commentators, "the annalist tradition", are shown to be largely futile by the marked disagreements among scholars who try to do this sort of thing.[11] In any case, even if it can be shown, or, in one or two instances, it is known, what source was being used by Polybios, for example, that is not the end of the matter, as some scholars seem to think, since there is no proof that the source was right. In particular, although it is obvious that "Roman tradition" was biased in favour of Rome, and tended, for example, to exaggerate or even invent Roman successes, just to assume that because "Philinos" reflects the Carthaginian tradition, he is necessarily to be preferred, is quite unsound. For instance, we do not have to believe that Appius Claudius was defeated before Messana by both Hiero and the Carthaginians, because, according to Polybios (15.1–2), Philinos said so. Polybios himself did not accept this, and, according to him, Philinos was just as capable of bias in favour of the Carthaginians as Fabius Pictor was in favour of the Romans.

So in this book, on the whole, the existing source will be referred to or quoted, and little or no attempt will be made to say what evidence that source may itself have been using, unless it is particularly important or interesting. In the end, as good a principle as any is the one adopted by the "Father of History" himself, when he said that he felt he was obliged to say what was said, but not obliged to believe it (Herodotos 7.152.3).

So far we have been discussing the literary evidence for the war, but there is also a certain amount of archaeological evidence, for example the remains of places such as Agrigentum, Lilybaeum (Marsala) and Carthage itself, coins and one or two Roman inscriptions. Unfortunately the difficulty of dating coins means that attempts to relate them to particular episodes in the war are hazardous,[12] but they remain a witness, even if mute, to the sinews of the war. Most of the inscriptions are later copies, but they are usually assumed to be fairly accurate. They include lists of consuls (the various *Fasti*) and of those who celebrated triumphs, and more personal monuments such as the inscription in honour of Duilius, the victor of Mylae, on the *columna rostrata* (*CIL* i^2 2.25), and the funerary inscription of L. Cornelius Scipio, consul in 259 (*CIL* i^2 2.8 and 9).

Finally, there is the relatively unchanging nature of the terrain on which the war was fought and of the seas around it, that at least enables us, sometimes, to make an intelligent guess at the thinking behind various moves by the two sides; though, unfortunately, the lack of detail in the other evidence often leaves much to be desired in the study of the topography of the war – for example, it is not possible to tell where Regulus' defeat in Tunisia took place. But for a war at sea fought with largely oar-powered galleys, wind and wave played here an unusually important part, and present-day sailing conditions are thus relevant.

But, in the end, we must accept that we are never going to be able to study the First Punic War in even as much detail as the Second, let alone more modern conflicts. In particular, it is almost impossible to discern the personalities of those involved or the motives behind their actions. Some might even argue that because we have little or no contemporary evidence, and what evidence we have is untrustworthy, either because of the writers' approach to history, or just because of their remoteness in time, any attempt to write a history of the war is foredoomed. But that is a counsel of despair. We can, surely, work out what happened at least in outline, and on this basis arrive at some understanding of why the war broke out, what the basic strategies of the two sides were, and why, in the end, Rome won. To do so is the purpose of the following pages.

CHAPTER 2

Rome and Carthage

The two states that fought the war were very dissimilar, except, perhaps, in constitution. Rome controlled a tight-knit confederacy, based on a complex system of alliances, Carthage a sprawling maritime empire.[1] By the time the war broke out, the first comprised the whole of peninsular Italy as far north as Rimini in the east and Tuscany south of the Arno in the west, an area of some 50,000 square miles, with a total population of perhaps 3,000,000. Roman territory itself, the *ager Romanus*, comprised about a fifth of this area, with a population of perhaps one million. The adult, male citizens recorded in the census completed in 264, the year the war broke out, numbered 292,234 (Livy, *Per.* 16).

Within the area controlled by Rome there were essentially two groups of peoples, Roman citizens and their allies, each comprising two subgroups. Roman citizens included not merely the descendants of the original inhabitants of Rome, now widely spread through settlement on land annexed from defeated states and in the small colonies founded from 338 onwards to guard coastal sites, but those of a number of originally independent Latin communities that had been incorporated into the Roman state in 338, after the last war with the Latins.

The subgroup of Roman citizens were the "citizens without the vote" (*cives sine suffragio*), who had the same rights and duties as Roman citizens, apart from not being allowed to vote in Roman assemblies or hold Roman office. Unless the tradition that Caere was the first such community (Gell., *NA* 16.13.7), is correct, the earliest were some Campanian and Volscian communities in the 330s.[2] Originally the status seems not to have been

11

regarded as inferior, though later it was accorded to defeated peoples, like the Sabines in 290, as a kind of stepping-stone on the way to full citizenship. The Sabines, for example, received the latter in 268.

All the other communities in the area controlled by Rome were classed as "allies" (*socii*). Of these about a quarter were the "allies of the Latin name" (*socii nominis Latini*), made up of a handful of old Latin states, such as Praeneste and Tibur, that had not been incorporated into the Roman state after the war with Rome, and 24 Latin colonies, some established in the fourth century, some in the third. One more – Firmum – was to be founded the year the war broke out, and two more – Aesernia (263) and Brundisium (Brindisi, 244) – during its course. All these communities enjoyed special rights, and their citizens could even become Roman citizens by migrating to Roman territory. If in Rome, they could vote in any assembly that took place, though only in a single voting unit chosen by lot. Their main obligation was to supply troops.

Finally came the ordinary allies of Rome. Some of these had joined her more or less voluntarily, others only after lengthy and often bitter conflict. But it was characteristic of Rome that when all was over, even if some territory was confiscated, what remained would be treated as an independent entity, however closely now bound to follow Rome's behest. A view once held was that these allies also fell into two groups, depending on whether they had a *foedus aequum* or a *foedus iniquum* ("a treaty between equals/ unequals") with the Republic.[3] But although there may have been such a difference in practice, and the term *foedus aequum* is common enough, it is significant that the term *foedus iniquum* never occurs. This suggests, what is surely the case, that the Romans would never openly have admitted that an ally was not an "equal". It is also significant that what is held to be the characteristic clause in such a treaty, binding the other party to "pay due respect to the majesty of the Roman people" (*maiestatem populi Romani comiter conservare*), first occurs in the treaty between Rome and the Aetolian League, concluded in 189. Thus there is no reason to believe that any Italian state had ever been required to swear to such an undertaking.[4]

Again, whatever rights such allies might have, their main obligation was, like the Latins, to furnish Rome with troops. Exceptions may have been the southern Greek states, which are not listed by Polybios (2.24) as providing troops in 225. It has been suggested that instead they provided Rome with naval forces, and thus constituted what the Romans called *socii navales* ("naval allies").[5] We shall return to this problem later, when we consider the creation of the Roman navy in 260 (see below, pp. 65 ff).

All allies were probably theoretically obliged to help Rome with all their forces, but in practice their obligations may have been defined by what was known, at any rate later, as the *formula togatorum* (i.e. "list of adult males"), possibly a kind of sliding-scale requiring so many men for the number of citizen soldiers raised in any year.[6] But whether or not such a system already obtained at the time of the First Punic War is uncertain, though we can probably assume that already roughly half Rome's armies were made up of allied troops (cf. 6.26.6). However, there are only two references in Polybios' narrative to "allies" (σ ὑμμαχοι: 16.2, 24.3), and the second passage almost certainly refers to Sicilian allies; neither gives numbers. There are also very few references to Italian allies in the secondary sources: the most interesting is Diodorus' statement (24.3) that when trying to restore discipline in the army at Lilybaeum in 249, the consul, Claudius Pulcher, while inflicting traditional punishments on the Roman citizens, had some of the allied soldiers flogged, a punishment that was probably already at this date unlawful in the case of citizens.

We do not therefore know how allied troops, whether Latins or Italians, were armed or organized during our war. In the Second the infantry seems to have been grouped in "cohorts" (*cohortes*) of between 460 and 600 men (cf. Livy 28.45.20, 23.17.8 and 17.11), and one passage in Livy (30.41.5) seems to imply that there were normally 15 such cohorts attached to a legion. However, the passage in question refers to the slimming down of the army in Spain to one legion of citizen troops and 15 cohorts of Latins, and it is possible that a larger than normal number of allies was to be retained in this instance. If each legion was already divided into ten cohorts (see below), it is possible that ten allied cohorts were normally attached to it.[7] Allied contingents later had their own officers, but there were also Roman officers – "prefects of allies" (*praefecti socium*), later three per legion (6.26.5). Whether allied cohorts were further subdivided, and how they were armed, is quite uncertain, but the implication of Polybios' silence may well be that they were virtually indistinguishable from Roman troops. Allied cavalry units are never mentioned in connection with the First war, but were presumably present, perhaps, as was later the case (cf.6.26.8), in larger numbers than Roman citizen-cavalry.

In one passage, referring to 263, Polybios says that each year the Romans enlisted four legions "apart from the allies" (χωρὶς τῶν συμμάχων), each consisting of up to 4,000 foot and 300 horse (16.2). This more or less agrees with what he says later about the Roman army in his day (6.19 ff), except that there the total number of foot in each legion is 4,200, made up of 600 *triarii*, 1,200 *principes*, 1,200 *hastati* and 1,200 *velites* (6.21.6 ff). Probably the total given in the earlier passage is a round number.

Whether or not the "light companies" were already called *velites* at the time of our war, or still retained the old name *rorarii*,[8] there can be little doubt that there already were such troops, and Polybios' use of the term "javelineers" (γροσφομάχοι) for Roman skirmishers in 255 (33.9, cf. 6.21.7) confirms this. Such troops were primarily armed with light, throwing spears, though it seems unlikely that each carried seven, as Livy claims (26.4.4). Later at any rate, they also had a sword, and for protection wore a helmet, and carried a round shield (*parma*), 3 feet in diameter (6.22), but wore no armour.

In Polybios' account of the Roman army of his day (6.23), the "heavy" infantry, or infantry of the line – the *hastati, principes* and *triarii* – are said to carry a rectangular shield (*scutum*), usually 2½ feet wide by 4 feet long, with the long sides curving inwards, made of two layers of wood, faced with canvas and calfskin, but with iron rims at top and bottom and a central iron boss. They also wear bronze helmets, decorated with three 18-inch crimson or black plumes, bronze greaves and breastplates, or, if they belong to the wealthiest class, chain-mail corslets. All carry a short, cut-and-thrust sword (*gladius*), but whereas the *hastati* and *principes* also have a pair of throwing-spears (*pila*), the *triarii* are still armed with the old thrusting-spear (*hasta*), from which the *hastati* had originally derived their name.

Unfortunately, we do not know whether legionaries were already equipped like this at the time of the First Punic War. The *scutum* is usually thought to be Samnite (cf. e.g. Ath. 6.273f.), and, if so, was probably already in use, but the *gladius* and the *pilum* may in fact have been adopted by the Romans as a result of encountering Spanish mercenaries fighting for Carthage during this very war: the earliest reference to the *pilum* – ὑσσός (*hyssos*) in Greek – is in Polybios (40.12), referring to 251.[9] However, it is difficult to believe that soldiers would have been trained in the use of essentially different weapons in the midst of a war, and thus it is likely that Roman infantry weapons already consisted of something like a *gladius* and *pila* at the time of its outbreak, the Spanish weapons being simply better versions of the same kind of weapon.

Polybios' frequent references to the *triarii* in his account of the battle of Ecnomus (26.6 etc.), even if there it was a nickname (see below, pp. 85 ff), indicate that the legion was already divided into the three lines of *hastati, principes* and *triarii*, and the occurrence of his term for "maniples" (*manipuli*, i.e. "handfuls" – σημεῖαι in Greek), elsewhere in his account of the war

(33.9, 40.10) indicates that these subdivisions also existed. Later there were 30 such units in a legion, ten each of *hastati, principes* and *triarii*, with the *velites* being equally distributed among all the maniples. Thus a maniple of *hastati* or *principes* consisted of 120 heavy infantry and 40 light, a maniple of *triarii* of half the number of heavy infantry, but the same number of light (6.21.6–10). In one passage, referring to the battle of Ilipa in 206, Polybios says that the Romans called a group of three maniples, one each of *hastati, principes* and *triarii*, a "cohort" (11.23.2), which would mean that there were then, as later, ten cohorts to a legion. But he never uses the term in connection with the First Punic War, and it may have been a later innovation.

As for cavalry, it is very rarely mentioned, and when it is, no distinction is made between citizen and allied horsemen, the latter, in later times, usually being more numerous. Presumably, since cavalry was even transported to Africa (29.9), Roman armies were invariably accompanied by a body of horse, even when this is not specified, but the Roman cavalry does not seem to have been very efficient. According to Zonaras (8.9), it was routed by Hiero's in 264; in 262 it was lured into a trap by Hanno's Numidians before Agrigentum (19.2–4), and at Tunis it was swept from the field, though there, admittedly, it was heavily outnumbered (34.3).

Infantry officers already included "tribunes of the soldiers" (*tribuni militum*) at the time of the war, since Polybios uses the term "chiliarchs" (χιλίαρχοι: 23.1, 49.3), and this is his Greek equivalent for the Latin term (cf. e.g. 6.21.1). Even the names of a number of them are given by the secondary sources. Later there were six to a legion, but they were "staff officers" rather than commanders of specific units. Below them, again later, came centurions, of whom there were two to each maniple. They are not referred to in connection with the First Punic War, but they probably already existed. Tribunes were normally young men of the upper classes "doing their military service", before going on to higher things, and so would not be trained in any proper sense, though they might become experienced in the course of time. But the same would be true of all Rome's soldiers. Essentially we are dealing here with a militia army.

Overall command was usually vested in the annually elected consuls. They might or might not have seen action before reaching this, the highest office in the Republic, but in any case they owed their election primarily to their social standing rather than to any ability, military or otherwise. In our war, it was not uncommon for the same man to hold the consulship more than once – there are ten such instances – but there is no example of a man's holding the consulship more than twice or twice running, though there are examples of both in the Second Punic War.

Even more oddly, during our war the Romans do not seem to have made as much use as they did in the Second of the system of prorogation, whereby a man's authority (*imperium*) might be renewed for a further term, and there are no examples of a man's *imperium* being prorogued for more than one year, or until he had finished a particular task. They thus seem to have deprived themselves of the use of men of experience in favour of a strict rotation of office. The only case that is at all comparable to the use made of such men as M. Claudius Marcellus or both the elder and younger Scipios in the Second war is that of A. Atilius Caiatinus,[10] who was consul in 258/7 and 254/3, praetor in 257/6 when he celebrated a triumph, and dictator in 249 – the first dictator to command an army outside Italy (Livy, *Per.* 19). Even C. Duilius, the man who won the first naval victory in Roman history, was never used again, though he was still alive in 231. In a remarkable passage (8.16), presumably drawn from Dio, who would have known the Roman imperial army, Zonaras goes so far as to claim that the greatest mistake the earlier Romans made was to send out different commanders each year, depriving them of command just as they were learning the art of generalship, "as though choosing them for practice, not use".

Apart from the consuls, there were very few other officers of state at this time. There was one praetor each year until 242 – we know the names of several of them – and in that year a second was added (Livy, *Per.* 19). Thereafter, they were distinguished as the "city praetor" (*praetor urbanus*) and the "foreign praetor" (i.e. "praetor in charge of foreigners", *praetor peregrinus*). The first was originally appointed to relieve the consuls of some of their judicial duties, and this always remained the primary function of both. At this date the office was evidently regarded, in some ways, as the equivalent of a consulship, and of the three known praetors during our war, two had already held the consulship – A. Atilius Caiatinus (consul 258/7, praetor 257/6) and L. Postumius Megellus (consul 262/1, praetor 253/2). But an example of the later practice of holding the praetorship before the consulship was Q. Valerius Falto, who was praetor in 241/0 and went on to be consul in 239/8.

Despite their primary judicial role, however, both Caiatinus and Falto commanded military forces, the latter perhaps even being in effective command in the final and decisive battle of the war, and both celebrated triumphs, the one as praetor, the other as propraetor. Zonaras (8.11) says that the praetor of 260/59 was also sent to Sicily to take command of the army there, after one consul had been captured and the other had taken command at sea, and later (8.16) he implies that the praetor of 248/7 was in command of the army in Italy, again in the absence of both consuls.

Apart from consuls and praetors, we know of five pairs of censors during the war, though of those appointed in 253, one died in office and the other abdicated as a result. They had no military duties, their primary job being, as their title implies, to hold the census. But this involved deciding who was liable for military service, and also drawing up the list of senators and *equites* ("knights"), which gave the censors considerable political clout. Those of 252, for example, are said to have expelled 16 members from the Senate, and to have degraded no fewer than 400 *equites* to a lesser status for disobedience (Livy, *Per.* 18; Val. Max. 2.9.7; Front., *Strat.* 4.1.22).

The dictatorship, by its very nature, was an irregular office, and often the duties were quite trivial, though the appointment was a high honour. Cn. Fulvius Maximus Centumalus, for example, was appointed in 263, to carry out the religious ceremony of "banging in the nail" (*clavi fingendi causa*), and Q. Ogulnius Gallus in 257 to take charge of the celebration of the Latin Festival. But in 246 a dictator, Ti. Coruncanius, was appointed to hold the elections, presumably because of the absence of the consuls in Sicily, and in 249, as we have seen, the ubiquitous A. Atilius Caiatinus commanded an army as dictator. Whatever their duties, dictators had a lieutenant called the "master of horse" (*magister equitum*) during their term of office, which was six months at the most.

One very odd example of the dictatorship at this time was that of M. Claudius Glicia in 249. According to the sources, he was a low-born associate of the consul, P. Claudius Pulcher, who on being recalled by the Senate after losing the battle of Drepana, and ordered to nominate a dictator, demonstrated his anger by naming Glicia (Livy, *Per.* 19; Suet., *Tib.* 2). If this was all the evidence we had, we would be tempted to dismiss the story out of hand, but Glicia's name appears entire in the *Fasti Capitolini*, with the note that he "had been a scribe, and as dictator without a Master of Horse, was compelled to abdicate". It was presumably to replace him that Caiatinus was appointed.

Below the consuls and praetor(s), came the four aediles, two "curule", two "plebeian", whose job was mainly to administer the city of Rome itself. Only three curule aediles and two plebeian aediles are known from the period of our war, and they played no part in military affairs. Similarly, the names of only two "tribunes of the plebs" (*tribuni plebis*) are known, and they are both very uncertain:[11] they are said to have prosecuted Claudius

Pulcher for *perduellio* (treason) after his failure at Drepana. There were also already eight officials known as "quaestors" at this time, two of whom acted as lieutenants of the consuls, but they are only once referred to during the period of the war, when two or more of them – possibly *quaestores classici* in this instance (see below, p. 137) – commanded part of the Roman fleet in 249. There is, finally, only one known case of the later practice whereby elected officials themselves appointed lieutenants to whom they delegated authority – hence the term *legatus* – and that rests only on the dubious evidence of Plutarch (*Par. Min.* 23G), though there were probably more in reality.

Finally, a word must be said about the part played by the ordinary people of Rome. By this date most of the internal political problems that had beset the early Republic had been resolved, and there are even fewer signs of such problems in our war than in the Second, though this may well simply be due to our lack of Livy's narrative. The only times the People seem to have played an important part in the first war are right at its beginning and right at its end. Polybios alleges that the decision to go to war was taken by the People, despite the serious doubts of many in the Senate (11.1–3), and that they also at first rejected the draft peace treaty negotiated by Lutatius Catulus (63.1).

We shall consider the former at greater length when we come to discuss the causes of the war (see below, pp. 37 ff), but here we should perhaps note that the republican machinery of government was not really "democratic" in any proper sense of that term.[12] Thus the assembly that usually had the responsibility for declaring war was the "assembly in centuries" (*comitia centuriata*), which was also used to elect the chief officials – consuls, praetors, censors and curule aediles. At this date it was probably already made up of 193 "centuries", to which citizens were assigned in accordance with their wealth, the richest belonging to the 18 centuries of *equites*, the next richest to the 80 centuries of the First Class, and so on, with the very poorest, those who had no property and were simply classified "by head" (*capite censi*), belonging to the single century of the *proletarii*.

Since voting was by the block system, whereby the vote of the majority within each century counted as one vote, it follows that the system was heavily weighted in favour of the wealthier members of society, and that provided that these were united, there was very little the poor could do, even if they formed an actual majority in any given assembly. In other words, one suspects that conflicts that appear in the sources as conflicts between Senate and People, were very often, if not always, really conflicts between different factions in the Senate, perhaps using "popular" support to sway waverers amongst their own class.

Other assemblies were the "assembly by tribes" (*comitia tributa*), divided at this time into 33 blocs called *tribus*, and the similarly structured "council of the plebs" (*concilium plebis*). Since the blocs here consisted of 29 "rural" tribes and four "urban", but all voting took place in Rome, it is probable that the wealthier members of the rural tribes, who would have tended either to be domiciled in Rome, or to be able to get there for important votes, would have swamped the urban proletariat. The *concilium plebis*, under its presiding officials, the "tribunes of the plebs", had achieved parity with the other assemblies by the Hortensian Law of 287, which made its decrees – *plebiscita* – binding on the whole state, but it had never really been a truly "popular" assembly, and in any case we know nothing about its activities at this time. As we have seen, even the tribunes are only once said to have done anything during the war. We should remember that in Rome the distinction between patricians and plebeians was not a distinction between rich and poor or even upper and lower classes, but purely a matter of birth: certain families were patrician, the rest plebeian, but by the time of this war some plebeian families were as rich and powerful as the patrician ones. Apart from anything else, one consul each year had to be a plebeian.

All in all, one has the impression that the Romans fought this war – which was, after all, on a scale quite new to them – with a machinery of government more appropriate to their relatively parochial wars in Italy. It may indeed be the case that it was as a result of the lessons learned now that they fought the Second war in a different kind of way, though the differences may be more apparent than real. We must constantly bear in mind that mainly because of the loss of the relevant books of Livy, the evidence we have for the two conflicts is very different.

But the Romans already had one priceless asset in the First war, and that was the Senate. This was a body made up of anybody who was anybody in the Roman Republic. At this date it probably included men who had not yet held office, for Livy implies that this was true of some senators even as late as 216, when he says that those killed at Cannae included 80 men who were "either senators already or who had held those magistracies that gave them the right to be selected for the senate" (22.49.17). But we can be sure that at least those who had held the highest offices – consulships and praetorships – would have been members of the Senate, and probably many of those who had been aedile, quaestor and tribune of the plebs, and it would thus have been the repository of all their collective experience.

Although for this war we lack Livy's year-by-year account of how commands and forces were assigned, there can be little doubt that it was already the Senate that decided these things, as it was later. As we shall see, the strategy Rome pursued, if perhaps over-cautious at times, was on the whole sound, and, in the end, triumphant. Above all, it would have been the Senate that decided to build a fleet in 261/0, and thereafter to renew the naval effort, time after time, despite all the disasters suffered at sea, right up to the final decisive naval battle in 241. If there was no single Roman to match Scipio Africanus in this war, collectively the Romans already had a war-winner in their supreme governing body.

Constitutionally there were certain resemblances between Rome and Carthage, as Greek political theorists recognized by categorizing both as having "mixed" constitutions (cf. e.g. Arist., *Pol.* 1274b24 ff; Plb. 6.51–6), though in practice both were essentially oligarchic.[13] The titular heads of the Carthaginian state, in the third century, were probably two annually elected officials called *sufetes* in Latin, who obviously resembled the Roman consuls. For example, as was the case with the consuls if they were in Rome, one of the *sufetes* apparently presided over the Carthaginian "senate" (cf., e.g., 3.33.3), and probably also over the popular assembly. Moreover, as their title – which probably means "judge" (cf. the Hebrew "*shophet/shophetim*") – implies, they also had a judicial role. But the powers of the *sufetes* were by this time significantly different in one important respect: unlike consuls, they no longer had any military function. There was also a state treasurer and a moral censor (Livy 33.46.00; Nepos, *Ham.* 3.2), and presumably other officials to take care of day-to-day administration.

Military command, however, was in our period vested in men appointed specifically for the purpose, possibly elected, formally at any rate, by the popular assembly (cf. e.g. 3.13.4). This separation of civil and military powers was extremely unusual, if not unique, in the ancient world, but probably owes more to the nature of the Carthaginian armed forces than to any fears that it was dangerous to give high officers of state military power. Since there was apparently no limit to the length of time a general might serve, the system had the advantage that many Carthaginian commanders became highly "professional". But one should not imagine that they owed their appointment, in the first instance, to any military ability they had shown. They, like their Roman counterparts, were aristocrats, as far as we can tell, who owed their positions to their social standing. But unlike Roman consuls, who, as we have seen, were lucky if they served for more than one term at this period, and rarely commanded continuously for much more than a year, Carthaginian generals did at least have the opportunity of learning from experience.

On the other hand, there were also disadvantages to the system. In particular, perhaps because the generals, like their armies, were regarded as employees who had a job to do, there was a tendency for them to be left to their own devices, and not to be supported as strongly as they might have been. This is particularly noticeable in the Hannibalic War, when, for example, Hannibal only once received reinforcements from home, though his theatre of operations was obviously the crucial one. But it also, from time to time, affected operations in the first war. Hannibal's father, Hamilcar, for example, was largely left to carry on the struggle in Sicily from 247 to the end of the war on his own, when a wholehearted and concerted effort might have won the war for Carthage. What effect the savage punishments inflicted on unsuccessful generals may have had is unclear: they do not seem to have made them noticeably cautious.

Deliberative and legislative functions within the Carthaginian state were exercised by a number of bodies, of which the largest was what Roman writers called the "senate" (e.g. Livy 21.18.3), while the Greeks used various terms, including *gerousia* (which has the same meaning – "council of elders": e.g. Arist., *Pol.* 1272^{b}37) and *synhedrion* (e.g. 3.33.2 and 4). It apparently had several hundred members, who probably held office for life, but whose method of appointment is uncertain. Within the "senate" there was a smaller body of 30 councillors that probably acted as a steering-committee, and perhaps, in effect, decided much of the main body's policy in advance. In addition, there was a body of 104 judges, often referred to as the "hundred" (cf. e.g. Arist., *Pol.* 1272^{b}35 and 1273^{a}15), which is compared to the Spartan board of ephors by Aristotle (*Pol.* 1272^{b}35). If the comparison is at all exact, this implies that the "hundred" had a wide measure of control over all officials, and Aristotle in fact describes them as the "supreme council". He also says it was chosen by groups of five officials (πενταρχίαι), who were co-opted (*Pol.* 1273^{a}12 ff), but quite how is not clear. Nor is it clear what was the relationship between the "senate" and the "hundred", though it is usually assumed that the latter were members of the former.

If anything, the people of Carthage probably had even less say in their affairs than those of Rome, though Polybios believed that the situation had changed by the time of the outbreak of the Hannibalic War (6.51). According to Aristotle (*Pol.* 1273^{a}7 ff), if the *sufetes* and senate were in agreement, they could decide whether or not to bring a matter before the people, and

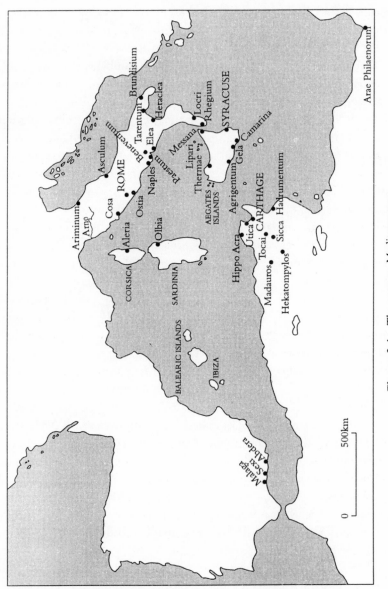

Figure 2.1 The western Mediterranean.

although in Rome many matters were no doubt in practice decided by the Senate, there would be no question of its deciding, for example, to go to war without consulting the people. Yet this is precisely what happened at Carthage in 218, if Polybios' account is to be pressed (3.33.3–4). Even the composition of Carthage's "senate" may have been decided by co-option, whereas although the membership of the Roman senate was theoretically decided by the censors, at least these officials were themselves elected by the people, and in practice they probably mainly chose men who had been already elected to office by the people, as we saw.

It is true that Aristotle (*Politics*) says that if a matter was referred to the people of Carthage, any one could oppose it, whereas in Rome, only the presiding magistrate or someone invited by him was permitted to address the people. In Carthage, too, at least some generals were, in some sense, elected by the people, again if Polybios' account of how Hannibal came to be appointed (3.13.4), is to be pressed. Nevertheless, in general, one suspects that Carthage was a narrower oligarchy than Rome. This could obviously have certain advantages in wartime, but one has the impression that it sharpened differences in the ruling class, whereas in Rome, though there were disagreements about policy, there was also more cohesion at the top, and perhaps a wider measure of support for the leading men from below.

What of the Carthaginian empire?[14] By the end of the fourth century she almost certainly controlled the whole of the Cape Bon peninsula, and much of the fertile land watered by the Oued Medjerda (the ancient Bagradas) and Oued Miliane to the southwest, more or less as far as the present frontier between Tunisia and Algeria. Thus a place called "Tocai", almost certainly the modern Dougga, is said to have been subject to Carthage in 310 (DS 20.57), but Hekatompylos (Tébessa in modern Algeria) was only captured in the 240s (DS 24.10.2, cf. Plb. 1.73.1); similarly, it is implied (66.10) that Sicca, the modern El Kef, had been in Carthaginian territory for some time in 241, whereas Madauros, the modern M'Daourouch in Algeria, was outside it (Apuleius, *Apol.* 24).

In addition, by the time of the outbreak of our war, Carthage controlled the whole coast of northern Africa from Cyrenaica to the Atlantic, partly through her own colonies, partly through having "taken under her protection" other Phoenician colonies, such as Utica and Hadrumentum (Sousse). Though numerous, these colonies were mostly quite small, as is indicated by the term *emporia* used of many of them by the Greeks (e.g. pseudo-Skylax 111). They were able to survive because the coastal region was apparently otherwise sparsely inhabited. The eastern limit of the empire was at the place the Romans called *Arae Philaenorum* ("Altars of the Philaeni": the modern Al'Uqaylah or El Agheila), which marks the boundary between Tripolitania and Cyrenaica. To the west, Carthaginian influence extended beyond the Straits of Gibraltar and down the west coast of Africa at least as far as the Spanish Sahara.

Beyond Africa Carthage probably already controlled a few outposts in Spain, which, like herself, had been originally founded by the Phoenicians, including Gades (Cadiz), Malaga, Sexi (near Almunécar) and Abdera (Adra?). In the Balearic Islands there was a colony on Ibiza, and there was a string of such settlements round the coast of Sardinia. In Corsica Aleria, at least, was presumably in Carthaginian hands by 259 when the Romans attacked it (cf. *CIL* 12.2.8 & 9), while the Lipari Islands were at latest providing a base for the fleet by 264 (DS 22.13.7). In Sicily, finally, Carthaginian power had had a chequered career for centuries, and had reached a low ebb as recently as 277, when Carthage had lost all but Lilybaeum (Marsala) to Pyrrhus (see below, pp. 32 ff). But recovery had been swift with Pyrrhus' departure in 276, so that by the time of the outbreak of our war she had won back control of most of western Sicily, including Panormus (Palermo) on the north coast and Agrigentum (Agrigento) on the south. As we shall see, she was even in a position to intervene militarily in Messana (Messina).

Carthage treated her subjects and allies in different ways. In Tunisia, the Cape Bon peninsula was almost certainly largely given over to the estates of the Carthaginians themselves (cf. DS 20.8), but the interior was occupied by the people Polybios calls "Libyans" (Λίβυες), the Romans "Africans" (*Afri*), the ancestors of the present Berbers. These were obliged to pay tribute to Carthage, amounting, in the case of those outside the towns, to half their produce (72.2), and to furnish the troops that formed the backbone of Carthaginian armies. Beyond these Carthage extended her sway from time to time over the people Polybios calls "Numidians" (Νομάδες), living in remoter parts of Tunisia and Algeria, and these, too, furnished troops for the Carthaginian forces, in particular the light cavalry that was later to perform such sterling service for Hannibal.

The inhabitants of the various Carthaginian colonies and entrepots were termed "Libyphoenicians" by the Greeks, and seem to have had local officials and institutions similar to those of Carthage herself. Polybios implies (7.9.5) that they had the same laws as the Carthaginians, and this suggests that they also enjoyed the same rights. But Carthage exacted dues on imports and exports, possibly direct taxes as well in some cases, and there is also evidence that Libyphoenicians were liable for military service abroad (cf. e.g. 3.33.15), whereas Carthaginian citizens were apparently exempt (see below, pp. 26 ff). It also seems likely that men from these maritime communities helped to man the Carthaginian fleet, though nothing is known for certain about its crews.

Probably the settlers in Spain, on Ibiza, Sardinia and the Lipari islands, enjoyed similar rights, those in Gades and on Ibiza even issuing their own coins. Carthage's Sicilian subjects possibly enjoyed even more freedom, judging by the coins issued by both Phoenician and Elymian, Sican and Greek communities, and by the permission granted by Carthage's first two treaties with Rome for Romans to trade in the island (3.22.10, 24.12). But it is probable that all communities had to pay tribute to Carthage, possibly the tithe on produce later exacted by the Romans (Cic., *Verr.* 2.3.6), and there were Carthaginian garrisons in some of the towns, as there were in Sardinia.

The population of the Carthaginian empire was probably at least as large as that of the Roman confederacy, and possibly larger, but whereas the very structure of the latter meant that Rome could dispose of its manpower, the ties binding Carthage's subjects to her were altogether looser. Unless there were some kind of reciprocal rights with the Libyphoenicians – Diodoros says they had the right to intermarry with Carthaginians, for example (20.55.4) – Carthage made no attempt to grant her citizenship to her subjects, or even to extend to them similar rights to those enjoyed by the Latins.

How her subjects viewed her it is impossible to say. There was a tradition that they were harshly treated, particularly in the matter of tribute (Plut., *Mor.* 799d), and Polybios is critical of Carthage's attitude towards the Libyans in particular (72.1–4). There were certainly revolts among these latter from the fourth century onwards, culminating in their joining the mutinous mercenaries at the end of our war. On the other hand, if lack of revolts means anything, the Libyphoenicians seem to have been reasonably content, at any rate down to the second century. The exceptions are the defection of Utica and Hippo Acra (Bizerta) during the Mercenary War, and it is noticeable that although at first they remained loyal, even though under attack, when they did decide to join the rebels, according to Polybios (82.9), they showed "an inexorable anger and hatred towards the Carthaginians". Nor do the Sicilian communities seem to have hesitated to side with Carthage's enemies whenever the situation seemed to warrant it. Above all, it was the exaction of tribute that marked the Carthaginian alliance off from the Roman.

The enormous wealth deriving from this tribute and from trade also made it possible for the Carthaginians to employ mercenaries to do their fighting for them, and this was another fundamental difference between them and the Romans (cf. 6.52).[15] Whereas every male Roman citizen between the ages of 17 and 46 was liable for military service, and one may plausibly guess that something similar was true of Rome's allies, by the time of our war Carthage's citizens had ceased to serve in her forces overseas, except of course as officers. Thus there is no reference to Carthaginian soldiers in Polybios' account of the fighting in and around Sicily, though Diodoros appears to imply that the fleet defeated off the Aegates in the final battle of the war was partly manned by "Carthaginians" (24.11.2); in Sardinia, the Carthaginians who executed their commander in 259 (Plb. 1.24.6) were presumably officers. But Polybios twice (33.6 and 34.6) refers to "the phalanx of the Carthaginians", as distinct from the mercenaries engaged, in his account of the defeat of the Roman army in Africa.

Overseas, instead of using her own citizens, Carthage relied almost entirely on her Libyan subjects, who already formed a quarter of her army in 311 (DS 19.106.2), and on mercenaries. Thus, in Polybios' account of our war, we meet Ligurians, Celts, Spaniards, Numidians and Greeks (17.4, 19.2, 43.4, 48.3), and he also mentions Balearic islanders and Libyans at the beginning of the Mercenary War, the latter being said to be the largest group amongst the mutineers (67.7). Curiously enough, he does not mention either Sardinians or Corsicans, though they were allegedly already serving in a Carthaginian army as early as 480 (Hdt. 7.165).

How all these troops were armed and organized, it is impossible to say. Presumably the Balearic islanders were slingers, since they were famous for the use of that weapon, and the Numidians already provided cavalry (19.2). As for the rest, unless they were homogenized on entering Carthaginian service, and issued with arms by the Carthaginian state, one may guess that the Greeks, if they were "heavy" infantry, were armed as hoplites, i.e. that their main offensive weapon was the shorter hoplite thrusting-spear rather than the Macedonian *sarisa*, and that they still carried the characteristic hoplite shield, and wore helmets, greaves, and linen or leather corslets; if they were "light" infantry, they could have resembled classical "peltasts", being armed with javelins, and carrying the light shield (*pelta*) from which peltasts derived their name. The Spaniards, if they were "line" infantry, may have used the formidable, short, cut-and-thrust sword, which their descendants wielded at Cannae (3.114.3), and been dressed, like them, in short, crimson-edged tunics; Spanish skirmishers may have wielded the formidable *phalarica* (cf. Livy 21.8.10), from which the Roman *pilum* was allegedly derived. The Celts may similarly have carried their long, slashing swords, and fought naked, or in trousers and cloaks (cf. 2.28.7–8 and 3.114.4).

But what of the "Libyans"? All we can be certain of is that by Hannibal's time, at any rate, they were worse armed than Roman soldiers, for he issued his Libyans with captured Roman equipment after the battle of Lake Trasimene (3.87.3, 114.1). But does this mean that he just gave them Roman helmets, body-armour, greaves and shields, or that they now also took *pila* and *gladii*? If the latter, they had presumably been primarily swordsmen already, since it is very unlikely that Hannibal would have risked retraining his best infantry in the course of a campaign. Even if the former, it seems likely that they were already accustomed to fighting in something like the Roman manner, since it was for this that Roman equipment was designed. On the other hand, it is possible that when the practice of using Carthaginian citizen-troops, except in Africa, was given up in favour of using Libyans instead, these latter were armed and organized in a similar way, and that was almost certainly in something akin to the Greek way. Thus, as we have seen, Polybios refers to the formation of the Carthaginians who fought against Regulus as a "phalanx" (33.6 and 34.6). But certainty is not possible.

A word, too, must be said about elephants. These were used by the Carthaginians in considerable numbers in both Sicily and Africa, and at times proved quite effective, though it is possible that they were used for the first time only at Agrigentum in 262 (see below, p. 58). They played a large part in the defeat of Regulus' army in Africa (34.1–8), and as a result were greatly feared (39.11–12) until Caecilius Metellus defeated an army containing perhaps as many as 140 of them (cf. 38.2) before Panormus (40.3 ff). Almost certainly the elephants in question were at least mostly African, and belonged to the variety known as "forest elephants" (*Loxodonta africana cyclotis*), which is now largely extinct, but was still to be seen until comparatively recently in the Gambia; in ancient times they were probably still to be found north of the Sahara in the forests of the Atlas. They were smaller than Indian elephants, standing on average under 8 feet tall at the shoulder, and carried a single rider, not a howdah; the elephant itself was the main weapon.[16]

At sea, once the Romans had decided to try to match the Carthaginians, the two sides evidently mostly employed the same types of vessel – indeed, the Romans are said to have built their new fleet on the model of a captured Carthaginian ship (20.15: see below, pp. 63 ff). The main battleship of the war was what the Romans called a "quinquereme" (*quinqueremis*, in Greek πεντήρης), though both smaller and larger vessels were also used, for example triremes (e.g. 20.14), the two *hexereis* (ἑξήρεις: "six-fitted") that served as the consuls' flagships at Ecnomus (26.11), and the *hepteres* (ἑπτήρης: "seven-fitted"), that had once belonged to Pyrrhus and served as the Carthaginian flagship at Mylae (23.4). All these terms seem properly to refer to the number of files of rowers from bow to stern, on each side of the ship, rather than to the number of "banks" of oars, though in the classical trireme, in which each man rowed a single oar, it amounted to the same thing.

In the case of larger vessels, it is not known how the oars were manned (see below, pp. 64–5). All that is certain is that a quinquereme was a larger vessel than a trireme, probably in its dimensions, and certainly in the numbers of its crew. Whereas from Herodotos' time the normal complement of a trireme was 200 men (cf. 3.14.4–5; 7.184.1 and 185.1; 8.17), probably consisting of 170 rowers and 30 marines and crew, at Ecnomus, for example, each Roman quinquereme is said to have carried 300 "rowers" and 120 marines (26.7), where the "rowers" probably included some deck-crew, for example to handle the sails and rigging, to steer, and to give the beat to the oarsmen. At that battle Carthaginian quinqueremes are implied to have had the same complements, though, if they relied more on ramming (see below), they may normally have carried fewer marines. As we have seen, we do not know who manned the Carthaginian ships, but it was possibly men from the maritime towns of the empire. There is similar doubt about the Roman navy, but it seems likely that the oarsmen were drawn from the allied communities of southern Italy and from the poorest section of the Roman citizen population, the *proletarii* (see below, pp. 65 ff). Neither side normally used slaves, except in dire emergencies.

Although catapults had been mounted on warships since the fourth century, they were "man-killers", not designed to destroy enemy ships, and the two ways of fighting at sea remained ramming and boarding. The Carthaginians, with a long naval tradition behind them – their earliest recorded sea-fight was against the Phokaian colonists of Alalia in Corsica in about 530 (Hdt. 1.166) – relied mainly on ramming, as is apparent from Polybios' description of the battles of Mylae and Drepana in 260 and 249 (23.5–10, 51). The Romans, famously, devised the boarding-bridge known as the *corvus* ("crow") to nullify the Carthaginian tactics in the early sea-battles of the war, though they later abandoned it, perhaps as a result of their experiences in bad weather (see below, pp. 68 ff). In the final battle of the war, off the Aegates in 241, the positions were reversed (60.9ff).

These oar-powered ships were not capable of remaining at sea for any length of time. They were designed to pack as many rowers as possible into a given size of hull, and were thus extremely crowded. There was little or no room to carry food, and, even more important, the huge quantities of water the rowers would have required; they would also have been very insanitary. This meant that there were severe limitations to the uses of seapower. In particular, blockade of even single sea-ports, let alone lengthy coastlines, was not really possible, and single ships or even whole squadrons could usually break through, if they were boldly handled. Thus, at the beginning of the war, the Romans were able to transport their army across the straits of Messina in the face of an almost complete Carthaginian command of the sea, even though the Carthaginians attempted to interfere (20.15); and later on in the war, the Carthaginians were able to run as many as 50 ships into Lilybaeum and out again when it was under siege by both land and sea (44, 46.1), to say nothing of the exploits of Hannibal "the Rhodian" (46.4 ff).

The two powers were, then, fairly evenly matched (cf. 6.52). If Rome had the advantage of numbers, or at least of numbers that could be mobilized, Carthage perhaps had the advantage of more "professional" troops and officers on land, and initially at least, what Polybios calls "undisputed command at sea" (20.12). Carthage also, perhaps, had the advantage of having fought wars overseas for centuries, whereas, as Polybios repeatedly emphasizes (5.1, 12.5), the Roman crossing to Sicily was their first venture outside Italy. Carthage was also the wealthier state, though this, perhaps, made less difference than it would have done in a more modern war, since Carthage needed her wealth to pay her mercenaries, whereas although Roman troops were probably paid, they were probably not paid so much.[17] But both states experienced financial difficulties. Rome had to raise a loan from her wealthier citizens to pay for the building of her last fleet in 243/2 (59.6 ff), but Carthage tried, without success, to negotiate a loan from Ptolemy II of Egypt (App., *Sic.* 1), and faced severe trouble because she could not afford what her mercenaries demanded, after the war was over (66 ff).

Polybios believed (cf. 6.52) that the crucial difference was that Rome fought with her own citizens and with those of her allies, whereas Carthage fought mainly with mercenaries. But apart from one or two incidents, there is no evidence that Carthage's mercenary soldiers fought less hard for her than Rome's citizen-soldiers for the Republic. Let us not forget that some of the best troops who have ever fought for Britain, the Gurkhas, are, strictly speaking, mercenaries, since Nepal has never been part of the British Empire, and one should not assume that Numidians, Spaniards, Celts, Balearic islanders, Ligurians and Greeks were any the less loyal. It was certainly not for lack of fighting spirit in her soldiers and sailors that Carthage lost the war.

CHAPTER 3

The origins of the war

For two states that were about to embark on over a century of warfare, Rome and Carthage had had not only a long relationship, but on the whole a not unfriendly one. In a long digression in his discussion of the causes of the Hannibalic War, Polybios lists three treaties between the two states concluded before the outbreak of our war (3.22 ff). There are problems with the treaties, but on the whole they do not concern us.[1] The only important question for us is whether there was another treaty, omitted by Polybios, that specifically debarred the Romans from Sicily (see below, pp. 32 ff).

The first of Polybios' treaties is dated by him to the consulship of L. Iunius Brutus and M. Horatius, the first consuls after the expulsion of the kings, 28 years before Xerxes' invasion of Greece – in our terms, probably, 508/7. Here we can ignore the question of the date, and although doubts have been raised about the authenticity of the treaty, Polybios' remark about the antiquity of the Latin in which it was couched (3.22.3) is its best guarantee. Possibly it was a renewal of a treaty between Carthage and the Etruscan kings of Rome, for Carthage and the Etruscans were certainly on friendly terms in the sixth century (cf. e.g. Hdt. 1.166). Basically the treaty appears to have been an attempt to restrict Roman trade with Africa and Sardinia, though not with Carthaginian Sicily, and to protect Rome's interests in Latium.

The second treaty is not dated by Polybios, but is probably to be equated with the one dated by Livy (7.27.2) and Diodoros (16.69.1) to 348, though they regarded this as the first treaty. Its chief interest is that it implies that Utica was now in the Carthaginian sphere, and apparently adds southern

Spain to the areas where Romans were forbidden to trade, while further restricting their activities in Sardinia and Libya, but again safeguarding their interests in Latium.

Polybios' third treaty is the most important from our point of view. It is evidently the one Livy (cf. *Per.* 13) dated to 279/8, and was concluded when Rome was engaged in her struggle with Pyrrhus, King of Epirus. The background to it is that Rome had become embroiled in war with Tarentum (Taras, Taranto), and that the latter had summoned Pyrrhus to her aid. After defeating Rome in two "Pyrrhic" victories at Heraclea and Asculum, the king had then received a request for help against the Carthaginians from some of the Greek communities in Sicily, and, in order to free his hands of his Italian commitments, had entered into negotiations with Rome. It was obviously in Carthage's interests to keep Pyrrhus in Italy, and this explains why she was evidently prepared to offer Rome favourable terms.

Polybios' version of the resultant treaty (3.25.2–5) is somewhat obscure,[2] but, while reiterating previous agreements, it was clearly designed to provide for mutual aid if either party was attacked. Although each party was to pay its own forces, Carthage was to provide the transports for any movement of troops by sea, and was to come to Rome's aid with naval forces, if a necessity arose, though the ships' crews were not to be compelled to land against their will. In other words, neither side was obliged to help the other, but had the option of asking for help, and in particular Rome could call upon Carthaginian naval help, if she so desired. The benefit to Carthage was presumably that Pyrrhus might be deterred from going to Sicily by the possibility that Rome might help Carthage there, though in the event the treaty did not have this effect, and Carthage did not ask for any help, despite Pyrrhus' successes against her. The chief interest of the treaty, from our point of view, is the lack of Roman naval forces it implies.

After discussing this treaty, Polybios goes on to condemn Philinos for saying that there was also a treaty that obliged the Romans not to interfere anywhere in Sicily, and the Carthaginians anywhere in Italy (3.26). This is often equated with the treaty mentioned by Livy under the year 306 (9.43.26), though it is somewhat difficult to reconcile its terms either with the then extent of Roman power in Italy or with that of Carthage in Sicily, and all Livy actually says is that "the treaty with the Carthaginians was renewed for the third time", implying that no changes were made.[3] Nevertheless, Livy evidently did know – possibly from Philinos – of a treaty supposedly debarring the Carthaginians from interfering in Italy, because he claimed that the alleged Carthaginian interference at Tarentum in 272 was a breach of such a treaty (*Per.* 14: see below). This is made clear by the speech he gives Hannibal's enemy, Hanno, in 218, where Hanno admits that the Carthaginians "had not kept away from Tarentum, *that is Italy*, according to the treaty" (21.10.8). For good measure, the Vergilian scholar, Servius, commenting on a line from the *Aeneid* (4.628), also mentions some such treaty, though in much vaguer terms.

However, it is difficult to believe that Polybios was mistaken, when he obviously took such care to examine the records of treaties between the two powers, and it is just as likely that Philinos was misled by Carthaginian propaganda, as it is that Polybios was misled by his Roman friends. A compromise solution is either that the treaty of 279/8 itself was held to imply a recognition of the Carthaginian and Roman "spheres of influence", or that the recognition of such spheres implied by Polybios' first and second treaties, and reaffirmed in that of 279/8, was held by the Carthaginians to preclude Roman interference in Sicily. The vague language Servius uses of his "treaty" possibly supports such a hypothesis. The agreement, he says, was that "the Romans should not approach the shores of the Carthaginians, nor the Carthaginians the shores of the Romans". Philinos' "treaty" would then be a product of such propaganda. Indeed, one might go so far as to say that although Polybios was formally right that there was no such treaty as Philinos claimed, nevertheless the latter's "spheres of influence" were implied by existing treaties.

But to return to the treaty of 279/8, it is unlikely that anything practical ever came of it, and it certainly did not amount to much. According to Justin (18.2), the Carthaginians sent one Mago, with 120 ships – Valerius Maximus (3.7.10) says 130 – to aid the Romans, but the implication is that this was not because of any new treaty, but rather, perhaps, in accordance with the "friendship" (φιλία in Polybios' Greek: 3.22.4 and 24.3) that already existed between the two powers as a result of the previous treaties. In any case, although, according to Justin, Mago himself addressed the Senate – Valerius Maximus says the Senate sent a delegation to him at Ostia, which seems more likely – the Romans, while expressing their thanks, rejected the aid, whereupon Mago sailed away to meet Pyrrhus. The treaty between Carthage and Rome would thus appear to have been negotiated at a later date, perhaps after Pyrrhus had rejected some offer by Mago.[4]

The only other possible result of the treaty is an operation involving either Rhegium or Locri. According to a fragment of Diodoros (22.7.5), after making an alliance with the Romans, the Carthaginians "took 500 men on board their own ships and sailed to Rhegium (now Reggio di Calabria)", and it has been suggested that these were Roman legionaries sent to reinforce the garrison. However, if what Diodoros said has been correctly reported, he seems to be talking about an abortive attack on Rhegium, which does not make sense at this date, when it was probably still held for Rome. An alternative is that the epitomator incorrectly reported what Diodoros wrote, which was that Locri, not Rhegium, was the subject of the attack.[5]

Apart from this, there is no evidence that either side gave any concrete help to the other, even when, as a result of Pyrrhus' successes, only Lilybaeum remained to Carthage of all her possessions in Sicily. However, in the end, Pyrrhus' continuous demands for men, ships and money, and harsh measures against those who refused, alienated the Sicilians, and after one last victory, he returned to Italy in 276. On the way, he was heavily defeated by the Carthaginians at sea, losing 70 out of his 110 ships (Plut., *Pyrrh.* 24). Subsequently, he fought a third battle against the Romans at Beneventum (Benevento), in which he was even less successful than previously, and returned to Greece.

It was after his departure that another and potentially explosive incident possibly occurred. Livy apparently recorded (*Per.* 14) that in clear breach of "the treaty", a Carthaginian fleet came to the aid of Tarentum, which was still held by Pyrrhus' lieutenant, Milo, and was now under siege by Rome. Later, as we have seen, he has Hannibal's opponent, Hanno, refer to the incident when attempting to dissuade his fellow-countrymen from going to war in 218 (21.10.8). This tradition also appears in Cassius Dio (fr. 43, cf. Zon. 8.8) and Ampelius (46.2), and Orosius (4.3.1–2) even goes so far as to claim that the Romans defeated the Carthaginians in a battle.

In another passage (8.6), Zonaras has a different and perhaps more plausible version. According to this, the Tarentines were angry at Milo's continued presence, and were harassed by a faction that had first tried to murder him, and had then withdrawn to a near-by stronghold to continue their attacks. As a result the Tarentines asked the Carthaginians for help, and it was then that Milo, under siege by the Romans from the landward side, and now under attack from the Carthaginians by sea, decided to surrender to the former. Possibly the truth of the matter is that the Carthaginians came to see if they could help, in accordance with the recent treaty, but that the Romans were suspicious since no help had been requested. According to Orosius (4.5.2), they even sent ambassadors to Carthage to complain, but the Carthaginians simply denied the incident.

This episode is sometimes regarded as unhistorical,[6] but there really is no good reason to reject it, even though Polybios says nothing about it. In the volatile situation Pyrrhus left behind, the Carthaginians may well have been anxious to see exactly what was going on in Italy, and, in particular, whether Pyrrhus was likely to return. Tarentum, being still held for the king, would be the natural focal point of such interest. As we have seen, a perfectly plausible scenario can be reconstructed that would explain how the Carthaginian fleet came to be there, why the Romans could have regarded its activities as suspicious, but how they could subsequently have accepted the Carthaginian denial that any hostility towards the Republic was intended.

Summing up the relations between the two powers, then: as long as they seem to have been reasonably cordial, or at least not unfriendly, as long as their interests did not seriously clash. However, as Roman influence spread throughout Italy, and particularly to the southern end of the peninsula, the two states may seem almost literally to have been on a collision course. Roman troops in Rhegium were, after all, less than ten miles from the shores of Sicily, an island in which Carthage had had an interest for some three centuries. Mutual enmity of Pyrrhus might postpone the inevitable, but once that was removed, it was only, it may seem, a matter of time. Indeed, one modern commentator has gone so far as to declare that "once Pyrrhus had been defeated in Italy (275), the possibility of conflict with Carthage probably became clear", and to argue that a number of Rome's actions in the next ten years were taken with this in mind. Thus the new Latin colonies at Cosa and Paestum, founded in 273, were designed to protect the coast, and the same year saw the embassy to Ptolemy II of Egypt, seeking friendship with a power that might also have reason to fear Carthage. The seizure of forest land from the Bruttians at about the same time was with ship-building in mind (cf. DH 20.15).[7]

Nevertheless, however inevitable a clash between Rome and Carthage may seem, it requires a spark to touch off such a conflagration, and in this case it was something that happened in the north-east corner of Sicily. One of the few places there that had not gone over to Pyrrhus while he was in the island was Messana (Messina). This had been seized, sometime in the 280s, by Campanian mercenaries who had previously served Agathokles, ruler of Syracuse from 317 to 289. Calling themselves the "Mamertini" or "People of Mamers", the war-god whom the Romans called "Mars", the Campanians had been able to take advantage of the confusion then prevailing in Sicily to consolidate their position and to plunder cities as far removed as Camarina and Gela. Their position had also been strengthened by the similar seizure of Rhegium, across the straits in Italy, by a force of Roman troops made up of Campanian "citizens without the vote" (7.6 ff).

However, in 270 the Romans had recovered Rhegium for its citizens, possibly with the aid of a new and vigorous ruler of Syracuse, Hiero (Zon. 8.6), and savagely punished the survivors of the treacherous garrison. This was a blow to the Mamertines, and at about the same time they may also have come under direct attack from Hiero. The chronology of his rise to power is uncertain,[8] but his first, abortive move against the Mamertines and subsequent seizure of power (9.3–6) may have been in 270/69, at about the time of the Roman recovery of Rhegium. For our purposes, however, the important question is the date of his subsequent victory over the Mamertines on the river Longanus (9.7–9; DS 22.13).

Polybios says that it was this defeat that led the Mamertines to appeal first to Carthage and then to Rome (10.1–2: see below), and this implies a date in 265 or even 264. But he also says (9.8) that it was as a result of his victory that Hiero was proclaimed "king", and later (7.8.4) that when he died in 215, he had been king for 54 years, implying that the victory was in 270/69. But although some have accepted this and argued that it was then that the Mamertines appealed to Carthage, and only some four or five years later that they appealed to Rome, it is highly unlikely that Polybios was mistaken about something as important for his purposes as the coincidence of the Mamertine appeals to Carthage and to Rome. So either we should suppose that the 54 years of Hiero's "reign" dates from his first seizure of power, not from his actual proclamation as "king", or – which is less likely – we should divorce his proclamation as king from the battle of the Longanus. In either case, it seems probable that the battle took place shortly before the appeals to both Carthage and Rome.

If we are to believe Diodoros (22.13.6), the defeat was so severe that at first the Mamertines decided to throw themselves on Hiero's mercy. But it was then that things took a different and fateful turn. A Carthaginian fleet happened to be at the Lipari islands, and when its commander, Hannibal, heard the news of the Longanus, he first approached Hiero, ostensibly to congratulate him on his victory, but in reality, it appears, somehow to forestall further action on his part. Perhaps he was able to convince him that Carthaginian good offices would secure the surrender of the town, or alternatively he claimed that it was already an ally of Carthage.[9] At any rate, Hiero took no further action, and Hannibal was then able to persuade the

Mamertines to accept a Carthaginian garrison (DS 22.13.7; Plb. 10.1, cf. 11.4), whereupon Hiero withdrew.

So far Rome was not involved, but shortly afterwards the Mamertines also appealed to Rome. It is uncertain how this happened. Either not all the Mamertines were happy at the prospect of a permanent Carthaginian presence in their town, and preferred the Romans as a "kindred people" (10.2; Zon. 8.8), and perhaps a remoter one; or even, knowing that Carthage and Rome had recently been in alliance against Pyrrhus, they could see no harm in approaching both. But the potential for a clash between the two powers was now clearly there.

Polybios says (10.3 ff) that for a long time the Romans could not make up their minds whether to accede to the Mamertine appeal. The reasons he gives were that, on the one hand, to do so seemed inconsistent with their recent punishment of the Campanian troops who had been guilty of the same kind of conduct in Rhegium as the Mamertines had been in Messana. On the other hand, they were aware of the extent of Carthaginian influence in Africa, Spain and the islands between Spain and Italy, and were afraid that if they also came to control Sicily – which appeared likely, if Messana fell into their hands – "they would prove most troublesome and dangerous neighbours"; to abandon Messana might allow them "as it were to build a bridge for their crossing to Italy". In the end, Polybios concludes, the Senate was not prepared to accept the appeal, but the people were persuaded partly by the strategic arguments, but partly also by the prospect of plunder.

This account has come in for considerable criticism from modern commentators, but much of this need not concern us.[10] Whether or not there was one assembly or two, for example, whichever it or they were and whatever exactly was decided, it is clear that in the end the Mamertine appeal was in some sense accepted, and that it was decided to send them military assistance. It also seems clear that at latest when Appius Claudius Caudex, the consul appointed to the command, got to Sicily, he was empowered to make war on both Hiero and the Carthaginians if necessary, since, if we are to believe Polybios (11.11–12), after the failure of last-minute negotiations, he immediately proceeded to attack them both.

There is also no good reason to doubt that there was a debate in the Senate – perhaps more than one – and that in the end the matter was resolved by a vote of the People. But whether the arguments that Polybios implies were used were the main or only ones, we cannot be certain. It has, for example, been argued that the moral issue can hardly have arisen now, since the seizure of Messana by the Mamertines had occurred some 20 years before; and that in any case the parallel with Rhegium was not close, since there Rome had acted on behalf of an ally against mutinous troops of her own. But if there were senators opposed to the alliance, as there undoubtedly were, they could have made use of the moral argument, however dubious it may seem to us. In such a situation, men do not always, or even usually, use rational arguments. It is possible, indeed, that the argument was an on-going one, if it is true, as Valerius Maximus alleges (2.7.15), that the execution of the survivors of the Rhegium garrison had been opposed by the other consul of 264/3, M. Fulvius Flaccus, when tribune in 270. A possible echo of the arguments about the Mamertines may even be preserved in a fragment of the Augustan poet, Alfius, who, like the Mamertines, was an Oscan, and who claimed that they had only gone to help the people of Messana and had been invited to stay.[11]

A more serious criticism of Polybios is that he exaggerates Carthage's power, and, more particularly, the extent to which she was a danger to Rome. Here we must be careful not to confuse our perceptions of the situation with those of contemporaries. Thus arguments about whether or not Carthage was really a threat to Rome[12] are beside the point. What matters is whether the Romans thought they were, and here again there is no compelling reason to doubt Polybios, even if he does exaggerate. Nor need we doubt that it was Carthage Rome mainly feared, even if the immediate problem was rather with Hiero. The more the Romans came to regard the whole of peninsular Italy as in some sense "belonging" to them (cf. 6.6), the more they were bound to be suspicious of a power that had similar "possessions" in Sardinia, possibly Corsica, the Lipari islands and Sicily. In particular, they may well have feared the naval strength of the Carthaginians, especially if it is true that a Carthaginian fleet of 120–30 warships had appeared at Ostia and subsequently off Tarentum.

In particular, we should remember that Rome's control of southern Italy was very new: Tarentum had only finally surrendered in 272, and as recently as 267/6 there had been a war against the Sallentini and Messapii of the "heel" of Italy. Thus the appearance of a Carthaginian fleet off Tarentum would have appeared particularly ominous, and now there was a Carthaginian garrison in Messana, from where the Mamertines had already interfered at Rhegium (7.8). More generally, Rome might well have feared that in any subsequent quarrel with her new "allies", they might turn to Carthage for support. Alternatively, if Carthage were to seek to extend her trade monopoly to the detriment of those allies, the Romans might feel that they would have to protect their interests or again see them turn to Carthage.[13] In view of all this, there is no reason to believe that the foundation of the Latin colonies at Cosa and Paestum, or even the seizure of the Bruttian forests and the embassy to Ptolemy II, were aggressive in intent. On the contrary, if anything, they bear out Polybios' contention that the Romans were afraid of Carthage.

Similarly, Polybios' account of what went on in the Roman assembly is not as implausible as has sometimes been claimed. In the first place, when he says that the masses (οἱ πολλοί: 11.2) were persuaded by the arguments of the *stratêgoi*, although this word can mean "generals", this does not make sense in a Roman context. In such a context Polybios usually uses it to mean "consuls", and in this instance, since one of the consuls, M. Fulvius Flaccus himself, was probably away commanding against Volsinii in Etruria, over whom he celebrated a triumph on 1 November 264, the presiding magistrate will have been the other consul, Ap. Claudius Caudex. As we have seen, it was he who was eventually given the Sicilian command, and it makes sense to suppose that he was the principal advocate of accepting the Mamertine appeal.[14]

The arguments used to persuade the people, according to Polybios, included a reference to the common good – i.e., presumably, to the dangers of allowing Carthage to control Messana – and to the individual profits that might accrue from helping the Mamertines, almost certainly in the way of plunder. It has been held that these arguments are both inconsistent in themselves, and with Polybios' description of the Roman masses as "worn out by the previous wars", for if Carthage was so dangerous, would war with her be lucrative, and if the masses were worn out with previous wars, would they want another one?[15] But if there are inconsistencies here, they are not the kind that would have been immediately apparent to a mass audience. Ap. Claudius, if it was he, could well have stressed the danger to Rome's interests of a Carthaginian presence in Messana, and even the potential menace of her empire in general, without making too much of her military power. After all, even a weak enemy may be said to be menacing if he encroaches on one's interests. As for the war-weariness of the people, the consul could have said that, while he was aware of this, he thought the common interest outweighed it, and that, in any case, one more effort would produce rich pickings.

However, this is not to say that these were the only considerations that weighed with the Senate and People. In particular, the motive of greed, which Polybios attributes at least to the Roman masses (11.2), and which looms larger in some later sources (cf. Flo. 1.18.2–4; Dio 11, fr. 43.1–4; Zon. 8.8; Amp. 46.2), raises the question whether "imperialism", in the broadest sense, lay behind the Roman attitude. It has, for example, been suggested that there was what might be called a "Campanian connection", represented by families such as the Decii, Atilii and Otacilii, and led, at least until the time of the war with Pyrrhus, by Ap. Claudius Caecus, the consul of 307/6 and 296/5 and the man who built the *via Appia* from Rome to Capua. One late source claims that Ap. Claudius Caudex was his brother (*de vir. ill.* 37.1), and it has even been suggested that the name "Caudex" means "dinghy" and refers to this man's advocacy of the building of a fleet.

More broadly, such men are sometimes categorized as "popular" or "democratic" leaders, as opposed to the "conservative element" in the Senate supposedly represented by the Fabii, but now in temporary eclipse because their leader, Q. Fabius Maximus Gurges, the consul of 265/4, had died in office as a result of wounds received in the war against Volsinii. The "Campanian connection", it is held, saw in Sicily a fertile field for exploitation, in the first instance by those who aspired to command Roman armies there, but also by Roman and Italian businessmen who would follow in their wake.[16]

Some of this is far-fetched. Ap. Claudius Caudex, for example, was certainly not Ap. Claudius Caecus' brother, since he bore the same first name, and he was probably too young in any case. As for the name "Caudex", there is no reason to think that it meant "dinghy" – if anything it meant "Blockhead". Nor are the supposed family links at all certain, and even if there were family ties between Roman and Campanian nobles, it is by no means certain that such men would promote the interests of Campanian manufacturers and traders. If there were particular men in the Roman senate who wanted a war in Sicily, it is much more likely that they saw there a chance of winning the military glory that was their principal means of winning influence for themselves and their families.

One modern view, indeed, is that the driving forces behind Rome's expansion both in Italy and outside it were the desire of her leaders for "glory", and the simple acquisitiveness of both them and the people they led.[17] In the case of the First Punic War we have Polybios' word for it, as we have seen, that the "clear prospect of considerable profits" (ὠφελείας προδήλους καὶ μεγάλας: 11.2) was dangled before the People, when the "consuls" were seeking to persuade them to go to war, and the same word, "profits" (ὠφελείαι), crops up again in his later narrative. Thus the decision to drive the Carthaginians entirely out of Sicily was because the Romans were no longer satisfied with "the existing profits from the war itself" (20.1), and the marines who fought at Drepana in 249 were eager to volunteer because of the likelihood of easy "profit" (49.5). What form these "profits" might take is revealed in particular by Diodoros when he talks about the sale of prisoners as slaves – 25,000 from Agrigentum (23.9.1), for example, and 13,000 from Panormus, where another 14,000 people were forced to ransom themselves (23.18.5).

In any case, there is no need to posit special interest groups in the Senate to explain why the Mamertine plea was accepted. It had long been Roman practice to accept such pleas, and in the case of the Mamertines the onus was probably on those who thought the Republic should reject it.[18] This may explain why the moral objection was raised, however illogical it may seem to us. Allies were often said to have "sought the protection of the honour of the Roman People" (*in fidem populi Romani se dedere*), but would not that "honour" be sullied by accepting the plea of such people as the Mamertines? Similarly, the illogicality of Ap. Claudius' apparent combination of fear of Carthage with the prospect of rich pickings, may owe something to the objections of those in the Senate who had warned of the dangers of accepting this plea. The real doubts they had possibly concerned Rome's lack of preparedness for a war against a naval power, though, if so, it is perhaps surprising that it was not until 261/0 that a fleet was built.[19]

"Imperialism" may well lie behind the Roman decision to help the Mamertines, but this does not mean we should reject Polybios' view in its entirety as simply due to his having swallowed the propaganda of Roman apologists. The causes of any war are immensely complex, and lust for glory and simple greed do not preclude fear. We are simply not in a position to know even what was actually said in the Senate and before the People, let alone what was really going on in the minds of the speakers, but Polybios' version is all we have, and at least goes back to some extent to contemporary sources.

We should also remember that however aggressive we may feel Rome's behaviour to have been, she was not acting entirely in a vacuum. It may not always take two to make a war, but it certainly did here, since, after all, Hiero and the Carthaginians could have acceded to Rome's demands, however outrageous. We should therefore also ask ourselves what motivated both the king of Syracuse and Carthage to reject those demands, even at the risk of war, unless we are to understand that they simply did not grasp what was happening. Presumably Hiero, having won his victory at the

Longanus, was not prepared to let slip the opportunity of dealing with the Mamertines once and for all, and, possibly, regarded the prospect of a Roman presence in Sicily as if anything rather worse.

Carthage's position, however, was presumably rather different. She had no reason to fear the Mamertines – on the contrary, they had refused to side with Pyrrhus against her and had accepted a Carthaginian garrison. But once that garrison had been expelled (see below, p. 43), why risk war with Rome over a town remote from the Carthaginian sphere of influence in Sicily? Perhaps she simply could not see why she should accept any Roman demands, and again, possibly, like Hiero, was worried at the prospect of Roman interference in the island. But we should also remember that it was probably Carthage that took the first overt military action against Rome, when she tried, however feebly and, possibly, apologetically, to prevent Roman forces crossing the straits of Messina, and she also joined Hiero in laying siege to Messana, knowing that it was under the protection of Rome's *fides*, however specious Rome's attitude may have been.

All this should remind us that when embarking on a war, no one knows what is going to happen. As a character in Euripides' *Suppliant women* (481–3) remarks, "whenever war comes to the vote of the people, no one reckons on his own death – that misfortune he thinks will happen to someone else." In similar vein, in August, AD 1914, the Kaiser told departing troops that they would be home before the leaves had fallen, while, conversely, an officer of the Russian Imperial Guard wondered whether he should take his full-dress uniform with him, for the triumphant entry into Berlin, or leave it to be brought by the next courier.[20] In 264, one imagines, no one on either side anticipated a war lasting for 23 years, with colossal destruction and loss of life on both sides.

Because we can view any war as a whole, once it is over, we are in danger of distorting its "causes". Thus here we should be asking what led the Romans to interfere in Sicily, and Hiero and the Carthaginians to oppose them, not what the causes of "the war" were. The initial Roman moves and the Syracusan reaction led to further moves and further reactions, as we shall see. If we are to believe Polybios (20.1–2), it was not until after the fall of Agrigentum in 261 that the Romans even began to think in terms of driving the Carthaginians out of Sicily as a whole, and Hiero and the Carthaginians may initially have doubted whether the Romans could even get to Sicily. It is in the light of this kind of consideration that we should seek to understand what happened, not in the light of hindsight.

CHAPTER 4

Early rounds

Polybios follows his account of the Roman decision to help the Mamertines and of the appointment of Ap. Claudius to the command, by simply saying that the Mamertines managed to eject the Carthaginian officer already occupying their citadel "partly by frightening him, partly by tricking him", and then "were for inviting Appius in and entrusting the city to him" (11.4). The unfortunate Carthaginian officer was crucified by his fellow-countrymen "both for lack of sense and lack of courage" (11.5), and they then proceeded to station their fleet near Cape Pelorias (Capo di Faro) and to threaten Messana with their land forces based around a place called "Synes" (11.6). The whereabouts of this place is unknown, but it presumably lay near Messana, and perhaps on the coast between it and the cape to the north.

Since these details are also in Diodoros (23.1.3), though he calls the Carthaginian land base "Eunes", it looks as though Polybios got them from Philinos.[1] However, Diodoros makes the Carthaginian moves follow an agreement with Hiero and coincide with the latter's renewed advance on Messana (23.1.2), whereas Polybios implies that the Carthaginians moved first and that only then did Hiero conclude an alliance with them and join in the attack (11.7–8). More seriously, Diodoros says that the agreement between Hiero and the Carthaginians was "to make war on the Romans unless they left Sicily as quickly as possible", and this seems to imply that some Romans were already in Sicily.[2]

A possible explanation is provided by the fragments of Cassius Dio (11, fr. 43.5–10) as amplified by Zonaras (8.8–9).[3] Their story is that Ap.

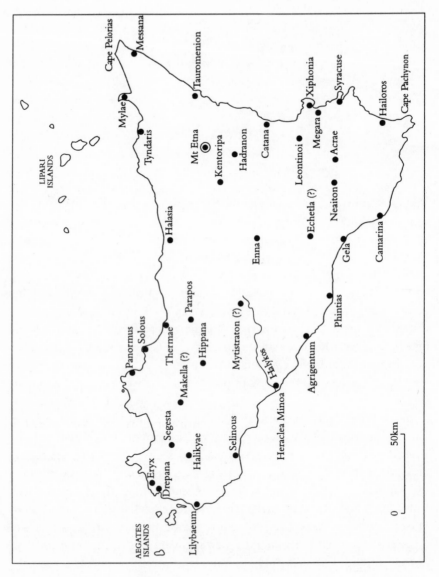

Figure 4.1 Sicily.

Claudius sent Gaius Claudius, a military tribune, ahead to Rhegium with a few ships, and that although at first he did not dare cross the straits in the face of a much superior Carthaginian fleet, he did manage to slip across twice in a small boat, on the second occasion receiving an enthusiastic response when he promised to help the Mamertines to secure their freedom. He then tried to force a passage, but having lost some of his ships, partly through enemy action, partly because of the current and a storm that blew up, was compelled to return to Rhegium.

The Carthaginian commander in Messana, Hanno, the story goes on, sent back the captured ships and was for restoring the prisoners in an attempt to persuade C. Claudius to end hostilities. When these moves were rejected, he threatened that he would not even allow the Romans to wash their hands in the sea. However, C. Claudius, wiser now to the effects of wind and current, managed to get across the straits without meeting any opposition. Calling an assembly of the Mamertines near the harbour, he persuaded them to send for Hanno, who had taken refuge in the citadel. At first the Carthaginian was reluctant to come, but eventually agreed to attend, evidently fearing that non-attendance would simply throw the Mamertines into Rome's arms. He was promptly imprisoned, but then apparently allowed to leave the city with his troops.

The main reasons for believing this story are that there is nothing intrinsically improbable in it, and that it is circumstantial – for example, the names of the enterprising Roman officer and of his less able Carthaginian opponent are given, the warships the former had at his disposal are called "triremes" (Dio 11.43.7; Zon. 8.9), which fits in with Rome's lack of a proper war-fleet at this time, and Carthaginian skill at sea is emphasized. It may also be thought likely that the Roman consul would have wanted to reconnoitre the crossing before trying it himself.

The main reason for disbelieving the story is that Polybios appears to know nothing of it, and this is always a serious objection, though it should not be elevated into a methodological principle. It is, after all, fairly obvious that Polybios' narrative is not even intended to be complete. The circumstantiality of the story may also be more apparent than real. For example, although it may seem plausible that the consul should have entrusted such a mission to a man who may have been a relative, the military tribune's name may be due to confusion with the consul, or even sheer invention. Similarly, if one were to invent the name of a Carthaginian officer, "Hanno" is among the half-dozen or so from which one would choose, and there is again the possibility of confusion with "Hanno, the son of Hannibal" whom Diodoros names as the commander of the Carthaginian land forces that later came to attack Messana (23.1.2). Finally, that the Romans would have preceded their invasion of Sicily with a reconnaissance, will appear "likely" only to those who habitually think of ancient warfare in modern terms.

Zonaras or his source also seems to have been guilty of some confusion. He says, for example, that it was after concluding an alliance with Hiero and reconciling him with the Mamertines "in order to prevent the Romans from crossing to the island" that the Carthaginians "began to guard the strait and the city under Hanno's command", and it has been suggested that the fighting between C. Claudius' ships and those of "Hanno" is really fighting between Ap. Claudius and the second Hanno. Similarly Diodoros (23.2.1) attributes the Carthaginian remark about not allowing the Romans to wash their hands in the sea to the negotiations with Ap. Claudius.

In the end certainty is not possible, and perhaps it does not really matter unless one is anxious either to pin "war-guilt" upon the Romans, or to exonerate them. It is probably best to follow Polybios, but if one is going to accept the story of C. Claudius' exploits, one should not then transfer some of the details to Ap. Claudius.[4] As for Diodoros' version of the agreement between the Carthaginians and Hiero, perhaps we should simply interpret it as an undertaking to expel the Romans from Sicily if they invaded the island, rather than to expel those who were already there.

On the timing of the agreement, however, Diodoros, presumably following Philinos, may well be right. It makes sense that neither of the parties to it would have been eager to move on Messana until there was some understanding between them. But when and where the agreement was made is unclear: all Diodoros implies (23.1.2) is that it was before Hiero's envoys met Hanno, son of Hannibal, the new Carthaginian general sent to Sicily, at Solous (see below). Possibly envoys had been exchanged between Syracuse and Carthage, or, alternatively, envoys from Hiero had met Hanno at Lilybaeum when he landed.[5] At all events, according to Diodoros (*ibid.*), having gathered his forces at Lilybaeum – presumably those already in the island, since he is not said to have brought any with him – Hanno advanced to Solous (now Solunto) on the coast east of Palermo, and if all this is true, it should be noted that Carthage reacted both swiftly and resolutely to the expulsion of the first Hanno from Messana. There is no hint that she was prepared to accept a *fait accompli*, and this should give pause to those who see Rome as solely responsible for the escalation of the conflict.

At Solous, Diodoros goes on, Hanno left his army, and himself made his way south to Agrigentum, presumably with a relatively small escort. Here he persuaded the people, who were already favourably disposed towards the Carthaginians, to form an alliance, and fortified the citadel. Though this may seem odd at first sight, it also makes sense. One of the best routes across Sicily from north to south leaves the coast just west of Solous and goes straight to Agrigentum. It is some 80 miles long by the modern road and Hanno could have made the journey there and back in less than ten days. Not only does Agrigentum command the southern end of this route, but it also lies athwart the one along the south coast of Sicily, and is at the southern end of another leading north-eastwards across the centre of the island towards Enna and then on to Catana (Catania) and the east coast. Again, if Hanno's journey to Agrigentum is historical, it shows that the Carthaginians were already thinking in wider terms than the mere recovery of Messana. It was on his return to Solous, according to Diodoros, that he was met by envoys from Hiero come to confer about their mutual interests.

We can only speculate about the motives of the two parties, and any view depends to some extent on whether we believe there were already Romans in Messana, or whether both the Carthaginians and Hiero knew they were likely to be coming. However, even if the story of C. Claudius' exploits is untrue, the Carthaginians will presumably have known that the expulsion of their force from Messana had resulted from a Mamertine plea to Rome, and they could have informed Hiero. There is thus no reason to doubt that the agreement included an undertaking to expel the Romans from Sicily, even if there were none there as yet. But Polybios merely says (11.7) that Hiero saw a chance to expel from Sicily the "barbarians" who were occupying Messana, with no mention of the Romans, and this may be right. Alternatively, if he knew the Romans were already in Messana or about to try to occupy the place, he may have felt that this would be even worse than allowing the Mamertines to do so; he may even have been annoyed at Rome's attitude after he had helped them to recover Rhegium.

But what did he and the Carthaginians propose to do with Messana? Modern commentators tend to assume that it was in the interests of both parties to suppress the Mamertines, though they had sided with Carthage against Pyrrhus and Syracuse, and that neither wanted the Romans in Sicily. But was Messana itself to be destroyed, and, if not, which party was to occupy it?[6] Presumably, if the Carthaginians had thought it worth their while to do so once, they would have thought it worth their while to do

47

so again, but would Hiero have been prepared to see a permanent Carthaginian presence in Messana in view of the age-old hostility between Carthage and Syracuse? Or did he think that the Carthaginians would be more congenial neighbours? Perhaps the future of Messana was glossed over in the discussions, or perhaps the two parties agreed to suppress the Mamertines and to restore the city to its original inhabitants.

The immediate task, in any case, was to secure control of the place, and Polybios and Diodoros are agreed on the Carthaginian and Syracusan positions once they had decided to co-operate. The Carthaginian fleet was off Cape Pelorias, their army perhaps between there and Messana at Synes (Eunes in Diodoros), Hiero's army at the "Chalkidian mountain", perhaps south of Messana (11.6–7; DS 23.1.3). Presumably when Ap. Claudius Caudex reached Rhegium, he was soon apprised of the position, whether or not the story of C. Claudius' exploits is true. To try to force a passage across the straits with his army was obviously extremely risky, even if the nature of ancient warships precluded a continuous blockade, so Diodoros (23.1.4) is again probably right that he first tried to get the Carthaginians and Hiero to lift the siege, by sending an embassy to both, though Polybios (11.11) says that this was after he had succeeded in getting to Messana.[7]

We do not know precisely what the Roman envoys said, but if Diodoros is right, Hiero's reply referred to the Romans' "harping on the word *fides* ('honour': θρυλοῦντες τὸ τῆς πίστεως ὄνομα: 23.1.4)", which would suggest that they made it clear that they regarded the Mamertines as under the protection of their "honour", and consequently they presumably demanded that both the Carthaginians and Hiero withdraw their forces. An unfortunately damaged passage in the fragment from Diodoros suggests that the message to Hiero, at any rate, may have been conciliatory. But Hiero's reply was intransigent, arguing that the attack on the Mamertines was justified by their past behaviour, and presumably the Carthaginian reply, which is not given in what survives of Diodoros, was equally firm.

Ap. Claudius now had to cross the straits of Messina, and it may seem surprising that he managed to do so with such apparent ease. According to Polybios (20.14), he had to borrow *pentekonters* (ships with 25 oars a side) and triremes from Tarentum, Locri, Elea and Naples, and it was on these that he took his men across. However, he presumably had an army of two legions, together with the usual contingents of allied infantry, and both citizen and allied cavalry, in all perhaps some 20,000 men, and it seems unlikely that he could have transported such a force on the warships alone.[8] Nor was the passage completely uncontested, for although Polybios first just states that he crossed "at night" (11.9), he later (20.15) says that the Carthaginians put out to attack him as he was crossing, and describes how one of their ships ran aground and so fell into Roman hands: allegedly it was on this model that the Roman navy was constructed four years later (see below, pp. 63).

Diodoros (23.2.1) also mentions a sea-battle between the "Phoenicians" and the Romans, and says that it was after it that the Carthaginians sent envoys to the Romans warning them that if they did not maintain friendly relations they would not dare even to wash their hands in the sea. This has been used to back up the theory that the fighting that Cassius Dio and Zonaras record between the Carthaginians and Gaius Claudius properly belongs to a first, abortive attempt to cross by Appius Claudius, and that it was after the Carthaginians had forced the latter to return to Rhegium that they handed back some of the captured ships, and tried to bring about a peaceful settlement.[9] However, it is doubtful whether we should reject or even supplement Polybios' account by reference to a much later and admittedly garbled tale, though Polybios' story of how the Carthaginian warship ran aground suggests that the Carthaginians were pursuing the Romans back to Rhegium. On the other hand, the ship might have run aground near Messana and thus fallen into Roman hands.

On the whole, it is better to accept Polybios' version that Ap. Claudius simply made a single, successful crossing at night, perhaps making use of the north-flowing current known nowadays as the "Montante".[10] Frontinus (*Strat.* 1.4.11) says that he put about a rumour implying that he could not carry on a war that had been begun without the authority of the Roman people, and pretended to sail back to Italy, whereupon the Carthaginians dispersed and he was able to land safely in Sicily. This is not totally impossible, but looks far-fetched. Zonaras (8.9), on the other hand, has him somehow make use of "the many Carthaginians often about the harbour on pretext of trading" to deceive the enemy, and this does suggest the spreading of false rumours. In any case, the fact of the crossing again demonstrates the ineffectiveness of ancient warships when it came to blockades.

Unfortunately there are also marked differences in the sources about what happened next.[11] After taking Ap. Claudius across the straits, and probably mistakenly having him then try to negotiate, Polybios says that he first won a decisive victory over Hiero, which caused the king to withdraw to Syracuse (11.10–15), and then also defeated the Carthaginians, causing them to disperse among neighbouring towns. Finally, he advanced triumphantly on Syracuse and laid siege to the city (12.1–4). Later, however,

Polybios (15.1–5) tells us that Philinos had a different story. According to him, Ap. Claudius was defeated by both Hiero and the Carthaginians, and it was only after they had both then withdrawn that he was able to lay siege to Syracuse and a place called Echetla (perhaps Grammichele[12]), between Carthaginian and Syracusan territory (15.10).

Diodoros (23.3) has yet another story – that after the consul had crossed to Messana, Hiero fled to Syracuse, thinking that the Carthaginians had treacherously allowed the crossing, but that the latter were defeated. The consul then laid siege to "Aigesta" (presumably Echetla), but after suffering heavy losses, withdrew to Messana. Cassius Dio (11.11–15) and Zonaras (8.9) agree with Polybios that Ap. Claudius defeated both Hiero and the Carthaginians, adding details, and that he was able to lay siege to Syracuse, though without success, before he withdrew to Rhegium, leaving a garrison in Messana. Orosius (4.7.2–3) also has the Romans defeat both Hiero and the Carthaginians, while Livy apparently recorded a number of defeats of Hiero before the king sued for peace (*Per.* 16).

The most plausible way to solve this problem is to assume that both sides exaggerated what were at best minor successes. On the one hand, Polybios has a point when he argues (15.6 ff) that the retreat of Hiero and the Carthaginians is difficult to explain if they had both won the outright victories Philinos claimed for them. On the other hand, it is equally difficult to explain why Ap. Claudius was not granted a triumph, if he had won the successes Polybios attributes to him. Admittedly, Silius Italicus (6.660–62) and Eutropius (2.18.3) do accord him a triumph, but it is not listed in the triumphal records and is almost certainly unhistorical. It is also significant that it was not Ap. Claudius, but one of the consuls of 263/2,. M'Valerius Maximus, who took the title "Messala", traditionally in honour of a victory involving Messana.

Perhaps, then, Ap. Claudius did attack Hiero first, as Polybios says, but, after an indecisive engagement, which both sides claimed as a victory, fell back into Messana. Here Zonaras may well be right in claiming (8.9) that it was the Roman cavalry that was defeated, but that their heavy infantry prevailed. Syracusan cavalry had been famous since the fifth century, but probably neither their hoplite infantry nor their mercenaries were a match for the legionaries, unless exceptionally well led. As a result, Hiero, realizing what he was up against, and possibly, as Diodoros says, distrustful of the ease with which the Romans had managed to cross the straits in the face of what should have been overwhelming Carthaginian naval power, withdrew to Syracuse.

It would then only have been natural for Ap. Claudius to turn his attention to the Carthaginians, and here again Zonaras may preserve the truth. He says (*ibid.*) that the Carthaginian position was on a kind of peninsula, with the sea on one side and marshes on the other, and that they had fortified the narrow neck of the peninsula. Ap. Claudius tried to force his way through, but had to retreat, and thereupon the Carthaginians foolishly sallied out, only to be driven back in their turn with heavy losses (cf. Dio 11.12). Zonaras adds that the Carthaginians subsequently did not venture to leave their camp while Claudius was in Messana, and perhaps we should assume that their forces were soon evacuated, possibly after they had learnt of Hiero's withdrawal, and dispersed among various towns, as Polybios says.

But what are we to make of the tradition that Ap. Claudius then advanced south and laid siege to Echetla and Syracuse? The simplest solution is to reject it out of hand as a confusion with the later campaign of Valerius Messala, and it must be admitted that an advance of some 100 miles to the south seems inconsistent with fighting around Messana that did not even warrant a triumph.[13] But unless Polybios completely misread Philinos, which is unlikely, Ap. Claudius' campaign to the south was also recorded by him, and perhaps the withdrawal of the enemy forces was enough to tempt the Romans to advance. Possibly the truth of the matter is that he did make some sort of tentative approach to Syracuse, as is suggested by Zonaras (8.9), but withdrew because he found himself unable to make much headway, and was facing problems with both supplies and the health of his army. Possibly he also suffered losses in an unsuccessful attack on Echetla.

Perhaps, then, Ap. Claudius did not deserve a triumph, though they were ten a penny in this war, for whatever his achievements, they were clearly not decisive. If he did manage to defeat both Hiero and the Carthaginians before Messana, he made skilful use of his position between the two to deal with them piecemeal, but even if he was not really responsible for their withdrawal, his period of command was not wholly unproductive. Above all, he deserved credit for getting his army across the straits of Messina, and for establishing a firm beach-head in the town. Without this the campaign in Sicily could never have got off the ground.

The following year (263/2) thus saw Rome vigorously on the offensive, with both consuls and their armies sent to Sicily, in all some 40,000 men (16.1–2). Indeed, since Ap. Claudius did not triumph, it is possible that most of his army was also left in Sicily – certainly a substantial garrison would have been left in Messana. Thus, allowing for losses, the new consuls may eventually have had nearer 50,000 men. A fragment of Naevius (fr. 3

Buechner) has been held to suggest that originally only one of the consuls, Valerius Maximus, crossed to Sicily, and certainly he receives all the attention. It was he who adopted the name "Messala", as we have seen, presumably in honour of some exploit involving Messana, he who triumphed and he who put up on the wall of the *Curia Hostilia* a painting depicting his victories over both Hiero and the Carthaginians (Pliny, NH 35.22). Our main sources are, however, unanimous that both he and his colleague, Manius Otacilius Crassus, went to Sicily (16.1; DS 23.4.1; Zon. 8.9).

Possibly the latter arrived too late to play any significant part in the campaign that culminated in the peace with Hiero, and as a *novus homo* he may in any case have been overshadowed by his patrician colleague. But the circumstances that led to Valerius' taking the *cognomen* "Messala" are difficult to determine. The simplest explanation is that it was he, and not Ap. Claudius, who relieved the siege of Messana, but it is hard to believe that all our sources, and Polybios in particular, got it all so wrong.[14] Possibly the title was bestowed upon him by the grateful Mamertines in recognition of the major part he played in compelling Hiero to make peace, and thus in ensuring the survival of their rule in Messana. The picture may signify nothing more than his own pride in his achievements, but the fact that he alone triumphed surely indicates that the public perception was that it was he who was responsible for the victory.

Of the campaign up to the peace with Hiero, Polybios (16.3) merely says that on the arrival of the consuls, most of the cities revolted from both the Carthaginians and the Syracusans, and joined the Romans. Diodoros (23.4) gives more details. First Hadranon (Adrano), south-west of Mt Etna, was taken by storm. Then, when Kentoripa (Centuripe) was under siege, envoys arrived from Halaisa (near the north coast, just east of Tusa), and these were followed by a large number of embassies from other cities, including Catana (Pliny, NH 7.214; Eutr. 2.19.1), and probably Enna and Camarina (DS 23.9.4). According to Diodoros (23.4), the total number was 67, but this may be an anachronism based on the later number of communities under Roman rule in Sicily;[15] Eutropius (*ibid.*) says 50. Having cleared the ground, the Romans then advanced on Syracuse.

All this was enough to convince Hiero that the Romans were far more likely to win than the Carthaginians (16.4), and he was possibly aware of a growing reluctance on the part of his people to continue fighting (DS 23.4.1). The upshot was that he sent several messages to the consuls with proposals for peace and an alliance. They, in their turn, were still worried about the supply situation, since the Carthaginians continued to command the sea. The first legions to cross had suffered from lack of supplies, and it was mainly for this reason that they were prepared to grant reasonable terms (16.4–7). The wisdom of their decision was confirmed if it is true that a Carthaginian squadron put in at Xiphonia (now Augusta), just north of Syracuse, to help Hiero, even though it sailed away when it realized what had happened (DS 23.4.1).

According to Polybios (16.9), Hiero agreed to hand over all his prisoners – presumably mainly those taken at Messana – without ransom, and to pay an indemnity of 100 talents – Eutropius (2.19.2) and Orosius (4.7.3) say 200. Diodoros (23.4.1) says that the peace was for 15 years, and although this was a Greek, rather than a Roman concept, Zonaras does claim (8.16) that a perpetual peace was signed only in 248, when the Romans "cancelled what they received from the king each year". This may mean that the indemnity was to be paid in instalments, in which case Diodoros' statement that it was only 25 talents may mean that this was the first instalment. But from Hiero's point of view the main thing was that he was to continue to rule an independent Syracuse, and an extensive area of eastern Sicily. According to Diodoros (23.4.1), this included Akrai (Acreide), Leontinoi (Lentini), Megara, Hailoros (Helorus) at the mouth of the river of the same name (now the Tellaro), Neaiton (Noto Antica) and Tauromenion (Taormina).[16]

Diodoros also records further military operations, probably towards the end of 263. He says first (23.4.2) that the Romans were repulsed from "the village of Hadranon" (Ἀδράνων κώμη) and from Makella, and then (23.5) that Segesta and Halikyae came over to them, but that they failed to take Ilaros, Tyrittos and Askelos. Finally, when Tyndaris also tried to come over, the Carthaginians took its leading men hostage and impounded its grain, wine and other stocks of food.

But all this is puzzling. "Hadranon" was evidently the name of the "city" (πόλις) said by the same author to have been captured by the Romans at the beginning of the campaign of 263 (23.4.1), and although he appears to distinguish between the earlier "city" and the later "village", one suspects some carelessness on the excerptor's part. Makella, on the other hand, if it is correctly identified with Macellaro, near Camporeale in western Sicily,[17] seems much too far west for the Romans to have been operating there at this early date – it is less than 40 miles from Lilybaeum – and it seems even more unlikely that Segesta and Halikyai, even further to the west, can have joined the Romans now.[18] Zonaras, however, also records the defection of Segesta at this point (8.9). The whereabouts of Ilaros, Tyrittos and Askelos are unknown, but Tyndaris might well have tried to defect – it is on the north coast less than 40 miles from Messana – and may have been prevented by the Carthaginian navy, if the latter was still based on Lipari some 25 miles to the north.

But whether or not the Romans won over further Sicilian communities at this time, the peace with Hiero completely changed the complexion of the war. Not only did the Romans no longer have to fight two enemies at once, but they now had a secure base in eastern Sicily, and did not need to worry any longer about the supply situation. Polybios, indeed, says (17.1–2) that when the peace was ratified by the Roman people, it was decided to make do with a force of only two legions for the future. Presumably we are to understand that those of the consuls of 263/2 were withdrawn when the consuls themselves left towards the end of 263 (17.6). Those of Valerius Messala, in particular, would have taken part in the triumph he celebrated on 17 March 262, by the Roman calendar, "over the Carthaginians and Hiero, King of the Syracusans", according to the triumphal records.

An anonymous Greek source (*Ined. Vat.* 4) claims that Valerius also already saw the necessity of making an effort at sea, "on the grounds that since they were fighting for an island and in an island, final victory was not possible unless they commanded the sea". This has been connected with a fragment of the first-century-BC historian, L. Piso, quoted by the elder Pliny (*NH* 16.192), to the effect that the Romans built 220 ships in 45 days for the war against Hiero. But as they stand, the two passages actually contradict each other, since the anonymous Greek implies that it was after he had made peace with Hiero that Valerius stated his opinion, whereas the Piso fragment alleges that the fleet was built for the war with Hiero. In any case, the latter looks like confusion with one or other of the later shipbuilding programmes, for example the 220 ships built in three months in 255/4 (38.5–6), or the 100 quinqueremes and 20 triremes of 260 (20.9). In any case, it is impossible to believe that the Romans possessed a powerful fleet in 262 and 261, since if they had done so, the war would surely have been fought in a different way, in those years. But Valerius may have been one of those who supported the idea of creating a navy in 260,[19] and if he did give voice to the opinion attributed to him by the anonymous source, he can lay claim to being one of the few ancient statesmen, let alone Romans, who really understood seapower.

If it is true that the Romans originally intended only to send two legions to Sicily in 262, it is possible that they would not have been too unwilling to negotiate a peace with Carthage at this juncture. After all, they had gone to war to protect the Mamertines, particularly from Hiero, and that had now been achieved. Admittedly, war had also been declared on the Carthaginians in 264, but, apart from what may have happened in the straits of Messina and possibly outside the city, there had been no serious fighting between them, and it is possible, as we have seen, that the Carthaginians had even made some conciliatory gestures at the outset. But it was they who now decided to increase their forces in Sicily, and it may have been this that induced the Romans, in turn, to change their minds and to send both consuls of 262/1 to the island (17.6).

The Carthaginians, Polybios says (17.4–6), hired Ligurian, Celtic and, above all, Spanish mercenaries, and sent them to the island, where Agrigentum now became their principal base. This looks as though they were reverting to their age-old strategy of inducing their enemies in Sicily to attack them in their half of the island. In the past, however much they had lost in the early stages of a campaign, they had always managed to cling on to their bases in western Sicily, and sooner or later to recover much of the ground.[20]

At the same time, however, they may have for once made use of the strategic flexibility their command of the sea gave them by sending forces to Sardinia. This is stated by Zonaras (8.10), but although he says that they sent "most of their army" (τὸ πλεῖον τοῦ στρατοῦ), this cannot be right – "most of their army" was clearly in Sicily. Possibly what Cassius Dio, Zonaras' source, actually wrote was "most of their naval force" (τὸ πλεῖον τοῦ ναυτικοῦ στρατοῦ). It is also not clear what Zonaras thought that the purpose of sending forces to Sardinia was. He says that it was "in order to attack Rome from there and thus either completely force them from Sicily or make them weaker when they crossed over", This seems to imply that the intention was to use the island as a base for attacks on Italy, in the hope of either diverting the Romans from Sicily or making them retain some of their forces to defend Italy. This might certainly have been an effective strategy, but there is no evidence that there were any attacks on Italy at this juncture, and if there were, they evidently did not have the desired effect.[21]

Far from being deterred, the new consuls for 262/1, Lucius Postumius Megellus and Quintus Mamilius Vitulus, also concentrated their forces on Agrigentum, camping about a mile from the city (17.8). It lay two and a half miles from the coast on a plateau surrounded by steep slopes on all sides except the west, and dominated by a higher ridge on the north, the western end of which, projecting beyond the west city wall, formed the

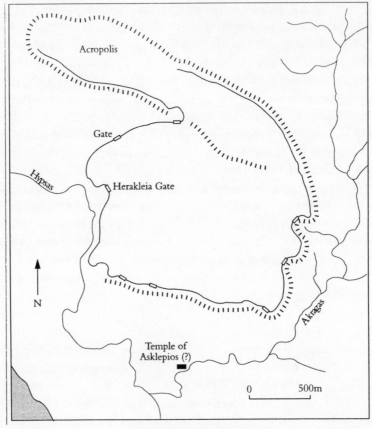

Figure 4.2 Agrigentum.

acropolis. The whole area including the acropolis comprised some 900 acres and was surrounded by walls pierced by nine gates. Further protection was provided by the river Hypsas (Drago) to the west and the Akragas (San Biagio) to the east, which met south of the city before flowing into the sea. As we have seen, the city commanded not only the main route along the south coast of the island, but also important routes leading northwards to Panormus and north-eastwards to Enna and on to Catana. It was thus a site of immense strategic importance and apart from Panormus – which was further from Carthage – the best jumping-off place for attacks on eastern Sicily.

On their arrival, the Roman troops were at first overconfident. Since it was harvest-time (i.e. June), and they knew that the siege was liable to be protracted, they scattered to forage, and were promptly attacked by the defenders. However, they had taken the precaution of posting a covering-force and this, although outnumbered, was able to put the enemy to flight as they were about to attack the Roman camp, and drive them back to the city with heavy losses (17.9–13). Polybios here notes that it was Roman discipline that saved the day, since the penalty for deserting such a cover-ing-force was death.

This skirmish induced more caution in both sides. The consuls divided their forces, the one taking up a position near the temple of Asklepios, pos-sibly to the south between the rivers, possibly to the east, the other to the west of the city covering the road to Heraclea Minoa. They linked the main camps with a double ditch, the outer one to guard against relieving forces, the inner against sorties, and placed guard-posts in the space between at suitable strongpoints (18.1–4). Supplies were brought in to a place Polybios calls "Herbesos", and which he says was "not far" from the Roman siege-works (18.5). It therefore cannot be the town of that name near Syracuse, but its whereabouts is uncertain.

For some five months (i.e. until November 262) there was stalemate, but then supplies began to run out in the beleaguered city, where, Polybios says (18.7), at least 50,000 people were now congregated. The Carthaginian commander – named as "Hannibal" by Polybios (ibid.), and as "Hannibal, son of Gisgo" by Zonaras (8.10) – was probably the man who had been responsible for despatching troops into Messana. He had been sending a stream of messages to Carthage, presumably by sea, appealing for help, and the Carthaginians responded by shipping the forces they had been collect-ing in Africa across to Sicily, Diodoros implies to Lilybaeum (23.8.1). There they were taken under command by Hanno, whom Polybios describes as "the other general" (i.e. apart from Hannibal: 18.8). He was probably the "Hanno, son of Hannibal" who had been sent to Sicily in 264, according to Diodoros (23.1.2–3), and after fortifying Agrigentum had joined Hiero in attacking Messana, though here (23.8.1) Diodoros calls him "Hanno the Elder".

Polybios gives no details of his army except that it included "about" 50 elephants, Numidian cavalry and mercenaries (19.2, 4 & 9).[22] Diodoros, here on the explicit authority of Philinos, says there were 50,000 infantry, 6,000 cavalry and 60 elephants (23.8.1), Orosius 30,000 infantry, 1,500 cavalry and 30 elephants (4.7.5). One could reconcile these figures by assuming that Diodoros included troops already in Sicily and that Orosius was talking about only the reinforcements brought from Africa. But the fragment of Diodoros actually says that the forces listed were those brought

57

over from Africa by Hanno, in which case Orosius' figures are probably just wrong.

Hanno advanced from Lilybaeum to Heraclea Minoa, at the mouth of the Halykos (Platani), about 25 miles west of Agrigentum, where he concentrated his forces, and was immediately able to achieve a considerable success by capturing the Roman supply base at Herbesos (18.9) – Diodoros implies that it was betrayed to him, which is quite likely. This meant that the Romans, too, began to suffer from severe shortages, and Polybios says they would have been forced to raise the siege but for the efforts of Hiero to keep them supplied (18.10–11).

Hanno, learning that the Romans were suffering from disease and privation, now moved on Agrigentum from Heraclea Minoa, ordering his Numidian cavalry to go ahead and try to provoke the enemy cavalry into leaving camp, whereupon it was to retire upon the main body. The ruse, which so looks forward to Hannibal's later use of his Numidians, here, too, worked to perfection. The Roman cavalry, issuing from one of the camps, pursued the Numidians back as far as Hanno's main body, whereupon the Numidians wheeled and, encircling the Romans, attacked in turn, then pursued the remnants back to their camp (19.1–4). After this success, Hanno took up a position on a hill called "Toros", just over a mile from the enemy, and desultory skirmishing continued for a further two months (i.e. into January 261, in our terms). This means that the siege lasted seven months in all, according to Polybios, though Diodoros (23.9.1) says six.

Eventually, however, in response to continuous appeals from the commander of the Carthaginian garrison in the city, by fire-signals and messengers, Hanno decided to risk a pitched battle, a challenge that the Romans accepted because of their own difficulties (19.7). Details of the battle are meagre, and the sources contradictory. Polybios implies that Hanno placed his mercenaries in front, with his elephants, oddly, between them and the rest of his army. Nothing is said about the cavalry, but it was presumably on the wings, as was usual, and in view of what had recently happened, one might have expected it to play a significant part. The odd position of the elephants may have been due to inexperience in their use, or, possibly, the idea was to use them for a decisive blow once the Romans had been disorganized by the fighting with the mercenaries.[23]

However, according to Polybios (19.9–11), after a long struggle the Romans drove the mercenaries back on the elephants and the troops to their rear, throwing the whole Punic army into confusion. A complete rout ensued, in which most of the Carthaginians were killed, though some managed to escape to Heraclea, and the Romans captured most of the elephants and all the baggage. Diodoros' account of the battle is lost, but he gives the Carthaginian losses in the two battles as only 3,000 infantry and 200 cavalry killed, and 4,000 men taken prisoner, and although he confirms the loss of most of the elephants, he says eight were killed and 33 disabled (23.8.1). He also says that the Romans lost 30,000 foot and 540 cavalry throughout the siege (23.9.1), and although both figures are dubious for different reasons – 30,000 surely too many, 540 too precise – the fact that no triumph was awarded for the victory and the subsequent capture of Agrigentum, despite what Eutropius claims (2.19.3), may well indicate that Polybios has exaggerated the Roman success.

Zonaras has a rather different version of the battle. According to him (8.10), after constant skirmishes, Hanno decided to fight, assuming that the Carthaginian garrison of Agrigentum would fall on the enemy rear, and when the consuls, divining his plan, remained inactive, he scornfully advanced on their lines. Somehow the Romans managed to place some men in ambush in the Carthaginian rear, and when Hanno finally attacked towards evening, he was taken in front and rear. The Carthaginian garrison did meanwhile sally, but was beaten off by the men left to guard the Roman camps.

This version is in some ways similar to an anecdote about the consul Postumius Megellus in Frontinus (*Strat.* 2.1.4). The Carthaginians, his story goes, made a habit of constantly deploying their forces before the Roman entrenchments, while the Romans responded by holding them in play with only part of their forces. Then, when the consul realized that the enemy was becoming careless because the same thing kept happening, he ordered the rest of his army quietly to prepare for battle within his encampment, while the troops as usual fighting outside it were to keep the enemy engaged longer than on previous occasions. After noon the Carthaginians, tired and hungry, began to retreat, whereupon Postumius set upon them with his fresh troops and routed them.[24]

It is impossible to say which version is correct, but Polybios' is to be preferred on *a priori* grounds, and the Roman attack from Hanno's rear in Zonaras seems improbable. On the other hand, it does seem likely that at least some attempt would have been made to concert operations between the Carthaginian relieving army and the beleaguered garrison. Frontinus' story is of a common type and may or may not be true.

In any case, whatever precisely happened, there is no doubt that the Romans won, at least to the extent of forcing Hanno to retreat. The

Carthaginian garrison commander also now decided to make use of Roman euphoria and fatigue to break out of the city. Filling the Roman trenches with baskets packed with straw, he was able to escape with his mercenaries the night following the battle (19.12–3), though Zonaras (8.10) improbably says that he alone escaped, some of his men being killed by the Romans, many by the people of Agrigentum. At daybreak the Romans realized what had happened, but after inflicting some slight losses on his rear-guard, turned back to seize the city. Encountering no opposition, they comprehensively sacked the place, selling its inhabitants – 25,000 according to Diodoros (23.9.1) – into slavery (19.14–15).

According to Polybios (20.1–2), it was the capture of Agrigentum that inspired the Senate to start thinking in terms of driving the Carthaginians entirely from Sicily, not just of ensuring the security of the Mamertines, and this in turn led to the decision to build a fleet. His view has been questioned on the grounds that the possibility of building a fleet is already implied in the diplomatic exchanges of 264 (DS 23.2.1), and that support for the policy is ascribed to Valerius Messala (*Ined. Vat.* 4).[25] This is not very good evidence, but it is possible that Polybios has exaggerated the offensive reasons for building the fleet, and so the significance of Agrigentum, at the expense of the defensive ones. There was certainly increased Carthaginian naval activity in 261, if not 262 (see Chapter 5), and it may have been ultimately this that led to the Roman decision to try to match Carthage at sea.

Nevertheless, and despite the failure of Postumius Megellus and Mamilius Vitulus to obtain a triumph, the capture of Agrigentum was important.[26] It meant that Rome's hold on eastern Sicily was finally secure, and perhaps did give her the confidence to begin thinking in terms of a wider victory.

CHAPTER 5

The Romans wash
their hands in the sea

One result of Polybios' close linking of the fall of Agrigentum to the Roman decision to build a fleet is that he almost entirely neglects the military operations of 261. All he says (20.3–6) is that although the new consuls, Lucius Valerius Flaccus and Titus Otacilius Crassus, appeared to be managing things in Sicily as well as possible, the war remained evenly balanced while the Carthaginians continued to enjoy uncontested control of the sea. This was because although many inland cities joined the Romans, even more coastal ones defected because of fear of the Carthaginian fleet.

Modern commentators have criticized the Romans for their treatment of Agrigentum, arguing that a more humane attitude to the Greek civilian population after the escape of the Carthaginian garrison would have paid dividends, whereas disgust at Rome's barbarous behaviour simply drove the Sicilians into the arms of the Carthaginians.[1] This may be true, but it is not what Polybios implies. On the contrary, in his view, what decided communities to adhere to Carthage or to Rome had nothing to do with the behaviour of either side, but was simply a matter of expediency, and this is just as likely to be true.

Some details of what happened in 261 may be culled from other sources, but the chronology is uncertain. Perhaps soon after the fall of Agrigentum, i.e. early in 261, belongs an episode related by Frontinus (*Strat.* 3.16.3), if the Carthaginian general involved was really Hanno, as seems to be confirmed by Diodoros (23.8.3), though Zonaras makes the general involved Hanno's replacement, Hamilcar (8.10). According to Frontinus' story, Hanno learned that about 4,000 of his Celtic mercenaries were plotting to desert to the Romans because they had not been paid for several months.

Not daring to punish them for fear of outright mutiny, he promised to make good the deficit, and undertook to allow them to go out foraging. But he then informed the consul, Otacilius, through a trusted agent, with the result that the Celts were ambushed and massacred. To about the same time may also belong another anecdote related by Frontinus (*Strat.* 4.1.19), in which a consul called "Otacilius" orders soldiers who had been "sent under the yoke" by a Hannibal and then released, to bivouac outside the camp.

Even if Hanno did enjoy some success, however, he was soon recalled to Carthage, where he was lucky to escape with loss of rights and a fine, for his failure to relieve Agrigentum (DS 23.9.2). He was replaced, probably in the first half of 261, by a "Hamilcar" (DS *ibid.*), who despite Cicero (*de off.* 3.99) and Zonaras (8.10) is not to be identified with Hamilcar Barca, the father of Hannibal. This Hamilcar is the one mentioned by Polybios (24.3) as "the Carthaginian general in command of the land forces" after the battle of Mylae, and the way in which the historian later introduces Hamilcar Barca as "Hamilcar, the one called Barca" (56.1) makes it quite clear that he is a different man.[2]

Immediately after mentioning the earlier Hamilcar's appointment, Diodoros records (23.9.3) an abortive Roman assault on Mytistraton (for its location see below, p. 75). This may have started in 261, though if the siege was really prolonged for seven months, as Diodoros says, it presumably continued into 260. In any case, Hamilcar's victory at Thermae, which comes next in Diodoros (23.9.3), certainly belongs to 260, or even early 259 (1.24.4: see below, pp. 72–3), and the other episodes related by Diodoros in this passage also clearly belong later.

Zonaras may, however, be right that Hamilcar's first action after his appointment was to order Hannibal, the admiral in charge of the fleet, and probably to be identified with the defender of Agrigentum, to raid Italy (8.10, cf. Oros. 4.7.7). The base for this operation may have been Sardinia (see above, p. 55), and there were possibly several such attacks, as is implied by Polybios (20.7), though Hamilcar's own raid on Italy, mentioned later by Zonaras (8.10) came after the departure of the consuls of 261, and so, presumably, in 260, if Zonaras is to be trusted. It was probably these Carthaginian raids on Italy and the defection of coastal towns in Sicily, at least as much as any growing "imperialism", that now led the Romans to make one of the most momentous decisions in their history – to create a navy.

Polybios probably exaggerates when he claims (20.9) that this was the first time Rome had built ships of her own. Even if we discount the

warship (*navis longa*: Livy 5.28.2) that allegedly carried envoys with offer-
ings to Delphi in 394, and Polybios' view that the first treaty between
Rome and Carthage referred to warships (3.23.2), for which there is no
warrant in his own version of the treaty,[3] it is unlikely that the Republic
was entirely without warships. In any case, in 311, a "Naval Board of Two
for the purpose of fitting out and repairing the fleet" (*duoviri navales classis
ornandae reficiendaeque causa*: Livy 9.30.4) was created, and it appears from
later passages in Livy (40.18.7; 41.1.2–3) that each of the *duoviri* commanded a squadron of ten ships.

However, the only known purely naval operation in which these vessels
participated ended in disaster. In 282, one of the squadrons lost five ships
rammed and disabled, and one captured, to the Tarentines (App., *Sam.* 7.1;
cf. Livy, *Per.* 12), and it seems that this led this early experiment with a navy
to be abandoned in favour of a system whereby Rome relied, if necessary,
on warships supplied by her southern-Italian allies. Thus, as we saw (above,
48), Ap. Claudius used ships from Naples, Elea, Locri and Tarentum, to
cross the straits of Messina in 264. It was possibly in connection with this
system that four extra quaestors were added to the existing four in 267
(Livy, *Per.* 15; Lyd., *de Mag.* 1,27). But their title *classici*, may not have had
anything to do with the fleet (*classis*).[4]

Rome was, thus, apparently without any warships of her own when it
was decided, late in 261 or early in 260, to build a fleet of 100 quinqueremes and 20 triremes (20.9), the latter, possibly, representing a revival
of the old duumviral squadrons. Tradition has not recorded the names of
those responsible for this new departure, but it may not be a coincidence
that of the consuls of 261/0, one – Titus Otacilius Crassus – was the
brother of the consul of 263/2, M'. Otacilius Crassus, and the other –
Lucius Valerius Flaccus – possibly a relative of Valerius Messala. As we have
seen (above, p. 54), there is some slight reason to believe that Valerius
Messala had already foreseen the necessity for a fleet. But in any case, the
frustrations of the campaigning season of 261 were probably enough to
convince the consuls of that year that a fleet must be built.[5]

Polybios tells a famous and exciting story about how it was done (20.10
ff). Since, he claims, no one in Italy had ever used quinqueremes, the
Romans took as a model the Carthaginian quinquereme that had run
aground and been captured at the beginning of the war (see above, p. 49).
They also trained the rowers on land, sitting them on benches in the same
order as they would have to sit in at sea. The story of the use of the captured
quinquereme as a model has been disbelieved because, it is thought, models

would already have been available from Tarentum and Syracuse, and later on in the war the famous quinquereme of Hannibal the Rhodian is said to have been used in a similar way (59.8).[6] But there is no guarantee that Tarentum possessed quinqueremes, in view of Polybios' denial that anyone in Italy had ever used such ships (20.10), and even if Syracuse did, the captured Carthaginian vessel may have been regarded as better for some reason. As for the land-based rowing practice, this has parallels (Polyainos 3.11.7; Ennius (Vahlen) 227–31; Dio 48.51.5), and seems entirely plausible.

Nor is there any good reason to disbelieve that the new ships were built within 60 days from the cutting of the timber, as Pliny the Elder says (NH 16.192, cf. Flo. 1.18.7 and Oros. 4.7.8). The remains of an actual Carthaginian warship, though a smaller vessel than a quinquereme, found off western Sicily, include timbers numbered with letters, suggesting prefabrication and mass production, and it is possible that the Romans copied this method.[7]

Where they were built it is impossible to say, but although one might assume that the necessary expertise was only to be found in the dockyards of maritime allies such as Naples and Tarentum, there is something to be said for the notion that it would have been easier to bring the shipwrights and raw materials to Ostia, where Roman officials could exercise a stricter supervision. Polybios' story suggests such a centralized building programme, and that the fleet was built near Rome is implied by his account of how it put to sea and sailed "along the coast of Italy . . . towards the straits", while the consul went ahead "to Messana" (21.3–4). There is no hint here that the fleet had first to be assembled from scattered dockyards. One would also very much like to know where the timber came from, and how its cutting and transportation to the shipyards was organized. It would have been a mammoth undertaking.[8]

Two questions remain: what exactly were the ships, and how were they manned? It is still not possible to answer the first question with any certainty. Since the triumphant reconstruction of an ancient trireme,[9] we now think we know at least what a Greek fifth- and fourth-century trireme was like, and we can probably assume that the 20 Roman triremes now built were much the same. But there is no such unanimity about the quinquereme. All we can be certain of is that such a vessel carried a bigger crew and could carry more marines than a trireme, that the number of its oarsmen was in a ratio of 5:3 to those of a trireme, and that since it is impossible to believe that each oar was rowed by a single man, as was the case in a trireme, some at least of the oars must have been rowed by more than one man. But this leaves two basic possibilities: a single bank of oars each rowed by five men, or more than one bank with some of the oars rowed by more than one man – for example, two banks with the upper oars rowed by three men, the lower by two, or three banks with the top two rowed by two men, the lower by one.[10]

Although the first of these possibilities has been accepted by a number of scholars, it would probably have meant abandoning the age-old method of rowing seated at a bench, in favour of the rowers' rising to their feet to dip the oar and then subsiding onto the benches for the pull. This is not precluded by Polybios' story of the training on land, but it seems unlikely. Of the other two possibilities, the last has the merit of making a quinquereme resemble a trireme, but would have meant that the top oars would have had to be rowed through an outrigger, as were those of a trireme. However, this was really a weakness in the trireme, brought about by trying to retain the principle of one man, one oar, while increasing the number of rowers. Once that principle was abandoned, it is possible that shipwrights also gave up the outrigger and reverted to a much easier arrangement whereby there were oars at two levels, one set rowed across the gunwales, the other through oar-ports. But certainty is not possible.

The question of how the Roman ships were manned is also difficult. One view is that the 300-strong crews (cf. 26.7: below, p. 85) consisted mainly of "naval allies" (socii navales), drawn from the towns of Italy bound to Rome by treaty. Those towns that were on the coast would have had a seafaring tradition, and could have provided skilled sailors and oarsmen, but for the huge fleets now required, numbering eventually several hundred ships, even men from inland communities would have had to be recruited, and there is evidence for Samnites' being called up for naval service (Zon. 8.11; cf. Oros. 4.7.12). In addition, the citizens of Roman maritime colonies – Ostia, Antium (Anzio), Tarracina (Terracina) – were also liable for naval service (Livy 36.3.4–6), and freedmen may also have been.[11]

On the other hand, Polybios (6.19.3) says that Roman citizens rated below 400 asses, i.e the proletarii, were liable for naval service, and although it has been argued that this means service in the marines,[12] a more natural interpretation of Polybios' words is that he meant service in the crews. This is borne out by two pieces of evidence. One is the famous story of how the sister of Claudius Pulcher, the man who lost the battle of Drepana in 249, was three years later punished for insulting the majesty of the Roman People by expressing the wish that her brother might come alive again, lose another battle and so reduce the crowd that was impeding the progress of her rickshaw (Livy, *Per.* 19; Suet., *Tib.* 2.3; Gellius, *NA* 10.6). Here Claudia was obviously thinking of the crowds in the city of Rome, and these can hardly have consisted just of freedmen, let alone Rome's naval allies.[13] The second piece of evidence is more roundabout. We know that Rome had considerable difficulty in manning her fleet in 214 (Livy 24.11.7–9), and this may have been due to the lowering of the qualification for legionary service at about this time, which would have had the effect of reducing the number of *proletarii*.[14]

Again certainty is not possible, but the warships were probably manned by a combination of *proletarii, socii navales*, citizens from maritime colonies and freedmen. The marines, or at any rate those permanently attached to each ship, may also have come from the *proletarii*. There is some reason to believe that the permanent establishment was 40, but that up to 80 more could be drawn from the legions, when battle was anticipated.[15] Sometimes, Polybios suggests, all the marines were picked men drawn from the legions, as at Drepana in 249 (49.5) and the Aegates (61.3).

The new fleet was launched as soon as it was ready, and after a brief period spent training actually at sea, proceeded south down the coast of Italy (21.3). At this stage its commander was Gnaeus Cornelius Scipio, one of the consuls of 260/59, and he went ahead with 17 ships to Messana, to arrange for supplies and other necessities for the main fleet (21.4). At Messana, however, he received an offer to betray Lipara, the main town of the island of Lipari, and sailed there with his ships. Lipara had become a Carthaginian base by the time of the battle of the Longanus (DS 22.13.7), but had previously been on friendly terms with Rome (DS 14.93), so the offer probably seemed perfectly genuine to the consul. But the Carthaginian admiral, Hannibal, then at Panormus, got wind of the plot, and immediately despatched Boödes, a member, probably, of the inner Council of Thirty, to deal with the situation. Boödes arrived at night and thus caught Scipio in the harbour. At daybreak, the Roman crews panicked and fled to shore, and their hapless commander, according to Polybios here (21.5–7), surrendered.

In a later passage (8.35.9), however, Polybios suggests that Scipio was somehow the victim of treachery, and this appears to have been the Roman version of what happened (cf. Livy, *Per.* 17; Flo. 1.18.11; Eutr. 2.20.2; etc.), perhaps put about by Scipio himself.[16] Some sources, indeed, suggest that the initial offer to betray Lipara was itself a trick (Zon. 8.10; Polyainos 6.16.5), which may be true. But it cannot be true that Scipio lost his life, as the later passage of Polybios implies, and as is stated by Florus (1.18.11) and

Orosius (4.7.9), for he was consul again in 254/3, having apparently been exchanged at some point (cf. Livy 22.23.6). Nor does his career seem to have been affected by the nickname "Asina" ("She-ass") he received as a result of the *débâcle,* if what the elder Pliny (*NH* 8.169) says is true, though it is a puzzle why he was called "*she*-ass".

Taking the captured ships and prisoners with him, Boödes rejoined Hannibal, according to Polybios (21.8–11), and a few days later Hannibal, hearing that the main Roman fleet was approaching, and wishing to find out its numbers and order of battle, sailed towards it with 50 ships. Rounding what Polybios calls "the cape of Italy" (21.11), perhaps the modern Cape Vaticano, he unexpectedly came upon the enemy and lost most of his ships, though he was able to escape with the rest.

This story told by Polybios has given rise to an elaborate theory that he was here following Philinos' account of the battle of Mylae, without realizing it, and even those who reject this theory still think that he probably exaggerated the Roman success.[17] But it is very difficult to believe that he can have made the mistake of taking Philinos' account of Mylae to be about a different engagement, and if this was Philinos' version of that battle, it can hardly be true. There is really no reason to doubt that Hannibal would have wanted to learn more of the Roman fleet than the information Boödes will have been able to supply, and this was not the first time, nor would it be the last, that two fleets unexpectedly collided. Perhaps Hannibal was combining reconnaissance with a plundering raid, as Zonaras suggests (8.11). As for the possibility that Polybios exaggerated the extent of the Carthaginian losses, there is no way of telling. The significant thing is, possibly, that Hannibal himself was able to escape with some of his ships, which suggests that they were faster, as the Romans are subsequently said to have realized (22.3).

Encouraged then, perhaps, by this success, but possibly dismayed at the handiness of the enemy ships, the Roman fleet reached Sicily – presumably Messana – where it learned of the capture of Scipio and his squadron. This meant a change of admiral, and, according to Polybios, the other consul, Gaius Duilius, who was in command of the land forces, handed them over to his military tribunes, and assumed command of the fleet (22.1, 23.1). Zonaras (8.11) implies that Duilius was still in Rome when the news of Scipio's humiliation reached the city, and says that first the *praetor urbanus* was sent to Sicily. The latter may be true, but on the question whether Duilius was already in Sicily or not, it is better to believe Polybios.

It is, indeed, possible that Duilius' operations on land preceded his naval victory, despite Polybios, who places them later (24.1–2). The famous inscription on the *columna rostrata* (*CIL* 12.2.25), put up to commemorate Duilius' achievements, records the land operations first, and the triumphal records also describe Duilius' triumph as having been "over the Sicilians and the Punic fleet" in that order. There is also the point that the preparations for the battle of Mylae may have taken some time, and it is possible that Duilius' land operations belong to this period. In the end it really does not matter which came first, but on the whole it is again perhaps better to follow Polybios, and it is possible that the inscriptions record the land operations first because it was normal for the Romans to think they were more important.[18]

At all events, there is no reason to doubt Polybios when he says (22.2 ff) that it was while awaiting the consul's arrival that the Roman fleet began to prepare for battle, and in particular now that, "since their ships were poorly built and difficult to move, someone suggested to them as an aid to fighting what later came to be called 'crows'". Here Polybios uses the Greek word *korakes* (κόρακες), but the Latin word was evidently *corvi* (*corvus* in the singular), and this is the word usually used for the device by modern commentators, though none of the extant Latin authors who wrote about the war actually uses the word. The device consisted, according to Polybios, of poles, 24-feet high, 9–10-inches thick, with a pulley on top, mounted on the prows of the ships. Round the pole was slotted a boarding-ladder of cross-wise planks nailed together, 4-feet wide and 36-feet long, the slot in it being oblong and set 12 feet from its near end. Along each side of it ran a railing as high as a man's knee, and at its end was fixed an iron spike with a ring at the other end. To the ring was attached a rope that enabled the end of the boarding-plank to be raised by means of the pulley on top of the pole, and then let down onto the deck of an enemy ship. The slot in the ladder enabled it to be swung round, so that it could be dropped either onto the prow or onto the side of the hostile vessel, depending whether it attacked head on or collided broadside. Once the spike was fixed in the deck of the other ship, boarders could then charge across.

The only uncertainty in this description is whether the boarding-ladder was hinged where it intersected with the pole. In favour of this view is the fact that since the slot began 12 feet from the in-board end, if there were hinges at that point, the remaining 24 feet, when raised, would exactly reach the top of the pole. But Polybios says nothing of any hinges, and they would have been a structural weakness. Moreover, if the ladder was so hinged, there was no point in having a slot where it intersected with the pole, since a round hole would have done. This is also an objection to the

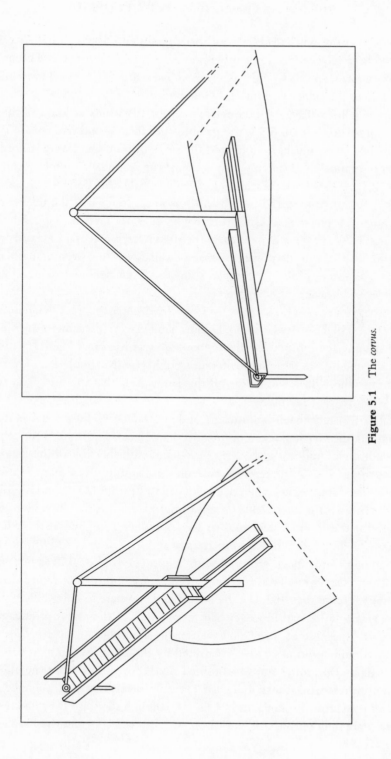

Figure 5.1 The *corvus*.

theory that the whole ladder was horizontally raised, which in any case would have required more than the one rope Polybios mentions. The only point of having a slot would seem to have been to make it possible to raise one end of the ladder without its being hinged.

Some scholars have even completely rejected Polybios' account of these boarding-ladders, mainly on the ground that they would have made the ships top-heavy, and have suggested that in reality the *corvi* were simply a form of grapnel, as is suggested by some of the secondary sources (Front., *Strat.* 2.3.24; Flo. 1.18.9; Zon. 8.11; *de vir. ill.* 38.1). But Polybios' description is circumstantial, and there is no reason to doubt that the device he describes was practicable. Unfortunately he does not say who suggested it, but it may have been a Syracusan, perhaps even Archimedes. However, one should not rule out the possibility that a Roman was the inventor, particularly if, as some think, the Roman ships had been deliberately designed broader and heavier for boarding.[19]

At all events, as soon as he learned of the disaster that had befallen his colleague, Polybios says (23.1 ff), Duilius handed over his army to the military tribunes and joined the fleet, presumably at Messana. Then, learning that the enemy was ravaging the territory of Mylae (Milazzo), he put to sea with his whole fleet, and it was off this latter place that the first great sea battle of the war took place.

Unfortunately, details are meagre and contradictory. Polybios says that Hannibal, the Carthaginian commander, had 130 ships, which is probably right, though Diodoros gives 200 (23.10.1). Presumably at least the majority of these were quinqueremes, though the flagship was a giant *hepteres* (seven-fitted ship) which had once belonged to Pyrrhus (23.4), and is probably mentioned in the *columna rostrata* inscription. But Polybios gives no figure for the Roman fleet, and so we are reduced to guesswork. It had originally numbered 100 quinqueremes and 20 triremes (20.9), but of these ships 17 had been captured with Scipio (21.4), though it is not said what type they were. Thus the Roman ships in Duilius' fleet cannot have numbered more than 103. On the other hand, if we are to believe Polybios (21.11), Hannibal had lost over half his 50 ships in the previous engagement off "the cape of Italy", and presumably a number of these had been captured and could now have been used by the Romans. Then, too, it is quite likely that some ships had joined the Roman fleet from the allied communities of southern Italy, for example those that had helped Ap. Claudius to cross the straits in 264 (20.14), though the ships they had provided were only *pentekonters* and triremes. It is thus likely that the Romans were slightly outnumbered in quinqueremes, but possibly had as many ships as the enemy overall.

Of the fighting Polybios says merely that the Carthaginians, full of confidence, sailed straight at the enemy, presumably in a single line abeam, which was the normal formation adopted by a fleet that considered itself superior, as was the case with the Carthaginians here. On the other hand, it has been suggested that the Romans must have been drawn up in two lines since the *corvi* would have been useless against attacks from astern, despite what Polybios implies (23.10), and yet subsequent Carthaginian attacks from astern were somehow thwarted. However, Polybios says nothing about a second line, and to argue that it "must" have been present is to go too far. It is true that a *corvus* mounted on the prow of a ship could not counter an attack from abaft the beam, and still less one from astern, and yet such attacks were apparently successfully countered by the Romans in the second stage of the battle. But we should not assume that the Roman ships were quite incapable of turning at least part of the way to meet such attacks, and in any case one can well believe that the sight of the *corvi* swinging round would have been disconcerting, even if cold calculation might have suggested that they could be avoided.[20]

We can well believe that the Carthaginians were at first puzzled by the *corvi*, as Polybios says (23.5), but they pressed home their attacks and were immediately grappled, losing their leading 30 ships, including the commander's *hepteres*, though he himself managed to escape in a skiff. Zonaras (8.11) says that his ship became entangled with a trireme, and this may be true, since, although if he was on a *hepteres* he would hardly have feared capture by the trireme itself, he could have feared the arrival of other Roman warships. But the rest of Zonaras' account is too vague to be worth anything. Presumably, if Polybios is right, the leading 30 ships had got ahead of the rest in their eagerness to engage, but when the remainder saw what was happening, they made use of their superior speed to veer aside in the hope of avoiding the *corvi* and being able to ram from abeam or even from astern. However, says Polybios (23.10), the *corvi* swung round and came crashing down in all directions, with the result that any ships that approached were caught. In the end, the Carthaginians gave it up and fled with the loss of 50 ships.

It is not certain whether Polybios intended the 50 ships he says the Carthaginians lost at the end to include the 30 he says they lost at the beginning, though this is probably the case. But, if so, this is probably a round number, for the secondary sources give 31 captured and 13 sunk

(Oros. 4.7.10), or 31 captured and 14 sunk (Eutr. 2.20) or 30 captured and 13 sunk (*de vir. ill.* 38), and there is some reason to believe that these figures may be derived from the *columna rostrata* inscription, though the surviving text has a gap at the vital point. Orosius and Eutropius also give 7,000 men killed and 3,000 captured on the Carthaginian side, which, if true, would mean that a considerable number managed somehow to escape either drowning or capture, since the total complement of 45 ships would have been of the order of 15,300 men, assuming crews of 300 and 40 marines – 18,900 if there were 120 marines on board each vessel.

But whatever the true figures for the Carthaginian losses, the battle was a tribute to Roman ingenuity and fighting spirit in the face of a more skilful enemy, and it was right and proper that Duilius should be honoured with the first naval triumph in Roman history, by the erection of the *columna rostrata* and by being accorded the right, on returning from dining out, to be preceded by a torch and flute-player (Livy, *Per.* 17). But it is puzzling that despite living until at least 231, when he was dictator, he never again held high command, though he may have taken part in a raid on Africa in 247 (Zon. 8.16; Front., *Strat.* 1.5.6: see below). He was, however, a *novus homo*, and his nobler rivals may have got tired of his boastfulness, if the tone of the inscription truly reflects his own attitude.

But his achievements were not ended by the victory off Mylae, if Polybios is to be believed, for after the battle he is said to have relieved the siege of Segesta and captured Makella (Macellaro? see above, p. 53: 24.1–2). Here we may also call in Zonaras, who describes how the new Carthaginian commander on land, Hamilcar, waylaid and destroyed a force commanded by the tribune, Gaius Caecilius, before Segesta, for this is borne out by Polybios' statement (23.1) that Duilius left the tribunes in charge of the army when he left to take command of the fleet. Zonaras may also be right that the *praetor urbanus* took over command of the army after this defeat, and a fragment of Naevius (fr. 39 Buechner) has been thought to refer to this, though it merely talks vaguely of an unnamed praetor receiving a good omen.[21] Another incident that may belong here is the abortive attack on Mytistraton, recorded by Diodoros (23.9.3). However, that is all we know of land operations this year, and it is clear that they took second place to those at sea.

It is also clear, however, that the battle off Mylae made no immediate difference to the course of the war in Sicily, though it did enable the Romans to attack Sardinia and Corsica in 259. In Sicily the earlier part of this year was probably marked by Hamilcar's victory between Paropos and

Thermae (now Termini), mentioned by both Polybios (24.3–4) and Diodoros (23.9.4). The victory was brought about by dissension between the Romans and their "allies" – presumably Sicilian allies – according to Polybios, and led to the death of 4,000 of the latter. Diodoros, who has the battle against the Romans, gives the losses as 6,000, but has the Romans capture a fortress called "Mazarin", probably Mazara in the territory of Selinous, at about this time.[22]

There has been some speculation by modern commentators as to why the Romans did not immediately follow up their victory off Mylae by at least using the fleet to take the war to the enemy in Sicily – for example by blockading Panormos and Lilybaeum – if not by invading Africa. Part of the answer is probably that they were only too well aware that the victory had not eliminated the Carthaginian navy. Hannibal had got away with at least 80 ships, even if Polybios' figure for his losses is accepted, and these were almost certainly not the only ships available to Carthage. It would thus take another effort to raise the number of ships to the kind of total that would finally give command of the sea, and the Senate may have been wary of asking for another such effort so soon after the first. It should be remembered that it would have required not just the building of new ships but their manning, and there is some evidence that there was in fact trouble with some of the Samnite naval allies precisely in 259 (Zon. 8.11; cf. Oros. 4.7.12).

But a more convincing reason is that – despite what Polybios claims – the Roman fleet had been built primarily for defensive reasons (see above, pp. 60 ff), and that it did not occur to anyone at this point that it could be used offensively against either Sicily or Africa. After all, the Romans were still very new to the sea, and the uses and limitations of seapower are not learned overnight. Even the operations against Sardinia and Corsica (see below) may have seemed defensive, if the Romans felt that the presence of Carthaginian forces in these islands menaced the shores of Italy, and particularly if some of the raids on Italy had in fact been mounted from Sardinia. As for Sicily, as we shall see, the Carthaginians took the offensive there in 258, and for a time it was touch and go whether the Romans could restore the situation. It would have taken an unusually bold strategist to suggest that it could be restored by the use of the fleet when most of the fighting was inland.

Of the consuls of 259/8 – Lucius Cornelius Scipio, the brother of Scipio "Asina", and Gaius Aquillius Florus – Polybios says absolutely nothing. However, of the former we know from the records of triumphs, a funerary inscription containing a two-line poem in his praise (*CIL* $1^2.2.8$ and 9) and the secondary sources, that he campaigned in Corsica and Sardinia, and of the latter from Zonaras (8.11) that he campaigned in Sicily. The fullest account of Scipio's operations is given by Zonaras (8.11) who says that he began by attacking Corsica, where he captured Aleria and subdued the rest of the island without difficulty. Possibly he chose to attack Corsica first because it was easier to get at, via Elba, without a long voyage in the open sea, and because the Carthaginian presence there was in any case minimal. But it seems unlikely that the island was really completely conquered in so swift a campaign.[23]

From Corsica, Zonaras goes on (*ibid.*), Scipio proceeded to Sardinia, encountering a Carthaginian fleet on the way, which fled before battle could be joined. He then came to Olbia, on the north-east corner of the island, but was alarmed by the reappearance of the Carthaginian fleet and sailed for home, allegedly because he was inferior in infantry. Valerius Maximus says that he took Olbia (5.1.2), Florus that he destroyed it (1.18.16), and since his triumph is recorded as having been over Sardinia, as well as the Carthaginians and Corsica, perhaps he did have more success in Sardinia than Zonaras allows. But whereas his funerary inscription (*CIL* $1^2.2.8$ and 9) mentions Corsica and Aleria, it says nothing of Sardinia. The first Carthaginian fleet he encountered may have been composed of ships already based on Sardinia, the second, possibly, a more powerful force commanded by Hannibal, son of Gisgo (see below, pp. 76–7). We do not know how many ships he himself had, but although they would probably have outnumbered any Carthaginian squadron permanently stationed on Sardinia, they would equally probably have been outnumbered by Hannibal's fleet.[24] Scipio triumphed on 11 March, 258, by the Roman calendar, so must have left Sardinia before that date, and on 1 June he dedicated a temple to "Storms" (*Tempestates*: *CIL* $1^2.2.8$ and 9; Ovid, *Fasti* 6.193–4), presumably in gratitude for some help from the weather.

Meanwhile his colleague Aquillius Florus had apparently been having a torrid time in Sicily. Probably with the departure of Valerius Flaccus and Otacilius Crassus at the end of 261, the forces in Sicily had been reduced to two legions, for this is implied by there being only one consul in command of the land forces in 260 – Duilius, probably both before and after his naval victory – and the same dispositions in 259. Thus Aquillius may not have had many more than 20,000 men with which to deal with the troops Hamilcar had taken over from Hanno and Hannibal after the fall of Agrigentum, perhaps numbering as many as 50,000 men. If so, he can hardly be blamed for failing to prevent Hamilcar from taking Camarina and Enna by treachery (DS 23.9.4); Hamilcar also fortified Drepana and moved thither the population of Eryx, which was demolished, apart from the sacred area around the temple (DS *ibid.*). According to Zonaras (8.11), if Aquillius Florus had not remained in Sicily over the winter – an unusual departure, since previous consuls seem to have returned to Italy before the winter – Hamilcar would have overrun the entire island.

The disposition of commands in 258 followed a similar pattern, Aulus Atilius Caiatinus being sent to Sicily, Gaius Sulpicius Paterculus – despite Polybios (24.9) – to Sardinia, as we know from the triumphal records. Polybios' mistake in thinking that both consuls operated in Sicily may be due to the fact that Aquillius Florus co-operated with Caiatinus, at any rate in part of the campaign, as proconsul. He certainly celebrated a triumph over the Carthaginians as proconsul, and had hardly earned this by any operations recorded of him as consul. His continuing presence also presumably meant that the Roman forces this year consisted of two consular armies, instead of one as in the previous two years.

According to Polybios, the Romans first attacked Panormus, where the Carthaginian forces were wintering, but then, when the enemy refused to be drawn into pitched battle, moved on to take Hippana, which may have been situated on the coast near Termini.[25] They then stormed Mytistraton, which had been unsuccessfully besieged twice before, according to Diodoros (23.9.4), burning it to the ground and selling its inhabitants; Zonaras, who has Atilius "Latinus" (i.e. "Caiatinus") join Florus before Mytistraton, says the Punic garrison escaped before the town surrendered (8.11). Since coins inscribed "MYTI" have been found near the modern village of Marianopoli, near Santa Caterina Villarmosa, Mytistraton probably lay in the vicinity.[26] Polybios (24.12) mentions Camarina as the next place taken by the Romans, but since he goes on to mention the capture of Enna, which lies only some 20 miles from S.Caterina Villarmosa, he or his source may have inverted the order of events. Both these places had been taken by Hamilcar the previous year.

A somewhat improbable story connected with the attack on Camarina appears in some of the secondary sources, according to which the consuls were ambushed on their way thither, and were only saved by a military tribune, who managed to draw the attack on himself and the 300 men he commanded, all of whom were killed, though he himself was captured alive. The fact that he was variously named as Laberius, Caedicius and Calpurnius Flamma, according to Frontinus (*Strat.* 1.5.15 and 4.5.10),[27] must cast some doubt on his historicity, and, after Thermopylae, one is always suspicious of heroic bands numbering 300 men.

Polybios adds (24.12) that after taking Camarina and Enna, the Romans also captured several other small towns from the Carthaginians, and these may include Kamikos and Herbes(s)os, mentioned by Diodoros (23.9.5), the former described as a "fortress" belonging to Agrigentum, and the latter presumably the Roman supply base at the time of the siege of Agrigentum (18.5). Diodoros, however, puts these operations in a slightly different order, placing the capture of "Sittana" – presumably the same as Polybios' "Hippana" – after the taking of Enna. Finally, Polybios mentions a Roman attack on Lipara (24.13), but although he says no more, according to Zonaras (8.12) it was forestalled by Hamilcar, and the Romans suffered heavy losses when he sortied.

The author of "*On famous men*" (*de vir. ill.* 39) credits Caiatinus not merely with the capture of Enna, but of Drepana, Lilybaeum and Panormus, which is obviously absurd, and even more absurd is his claim that having ravaged the whole of Sicily, he defeated Hamilcar in a naval battle. Roman successes at sea certainly continued, but it was Caiatinus' colleague, Sulpicius Paterculus, who was responsible. Polybios (24.5–7) merely records that Hannibal, the Carthaginian admiral defeated at Mylae, took the remnants of his fleet back to Carthage, and soon afterwards returned to Sardinia with additional ships and "some of the captains of repute". There he was blockaded in one of the harbours, and, after losing many of his ships, was arrested and crucified "by the surviving Carthaginians" – presumably, as we have seen (above, p. 26), officers of his fleet.

We can glean more about these naval operations from the secondary sources, though not all their information is trustworthy. Cassius Dio (11.18; cf. Zon. 8.11; Val. Max. 7.3. ext. 7; *de vir. ill.* 38) tells a tall story about how Hannibal avoided punishment for his defeat off Mylae by sending a message to Carthage to enquire whether he should risk a battle with the Roman fleet, as though he had not already done so. When the answer was in the affirmative, he then naturally claimed government authority for what he had done. More likely he escaped because the defeat was not held to be too serious. On the other hand, Polybios' statement that he took back with him "some of the captains of repute" may indicate that his competence was in doubt. His return to Sardinia may have led to the withdrawal of the consul of 259/8, L. Scipio, who, as we have seen, triumphed on 11 March 258 , by the Roman calendar.

This, then, may be why it fell to Scipio's successor, Sulpicius Paterculus, to deal with Hannibal. According to Zonaras, who has the fullest account (8.12), Sulpicius first overran the greater part of Sardinia, and then set out for Africa, whereupon the Carthaginian fleet also put to sea in pursuit, only for both to be turned back by contrary winds. Subsequently Sulpicius – Zonaras actually says "Atilius", but this is clearly a mistake – was able to lure Hannibal out to sea a second time by feeding him false information through deserters that he was again planning to sail to Africa. Because of a mist, Sulpicius was then able to surprise the Carthaginians and sink the majority of their vessels. With the remainder, Hannibal escaped to land, where he abandoned his ships and took refuge with his men in the city of Sulci (now San Antioco), on the south-west corner of the island. His abandoned ships were captured by the Romans, and his men mutinied and crucified him – Orosius (4.8.4) says stoned him to death. As a result, the Romans became over-bold in their operations on the island, and were defeated by one "Hanno". The only other evidence we have is a fragment of Dio (11, fr. 43, 32b) which at first sight appears to confuse the issue by having the storm and the mist occur at the same time, but which also mentions the deserters. Finally, there is the triumphal record that lists Sulpicius as having triumphed over the Carthaginians and the Sardinians.

It is difficult to know what to make of all this, but it seems unlikely that the Carthaginians would twice have been taken in by an apparent intention on the part of the enemy to sail to Africa, and although storms and mists do not usually occur together, it may be that the word Dio used for "storm" – χειμών – here means rather "wintry weather" or just "bad weather", without any implication that a wind was blowing. It would then be plausible that Hannibal was tricked just once into thinking that a raid on Africa was planned, and, on putting to sea, was caught by the enemy because of poor visibility. It may seem unlikely that he lost all his ships in the battle and subsequently in the harbour of Sulci, but it is not impossible, for we hear of no further naval operations off Sardinia, in subsequent years, though Carthaginian troops certainly remained on the island – they joined in the great mercenary mutiny after the war (79.1–7).

The year 257 saw a lull in operations in Sicily (25.6), although there were still two consular armies there, one commanded by one of the consuls, Gnaeus Cornelius Blasio, the other by Atilius Caiatinus, either as proconsul, or as praetor; he later celebrated a triumph for his victories of 258 on 18 January 256, by the Roman calendar.[28] Since Blasio had already been consul in 270/69, it may be that he was deliberately chosen for the Sicilian command because of his age and experience – probably no one wanted any serious operations to be set in train, in view of the huge new ship-building programme that was almost certainly begun this year (see below, p. 82). On the other hand, previous experience suggested the advisability of retaining sufficient forces to checkmate Hamilcar.[29]

The naval command was in the hands of the other consul, Gaius Atilius Regulus, and he was not inactive, though the sources are not very clear about the course of events. Polybios (25.1–4) merely records an engagement off Tyndaris, but a fragment of Naevius (fr. 37 Buechner) mentions the ravaging of Malta, and Orosius (4.8.5) that of both Malta and Lipari. Zonaras (8.12) mentions a campaign against Lipara and the battle off Cape Tyndaris (the modern Capo Tindaro), and Polyainos adds details (8.20).

It is not clear whether the operation against Malta occurred before or after the other operations, which are obviously linked, if not by Zonaras' explicit statement, then by geographical proximity. Since Malta was the farthest the Roman fleet had so far ventured, and seems to look forward to the invasion of Africa in 256, one is inclined to put the attack on the island after the other operations, and this is borne out by the fact that there had been an attack on Lipara in 258 (24.13).[30]

Zonaras, indeed, says that the first thing the consuls did on coming to Sicily was to attack Lipara, and it was then that they encountered the Carthaginian fleet off Cape Tyndaris. Although he is wrong in saying that both consuls were involved, it may well be the case that the battle off Tyndaris occurred as a result of a Roman attempt on Lipara, for although Polybios says no such thing, he does say that after the battle the Carthaginians withdrew to the Lipari islands (25.4). According to him, the Roman fleet was anchored off Tyndaris when the Carthaginian fleet was spotted sailing past in disorder. The consul then sped out with just ten ships, ordering the rest to follow, whereupon the Carthaginians turned upon him, and sank nine of his ships, though he managed to escape with his own. However, when the rest of his fleet came up, the tables were turned, and the Carthaginians lost eight ships sunk and ten captured before withdrawing to the Lipari islands.

Zonaras' version is different. According to him (8.12), both consuls planned an attack on Lipara, and, learning that the Carthaginian fleet was lying in wait off Cape Tyndaris, divided their forces. One doubled the promontory and Hamilcar, the Carthaginian admiral, thinking that this was all the fleet the Romans had, came out to the attack, only to be defeated when the rest of the Roman fleet approached. Polyainos (8.20) has an even more elaborate deception plan, whereby Sulpicius with 200 ships, realizing that the 80 Carthaginian ships would not come out to face him, towed 100 of his ships into battle with lowered masts concealed behind the spread sails of the rest.

Some of this is almost certainly untrue. Polybios (25.1) says that only one of the consuls, Atilius Regulus, was in command at Tyndaris, and this is borne out by the triumphal records, which list him as having celebrated a naval triumph, but not his colleague. In Polybios, too, it is Atilius Regulus who is anchored off Tyndaris when the Carthaginians appear, and not the other way round. However, it must be admitted that Zonaras' version, if anything, makes more sense here, since Regulus' impetuous attack with only ten ships in Polybios seems somewhat improbable. However, it is possible that the consul later pretended this was a ruse to draw the enemy into engaging a numerically superior fleet. But Polyainos' elaborate version of the ruse can hardly be accepted: to go into battle with sails spread would have been unheard of and dangerous, and it is very unlikely that the towed ships could have been concealed in this way.

But Polyainos' figures for the numbers of ships in the two fleets might be accurate since by now the Romans could have added considerable numbers of captured ships to their strength, whereas the Carthaginian fleet in these waters had been correspondingly reduced.[31] But, if so, it seems unlikely that Hamilcar would have engaged unless he thought either that he was faced by fewer ships than he really was, as the Zonaras/Polyainos version has it, or that he could deal with the leading Roman ships before the rest arrived, as Polybios suggests. He may appear somewhat foolhardy, but, in the event, the loss of 18 ships was not a disaster, and if the Romans had been about to attack Lipara, they were deterred. As was argued above, it was probably after the battle off Tyndaris that Regulus took his fleet down to raid Malta.

After the initiative and effort that had gone into the creation of a Roman navy, and its initial success off Mylae, it is perhaps surprising that so little was achieved in the following three years. On land, admittedly, the Carthaginian offensive of 259, which at one point had taken them as far as Camarina, only about 80 miles from Syracuse, had been contained, and they were now confined once again to the western end of the island. But they still held their main strongholds at Lilybaeum, Drepana and Panormus, and if the Roman navy had really been created to drive the Carthaginians completely out of Sicily, as Polybios implies (20.2), it had signally failed to do so – still less had it carried the war to Africa, as again Polybios implies was one of the reasons for its creation (20.7).

But if, as seems more likely, the navy had primarily been created as a defensive measure, then it could be said to have achieved more than had been expected of it. The decision to increase greatly its size and to attack Africa would then be another new and even more startling initiative.

CHAPTER 6

Ecnomus

The invasion of Africa, in the year 256, marks another clear stage in the conflict.[1] Since eight years of war had produced no decisive result, despite the creation of a Roman navy and its surprising success, the Roman strategy now, as Polybios says (26.1), was to strike at the enemy's heartland, and so bring the war to a definite conclusion. To us it may seem a simple and logical step, but in the circumstances of the time it was an astonishingly bold one, even if the precedent of Agathokles was known. It is worth repeating that the invasion of Sicily, only eight years before, had been the first time Roman troops had ever left the shores of Italy, and that operation merely involved crossing a narrow strait, less than ten miles from Rhegium to Messana. The voyage from Rhegium to Carthage via the south coast of Sicily was about 400 miles. One would dearly like to know who was responsible for the new strategy, and since it had been the one adopted by Agathokles of Syracuse in his war with Carthage, it is possible that it was suggested to the Romans by Hiero. But one would imagine that their leaders already knew enough about the history of Sicily at least to be aware of what Agathokles had done, and we should not assume that they were incapable of thinking of the strategy for themselves.

Since the invasion would have to be sea-borne, sufficient ships would be required not only to transport the invasion forces, but to defeat any attempt by the Carthaginians to dispute their crossing. A modern operation of this kind would involve transports escorted by warships, and this was sometimes the case in ancient warfare. The Athenian invasion of Sicily in 415, for example, involved 60 Athenian triremes acting as escorts, 40 as transports (Thuc. 6.43). But there is no reference in Polybios to transports in 256 –

only to "horse-transports" (ἱππηγοί: 26.14, 27.9, 28.2, 7 and 10) – and it appears that all the troops, including those destined for the "Army of Africa", were carried in warships.

This certainly required a larger fleet than before, though how large is a matter of controversy (see below). Some of the extra ships will have been captured Carthaginian vessels, but some at least would have had to be newly built, and this was presumably set in train in 257. If so, the consuls of that year probably deserve some of the credit for the new strategy, and Gaius Atilius Regulus' raid on Malta suggests that he was prepared to think in more far-reaching terms than were his predecessors. It may, then, not be just a coincidence that the man who eventually commanded the invasion of Africa was his elder brother, Marcus. However, the latter was not the first choice as consul in 256, being elected to replace Quintus Caedicius, who died soon after taking office, so too much should not be made of the relationship.

But just how many ships were there? Polybios says there were 330 "decked warships" (cf. μακραῖς ναυσὶ καταφράκτοις: 25.7), by which, judging by his later calculation of the number of men on board, he clearly means quinqueremes, though there were at least two larger vessels, the two *hexereis* (six-fitted ships) carrying the consuls; similarly, he gives the Carthaginians 350 "decked ships" (25.9). The only other evidence can be ignored, for Orosius repeats Polybios' figure for the Romans, and although Appian (*Lib.* 3) gives them 350 ships, this is surely just a mistake.

These figures have been doubted mainly on the grounds that although Polybios similarly says the Romans sent 350 ships to Africa in 255 (36.10), after capturing 114 at the battle off Cape Hermaia (36.11), they had only 364 in the subsequent storm off Camarina (37.2). Thus, even if we ignore the 40 that had been left in Africa the previous year (29.9), it looks as though the real figure for the battle off Cape Hermaia should be 250, and it is assumed that the figure for Ecnomus should similarly be something like 230 instead of 330. The larger figure, it has been suggested, was perhaps due to adding the horse-transports to the fighting ships.[2]

But all this is more plausible than compelling. In the first place, whatever is or is not wrong with Polybios' figures for Cape Hermaia, this has little or nothing to do with the figures for Ecnomus. Much of the speculation about ship numbers is vitiated by assumptions such as that ships that had once been launched remained in service until either captured or disabled, and that no more were built unless this is specifically stated. But there are all sorts of reasons why ships may have been laid up, or new ones built, without this being mentioned in sources that were largely interested in the main events. In this case, even if Polybios' figures for the operations of 255 should be reduced, which is by no means certain (see below, pp. 107 ff), this does not by any means prove that those of 256 should similarly be reduced.

Another argument that is sometimes employed is that Carthage usually seems to have manned about 200 ships in a crisis, that this would have been known to the Romans, and that therefore they would have tried to produce a few more, but not over a hundred more. Thus, again, the Roman fleet at Ecnomus would have consisted of more like 230 ships than 330.

But even if it is true that the Carthaginians usually only manned 200 ships in a crisis, is it relevant? By 257 both sides would surely have been increasingly aware that they were involved in a struggle the like of which neither had ever seen. It is a completely unjustified and most unlikely assumption that they would just have carried on as they had always done. The Carthaginians, with their long maritime tradition, may well have been determined to recover control at sea by a supreme effort. As Polybios says, "they were adapting most, if not all, their effort to the struggle at sea" (τὸ μὲν πλεῖον καὶ τὸ πᾶν ἡρμόζοντο πρὸς τὸν κατὰ θάλατταν κίνδυνον: 26.8, cf. 25.5, quoted below), and it is surely not beyond the bounds of possibility that they could have produced a fleet almost twice as large as usual. One should remember that they, too, still had some ships left in Sicilian waters – at least 62, even if their fleet at Tyndaris had numbered only 80, as Polyainos alleges (8.20), and they had there lost 18 (25.4). In fact one suspects that they had more, and one certainly does not have to believe that they had to build as many as 350 new vessels.

Finally, it is in fact very unlikely that there were anything like as many as 100 horse-transports at Ecnomus. We do not know how many horses each would have carried, but even converted triremes could carry 30 (Thuc. 6.43), and only 500 horsemen were eventually left in Africa (29.9). More may have been taken there and then brought home, but one would not have thought many more. In any case, since Polybios knew that horse-transports were present, why should he have made a mistake like this?

Nor is Polybios' figure of 350 for the number of Carthaginian ships at Ecnomus contradicted by his statement that after losing about 100 there (28.14), they had to build new ones before they could "man" (cf. συμπληρώσαντες: 36.9) 200 before the battle off Cape Hermaia. In the first place, not all the 250 that escaped from Ecnomus may have been repairable, though some evidently were (36.8); in the second, it is possible that some were already in use to cover the 40 ships that had been left with the Roman forces in Africa in 256; and in the third, when it came to the point, it may have been the difficulty of finding enough men that prevented more than 200 being manned.

As for whether or not the Romans would have known about the usual size of Carthaginian fleets, or the Carthaginians about Roman preparations, for that matter, modern commentators are far too prone to assume that intelligence was as good in ancient warfare as it is in modern. In reality, the history of ancient warfare suggests that both sides often proceeded in a state of blissful unawareness of what the other was doing. In 218, for example, Hannibal got as far as the Rhône before the Romans were even apparently aware that he had crossed the Pyrenees: they were assuming that the war would be fought in Spain and Africa and had made their dispositions accordingly (3.41.4 ff, 40.2).

But even if they acted in complete ignorance of Carthaginian naval preparations, it is more than likely that the Romans would also have made a greater effort than ever before to win complete control at sea; and to produce a fleet of 230 ships would hardly have required any effort at all. They had originally built 100 quinqueremes, and even if all 17 of those captured with Scipio Asina (21.4–7) had been of this type, they had presumably captured some off Cape Vaticano (21.11), about 50 at Mylae (23.10), some again at Sulci (see above, p. 77) and ten at Tyndaris (25.4). Although we cannot be certain how many these amounted to in all, or how many of them were seaworthy, it is not implausible to suggest that they numbered at least 100, possibly even more. Thus they would probably have had to build fewer than 50 to have a fleet of 230. To build as many as 150 would have been a considerable effort, but surely not an impossible one. After all, Polybios says that after Tyndaris, both sides "threw themselves more wholeheartedly into getting together naval forces and disputing command of the sea" (25.5). It will, therefore, be assumed in what follows that his figures for Ecnomus are correct.

In the summer of 256, then, the Roman fleet set out for Africa, putting in first at Messana, before rounding Cape Pachynon (now Passero) and moving along the south coast of Sicily to the vicinity of Ecnomus, a hill on the right bank of the river Himera (the modern Salso), either the one called today Poggio San Angelo or Monte Cufino, above Licata (25.7–8). There was a small town here, called Phintias, which had been founded in the 280s by the tyrant of Gela of that name (DS 22.2.2). It is described later by Polybios (53.10, cf. DS 24.1.7–8) as not having a harbour, but a roadstead protected by headlands. Here the Roman fleet joined up with the land-forces, from which the best men were selected for embarkation (26.5 ff). The whole fleet was then divided into four sections, which were called either "legions" (στρατόπεδα) or "squadrons" (στόλοι).

Another unnecessary controversy has arisen from what Polybios says here.[3] If there were four "legions" on board, it is argued, they can hardly have been selected from the troops available in Sicily, since there can at most have been four legions there in the first place. But this is absurd: it is surely clear from what Polybios says that he did not mean that each section of the fleet carried a legion of men in the technical sense, but that the men on board it were called a "legion". This is indicated by the nickname *triarii* given to the fourth "legion" (26.6), for on land every legion included *triarii*.[4] Nor do we have to assume that as many cavalry were taken on board as would normally accompany four legions and the allies attached to them, since only 500 cavalry were left in Africa.

In fact, from what Polybios says about the numbers of marines on board each ship at Ecnomus – 120 (26.7) – and bearing in mind that there would, presumably, have already been some on board before the additional ones were embarked, one can produce perfectly sensible figures. It is usually thought that the permanent complement of marines on a Roman quinquereme was 40, which would mean that the additional ones would have numbered 80.[5] Thus, if there were 330 ships, the number of marines already on board would have been 13,200, and the number of those taken on board at Ecnomus 26,400. Assuming that there were four legions in Sicily at the time, it is not unreasonable to believe that there were about 40,000 men available, including those in the attached allied cohorts, and although to take 26,400 away would have left the army in Sicily dangerously short of men, this was not a serious problem. No offensive operations were planned there, and, more particularly, it was only intended to leave 15,000 men in Africa (29.9). Thus, even if these were exclusive of the 1,600 marines permanently attached to the 40 ships left with them (*ibid.*), 11,400 men would revert to the Sicilian army when the main fleet returned. Finally, the overall total of marines on board at Ecnomus would have been 39,600, which is, in fact, about as many men as four legions and their attached allied cohorts would have contained at fullest strength on land. The total number of men in the Roman fleet, including the crews, would have been 138,600, allowing a crew of 300 in addition to the marines, for each ship – Polybios gives the total as "about 140,000" (26.7).

A minor problem is how there came to be an army of four legions in

Sicily, in the first place, and who commanded them.[6] Two of the legions were presumably those of the consul of 257, Cn. Cornelius Blasio, who had commanded in Sicily, and could have been left there as proconsul. But the other two legions can hardly be those that had been commanded by Atilius Caiatinus as praetor in 257, for, as we have seen, he celebrated a triumph on 18 January 256, by the Roman calendar, and a triumph could not be celebrated without the troops who had won it. However, on the assumption that the Romans planned the rendezvous for the fleet and army at Ecnomus in advance, it is plausible to assume that they sent two fresh legions to Sicily either when Caiatinus took his legions home, or early in 256. The reason for not embarking them before the fleet left Italy is presumably that it would have been difficult enough to provision 330 ships, without adding to the problems with extra marines, until absolutely necessary.

The Carthaginians, meanwhile, had also manned their fleet and sent it across to Lilybaeum, where it was presumably joined by any ships nearby in Sicilian waters. As we have seen, Polybios says the total number was eventually 350 (25.9), and he estimates the number of men as "more than 150,000" (26.8). It is usually assumed that he arrived at this figure by calculating on the basis of 300 crew and 120 marines to each ship, and this is probably right, though, if so, he should have said "fewer than 150,000 men" – the actual figure is 147,000. However, it has been argued that he was in any case mistaken in thinking that the Carthaginian ships had as many marines as the Roman, first because they were not carrying an invasion force, and secondly because they did not rely on boarding tactics, as the Romans did.[7]

However, they may have well have drafted extra marines on board in the light of their experiences with Roman tactics in previous engagements, and is it absolutely certain that they did not intend to land troops in Sicily? It is, after all, not immediately obvious why they chose to confront the Roman fleet off Sicily rather than off Africa. It has been argued that if they had chosen the latter course, they would have risked missing the Roman fleet altogether, since they had no means of knowing where the landing would be attempted, whereas the following year, they knew that the Roman fleet was coming to rescue the remnants of the army at Clupea, and could therefore safely wait for it off Cape Hermaia.[8] But even in 255 they could not literally have waited for the Romans there for any length of time, for ancient warships could not do this, and Polybios does not say or imply that they did – he merely says that the Romans encountered them off Hermaia (36.11). They would have required a base near by, and one suspects that it was

Carthage itself. But if they could do this in 255, why could they not have done it in 256?

The Carthaginian advance to Sicily may, then, have been not defensive, but offensive. In other words, the strategy of both sides may have been more similar than is usually appreciated. The Romans had decided to win the war by striking a blow at the Carthaginian homeland. The Carthaginians had probably not decided similarly to strike at Italy, but they may have been thinking in terms of wresting control of the waters around Sicily from the enemy, and, if successful, of landing a massive new army on the island that would go on to destroy the already weakened Roman forces there. For what it is worth, this is to some extent borne out by what the Carthaginian commanders allegedly told their men before the battle – that if they won, they would be fighting the war for Sicily, but if they lost they would endanger their country and their families (27.1).

Thus there is really no need to doubt that there may have been as many troops on the Carthaginian ships as there were on the Roman, and if this was the case, the battle involved nearly 290,000 men, a figure, as Polybios says (26.9), calculated to astonish anyone at the "magnitude of the struggle and the vast scale and power of both states". It was probably the greatest sea-battle ever fought, and possibly the largest ancient battle on land or sea.

Polybios goes on to describe the formation adopted by the Romans (26.11 ff). The two *hexereis* led the way, side by side, carrying the consuls, probably Manlius Vulso on the right, Atilius Regulus on the left (cf. 28.7 & 10). Behind them the first and second squadrons were arranged in line ahead, but *en echelon*, so that the distance between each pair of ships from front to rear was wider, and the prow of each pointed outside the one in front, the whole formation being wedge-shaped.[9] The third squadron was then stationed in line abeam behind the first two, forming the base of the wedge, with the horse-transports in tow. Finally the fourth squadron was stationed behind the horse-transports, again in line abeam, but slightly overlapping the ships in front at either end.

Inevitably this description has also been doubted, mainly on the grounds that such a formation could not have been maintained. In reality, it is suggested, the first and second squadrons were side by side in a single line abeam, and when the enemy came in sight, the centre, where the two consuls were with their flagships, got ahead of the wings, thus producing Polybios' "wedge" formation. Since, in the end, even Polybios' critics agree that the Roman formation became much as he describes it, perhaps it does not much matter whether he or they were right. But there really is no compelling reason to doubt that ships under oar could have kept to a formation such as he describes, and *ex cathedra* pronouncements such as that "no captains, let alone Roman captains, could have kept station",[10] are no substitute for rational argument. Each steersman would merely have had to keep his prow pointing at open water to port or starboard of the ship in front, exactly as Polybios says (ταῖς δὲ πρώρραις ἔξω νεύοντα τὰ σκάφη: 26.13), and not overlapping its stern.

There are also two reasons for believing Polybios – apart from the obvious one that he is the best source we have. The first is that if the Roman formation had originally been just a single line abeam, one would have expected the two consuls to have been not side by side in the centre, but probably on the right of their respective squadrons, which was usually regarded as the post of honour, or on the right and left. The fact that they were in the centre suggests that their squadrons were expected to keep station on them, and bears out Polybios' version of the formation.

Secondly, although he does not tell us why the Romans adopted this formation beyond remarking (26.16) that "the whole thing was effective and practical and at the same time difficult to break up", it is not too hard to see possible reasons for it. It is always easier for fleets to move in line ahead, rather than line abeam, if they are going any distance, since it is much easier to keep station in line ahead. But such a huge fleet could hardly sail in a single line ahead, and if it had been ranged in several such lines, it would have been very difficult to change into line abeam, or more than one line abeam, for battle. Ancient fleets did not fight in line ahead, since it was obviously desirable to present as many rams to the enemy as possible, and in the case of the Roman fleet it was even more desirable, since the *corvi* were also in the bows.

The *en echelon* formation of the first two squadrons may thus have been a simple and effective compromise between sailing in line ahead and line abeam. If the enemy appeared, the two flagships just had to slow down while the squadrons to port and starboard rowed forward, to produce a single line abeam, that would also protect the third squadron with its tows, while the fourth squadron continued to protect the rear. An added advantage was that while *en echelon* the ships of the first two squadrons could protect the sterns and sides of those in front. The ships of the third squadron prevented any enemy from attacking the whole inverted "V" from the rear, and they in turn, with the vulnerable horse-transports in tow, were protected from the rear by the fourth squadron. Only the sterns of the fourth squadron would be vulnerable, and they would at least be far in the rear.

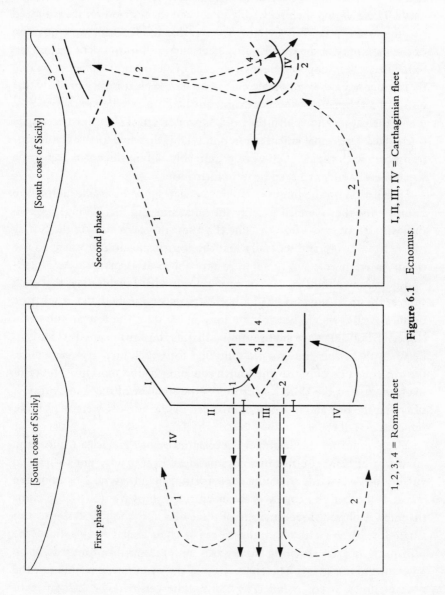

[South coast of Sicily]

First phase

I

II

III

IV

IV

1

2

1

2

3

4

1, 2, 3, 4 = Roman fleet

[South coast of Sicily]

Second phase

1

2

3

1

2

4

IV

2

I, II, III, IV = Carthaginian fleet

Figure 6.1 Ecnomus.

A more serious problem is why the Romans encumbered their third squadron with the horse-transports, when these could have been safely left at anchor off Ecnomus, under the protection of the army, until after the battle. There would then inevitably be a need for rest and repair, as indeed was the case (29.1). The obvious answer is that the Romans were unaware of the proximity of the Carthaginian fleet, and it is no argument against this to say that it "presupposes the total absence of a Roman intelligence service that in any way deserved the name": as we have seen, it is very unlikely that either the Romans or the Carthaginians had "an intelligence service".[11] Their formation shows that they did expect an attack, but not necessarily one so near their final embarkation point. Thus they had to take the horse-transports with them. They were presumably sailing ships, but had to be towed here in order to keep them in formation.

Speculation on the number of ships in each squadron is idle, unless one assumes that they were all roughly the same size, and that is belied by two things Polybios says – first, that the third squadron was towing the horse-transports (26.14), and secondly that the fourth squadron overlapped the third. As we have seen, there were probably not as many as 80 horse-transports, and although it is not certain from what Polybios says that each ship in the third squadron had a horse-transport attached, this is what he implies. Again, we are not told by how many ships the fourth line over-lapped it, but unless we are to suppose that its ships maintained wider gaps between them than those of the third line, for which there is no evidence, we can conclude only that the fourth squadron had more ships.[12] It seems likely, then, that the third squadron was the smallest of the four, and possibly that the first and second, commanded by the consuls, were the largest, which seems likely.

Meanwhile, the Carthaginian fleet had moved to Heraclea Minoa, and after a brief harangue from its commanders, it, too, now put to sea and sailed south-eastwards down the coast, presumably in several squadrons line ahead. But when the enemy came in sight, Polybios says (27.3), the com-manders deployed three-quarters of their fleet (i.e. about 260 ships) into single line abeam, stretching out to sea at right angles to the shore, the remaining quarter reaching shorewards and, presumably, forwards, at an angle to the rest (27.4). The right wing of the main line, consisting of the fastest ships, was commanded by Hanno, the general who had failed to relieve Agrigentum, the left by Hamilcar, the man defeated off Tyndaris; the name of the commander of the remaining 90 or so ships, forming the extreme left, is not given.

There is only one problem here, and that is how the Carthaginians were able to see what formation the Romans had adopted. It would have been easy enough to see from the air, but not so easy, one would have thought, from sea level. Possibly, there were spotters on the hills lining the shore, who would have had a bird's-eye view,[13] but it is difficult to see how they could have conveyed their information to the Carthaginian admirals, once embarked. Possibly the latter could see enough to realize roughly what the enemy formation was.

At all events, as the first and second Roman squadrons, perhaps now getting into single line–abeam as described above, swept forward to the attack, the Carthaginian centre (i.e. the left of the main line), under orders from Hamilcar, fell back, drawing the Romans further and further away from their third and fourth squadrons, the former of which was slowed by the horse-transports it had under tow (27.7–9). Polybios says later that when the ships of the Carthaginian centre finally engaged the Roman first and second squadrons, "they all turned together" (27.10), so evidently they withdrew by turning 180 degrees away from the enemy. It has been suggested that Hamilcar had devised these tactics as a result of his experience at Tyndaris, when the Roman admiral and ten of his ships had been drawn into a premature attack, and this may be right, though Tyndaris had not exactly turned out to be a happy experience.[14]

There is again a slight puzzle here. Polybios says that the battle began "when the Romans, seeing that the Carthaginians were spread thin, delivered an attack on the centre" (27.7). There is no problem about his use of the term "centre" (ἐπὶ μέσους), because he clearly meant the part of the Carthaginian fleet that Hamilcar commanded, and although he had originally described it as "the left" (τῶν δ'εὐωνύμων: 27.6), in terms of the main fleet it was the left, but in terms of the whole fleet, including the ships angled towards the shore, the centre. But if the Roman first and second squadrons were also, in effect, in single line abeam, albeit echeloned back from the flagships in the centre, why should they have thought the Carthaginian line "thin"? Probably all Polybios means is that the Carthaginian line appeared thin by comparison with the whole Roman wedge formation, which he had earlier described (26.16) as "effective and practical and at the same time difficult to break up".

When, then, the Carthaginians thought they had drawn the enemy first and second squadrons far enough away from the third and fourth, at a signal from Hamilcar's ship, they again turned 180 degrees, and attacked their pursuers (27.10). Polybios makes it clear that the Carthaginian ships were superior in speed and manoeuvrability, even though those under Hamilcar's command were not the fastest in the fleet, but it is not entirely clear how they used their advantage. The operative words literally mean that "through their speed they were far superior in sailing out and round and in easily approaching and swiftly retreating" (τῷ μὲν ταχυναυτεῖν ἐκπεριπλέοντες καὶ ῥᾳδίως μὲν προσίοντες, ὀξέως δὲ ἀποχωροῦντες, πολὺ περιῆσαν: 27.11).

Some modern translators take the word translated "sailing out and round" (ἐκπεριπλέοντες) just to mean that they outflanked the enemy line,[15] but this does not bring out the force of the preposition "out" (ἐκ), and is probably wrong. What was really going on is explained by both a sentence in Polybios' account of Mylae, and his description of the later battle of Drepana (23.9 and 51.2 ff, esp. 4–7), where he uses very similar language. At Mylae, he says that "relying on their speed, by sailing out and round (ἐκπεριπλέοντες), they hoped to make their ramming attacks safely, some from the side, some from the stern". At Drepana, he again emphasizes the superior speed of the Carthaginian vessels, here putting it down to the "different build of their ships and the state of their crews" (51.4). As a result, "if any found themselves hard pressed by their enemies, they were able to withdraw safely to open water because of their speed, and there, swinging round, rammed repeatedly and sank many of the leading pursuers, sometimes *sailing round them* (περιπλέοντες: 51.6), sometimes striking them side on as they tried to turn and got into difficulties because of the weight of the ships and the lack of skill of the crews."

Clearly in both passages Polybios is talking about individual ships, and this suggests that at Ecnomus, similarly, he means not that a whole section of the Carthaginian centre was able to outflank the first and second Roman squadrons, but that individual Carthaginian ships made use of their superior speed to break through the Roman line and turn to ram from the stern (ἐκπεριπλέοντες), or to advance and retreat from ahead. Those that broke through the line were, in other words, using the age-old tactics of the *diekplous*, a manoeuvre that he specifically says the Romans were unable to use at Drepana, again "because of the weight of their vessels and the lack of skill of the crews" (51.9). At Ecnomus, however, they were able to compensate for their lack of speed and manoeuvrability by the use of the *corvus*. If any enemy ship came within reach, it was immediately "hooked" and then the legionaries came into their own.

Meanwhile, the Carthaginian right under Hanno, keeping clear of the conflict, raced across open water to attack the fourth Roman squadron, the *triarii.* Hanno's ships presumably deployed into line-ahead for this manoeu-vre, since it required speed, deploying back into line abeam once they drew near the *triarii,* probably at an angle to the shore as the *triarii* turned to face them. Meanwhile, the Carthaginian left, which had evidently also been rowing forwards in line ahead near the coast, now, presumably, deployed to the right (i.e. to seaward) into line abeam, to attack the third Roman squadron (28.2). The latter cast off the horse-transports before engaging, and it later transpires that these remained near the fourth squadron (28.7).

Some modern scholars have made an unnecessary fuss about the trans-ports, one asserting that "they must have fled from the enemy (as transports have always done)", although he then has to assume that they had some oars of their own, despite Polybios' assertion that they were being towed, another denying that they can still have been under tow when the Car-thaginian left wing attacked. But Polybios says that the Carthaginian left had been reaching shorewards at an angle to the rest (ἐν ἐπικαμπίῳ νεῦον πρὸς τὴν γῆν: 27.4), at the outset, and this almost certainly means reaching *forwards,* i.e. in advance of their centre and right. Thus they may well have neared the third Roman squadron some time before Hanno and the right wing attacked the fourth. The commander of the third squadron then made the correct decision to cast off the towlines, since he could not fight so encumbered and the fourth squadron behind him was not yet under attack. All we have then to suppose is that the fourth squadron contrived to place itself in front of the transports before engaging Hanno's ships, to explain what Polybios says: all that would be necessary would be for any ships impeded by the transports to steer between them.[16]

Thus, as Polybios says (28.3), the whole battle dissolved into three sepa-rate engagements in which the two sides were fairly evenly matched, and he implies that all had gone according to plan for the Carthaginians. In reality, however, it has been suggested, all had gone wrong.[17] The plan had been to draw the first and second Roman squadrons away from the third and fourth so that the former could be attacked from the rear by the two wings of the Carthaginian fleet, thus avoiding the *corvi.* But, instead, Hanno on the right had gone racing off to attack the fourth squadron, and the left had attacked the third. This was due either to a misunderstanding of the plan, or to disagreement with it, or to the difficulty of implementing it when it was found that either by accident or design the Romans had adopted their wedge formation. An alternative suggestion is that the main target for the Carthaginians was the transports, and that their tactics were designed to expose these to attack.[18]

The latter suggestion at least has the merit of keeping to what Polybios implies, but it is almost certainly wrong. It presupposes that the loss of the transports would have been a crippling blow, whereas, if they were "horse-transports", as Polybios says, although their loss would have deprived the invasion force of its cavalry, this would hardly have been much of a problem, judging by the small number of cavalry eventually left in Africa.

A more recent suggestion is that Polybios misunderstood the Carthaginian plan, because he here largely based his account on Roman sources. The Carthaginian intention was to surround the whole Roman fleet by withdrawing their centre so that the two wings could take the enemy in the rear. Ecnomus, in other words, was intended to be a naval Cannae (see below). But the plan was ruined when the Roman third and fourth squadrons became separated from the V-formation of the first and second, because the third line did not immediately cast off the transports. This meant that the Carthaginian wings became fully engaged in separate battles and so were unable to relieve the pressure on their centre, which was consequently defeated. Thus the Romans "blundered to victory".[19]

This is ingenious and may be right, but there are two objections to it. First, it does presuppose that Polybios was wrong about the Carthaginian plan, and although this is not necessarily decisive, it is at least worth considering an alternative that adheres to his view that the intention was to draw the first and second Roman squadrons away from the third and fourth. The second objection is, perhaps, more serious: can we really suppose that the Carthaginian admirals seriously envisaged surrounding the Roman fleet? All we know of ancient naval warfare suggests that battles were largely hit-and-miss affairs, with admirals being capable of little more than getting their fleets to the right place, and deciding broadly on the formation in which they would fight. As a general rule, the simpler the plan we suppose them to have had, the more likely it is to be true. Here the intention was that the right wing should "encircle the enemy" (cf. ὡς κυκλώσαντες τοὺς ὑπεναντίους: 27.3), but that surely just means outflank it.

Too much has, in fact, been made of the supposed resemblances between Hamilcar's tactics at Ecnomus and Hannibal's at Cannae, even to suggesting that Hannibal learnt from the naval battle.[20] In fact the two battles were very different, and it is, in particular, most unlikely that Hannibal studied Ecnomus. At Cannae he advanced his centre, whereas Hamilcar withdrew his, and there was nothing at Ecnomus to correspond with Hannibal's Africans, the jaws of his vice. At Cannae, too, the left wing was more powerful than the right, whereas the reverse was true of Ecnomus, and, more importantly, the job of the Numidians on the right at Cannae was merely to hold the Roman allied cavalry in play, while it was Hasdrubal from the left who first destroyed the Roman citizen cavalry in front of him, then rode round to attack the allied cavalry from the rear, and finally fell upon the rear of the Roman infantry line. Hannibal's tactics were altogether more refined than the ones used by Hamilcar at Ecnomus.

After their experiences at Mylae and Tyndaris, the Carthaginians here knew that they had, somehow, to bring about a battle of manoeuvre, in which their faster ships would have the advantage and the *corvi* be rendered useless. If so, the simplest explanation of their tactics is that they were designed to do just what they did do – to split the Roman array up into scattered units spread over miles of sea where there would be room to manoeuvre. The horse-transports and their accompanying tow-ships were a target, but not an important one, and so they were left to the smallest section of the fleet, the ships of the extreme left, whose commander, appropriately, is not even named.

What went wrong had nothing to do with a failure to carry out a masterly plan. The Carthaginians lost because they really had no answer to the *corvus*, and this, in turn, was because of the nature of ancient sea battles. There were only two ways of eliminating enemy warships – ramming and boarding – and even the successful ship risked damage, loss of marines, and, at the very least, being left with a captured ship on its hands.[21] In short, every enemy ship put out of action tended to mean one of one's own also out of action. The only way to avoid this was to cripple an opponent by shearing away his oars, or by ramming him in the side or stern and backing away without damaging one's own ship. But shearing away an opponent's oars was difficult without damaging one's own, since there was no possibility of being able to ship oars in the last seconds before collision. Ramming an opponent involved some contact, wherever it occurred, and the *corvus* was precisely designed to take advantage of any mistake.

Of course, ramming from the stern, or even the side, abaft midships, would avoid the *corvi*, but to achieve this was not as easy as it sounds. Slow Roman ships might be, but they were not stationary, and even when their formation was broken up and the fighting became like a dogfight between aircraft, slower ships could still turn to meet an attack from abeam or astern. It goes without saying that faster ships could turn faster, and the trick was to out-turn your opponent. But in the maelstrom of an ancient sea-battle, there will always have been enemy ships waiting to pounce – there was no question of two circling opponents being left to have the ring to themselves.

So, at Ecnomus, Hamilcar's squadron was the first to find itself in difficulties, and took to flight, whereupon Manlius Vulso's first squadron occupied itself with taking the prizes in tow, while Atilius Regulus hastened to the relief of the third and fourth squadrons with all the undamaged ships of his second squadron (28.6–7). The fourth squadron, the *triarii*, took heart as the second came up to their assistance, though they had so far been having the worst of it, and Hanno, attacked in front and rear, began to withdraw out to sea (28.8–9).

Finally, both the first and the second squadrons went to the relief of the third, which had been penned up against the shore by the Carthaginian left wing. Presumably the latter had gradually forced the Romans back from the right, or the Romans had raced for the shore in the first instance.[22] Significantly, however, though in great danger, the ships of this squadron had been able to keep the enemy at bay with their *corvi*, and it was now the turn of their opponents to be surrounded, losing 50 ships. It may be here that some Carthaginian ships pretended to have run aground on shoals, in order to shake off their pursuers, who dared not close for fear of doing the same. However, there is really no proof that the anecdote that describes this (Front., *Strat.* 2.13.10), should be referred to Ecnomus, and it seems improbable in itself.[23] In all, according to Polybios (28.10–14), the Carthaginians lost 64 ships captured, and more than 30 sunk, the Romans 24 sunk, and these figures are repeated, with slight variations, in the secondary sources (Oros. 4.8.6; Eutr. 2.21.1; *de vir. ill.* 40.1). The result was once again a triumph for Roman ingenuity and fighting spirit. The way to Africa was open.

CHAPTER 7

Regulus

After the battle of Ecnomus, Polybios says (29.1), the Romans laid in more provisions, repaired the captured ships, and "having given their crews the care befitting their successes", set sail for Africa. Zonaras (8.12) has them set out from Messana, and this is not impossible: it seems to have been the main Roman fleet-base in Sicily.[1] The defeated Carthaginian fleet presumably rallied at Heraclea Minoa or Lilybaeum, and, according to Zonaras (*ibid.*, cf. Dio 11, fr. 43.21; Val. Max. 6.6.2), Hamilcar sent Hanno to the Romans, ostensibly with peace proposals, but in reality to gain time. If it is true, as Zonaras also says, that some of the Romans clamoured for Hanno's arrest in retaliation for the treacherous seizure of "Cornelius" (presumably Cornelius Scipio Asina), it is interesting that the Roman version of what had happened at Lipara in 260 had already taken hold. Hanno is said to have responded by saying that if the Romans did arrest him, they would "no longer be better than the Africans", and thus, by flattering them, escaped.

When the Romans eventually set out from Messana, Zonaras says, the two Carthaginian commanders, who had divided their forces, considered again bringing them to battle. But the odds were clearly unacceptable, since although, if they had gone into battle at Ecnomus with 350 ships, they would still have had some 250 left, some of these will probably have been damaged beyond repair, and they will have known that the Romans, if they had been able to repair most of their own and the captured vessels, would have had some 370 ships available. The morale factor was also crucial. It would have been asking a lot of the Carthaginian sailors and marines to fight again so soon after their defeat, even if the fleets had been more evenly matched – one thinks of the Athenians at Syracuse in 413 (Thuc. 7.72). So eventually Hanno returned to Carthage, according to Zonaras, while

Hamilcar remained in Sicily. This is consistent with Polybios' later statement (30.1) that Hamilcar was sent for from Heraclea, but he also says that those who escaped from Ecnomus sailed home (29.4), which implies that if Hamilcar remained in Sicily, he retained few, if any, ships.

According to Polybios (29.2), when the leading ships of the Roman invasion fleet reached Cape Hermaia (now Cape Bon or Rass Adder), they waited for the rest of the fleet, and then all proceeded down the coast to "the city called Aspis". This is the Roman Clupea – both words mean "shield" – and is probably the modern Kelibia. Diodoros (23.11) has a peculiar passage which, if the text is right, appears to talk of the Romans approaching the shore with a mere 30 ships in no sort of proper formation because of the violence of the wind. This may refer to Polybios' story of the rendezvous off Hermaia.[2]

Having reached Aspis, the Romans beached their ships and surrounded them with a trench and a palisade, then set about besieging the town (29.3). Meanwhile the Carthaginians, realizing that there was no longer any danger of an attack on their city from the sea, "having united their forces", Polybios says (29.5), took measures to protect both city and the surrounding countryside. Presumably this means that they laid up their fleet and brought the marines ashore to join the troops already available. Having taken Aspis, the Romans garrisoned the town, and sent to Rome for further instructions, possibly because winter was drawing near, and it might be felt better to withdraw to Sicily and return the following year.[3] In the meantime they contented themselves with a widespread *razzia* that led to the destruction of the luxurious manor houses of the Carthaginian nobility in the vicinity, and netted a quantity of cattle and more than 20,000 slaves (29.5–7), including, according to Zonaras (8.12), many Roman and Italian prisoners of war.

When messengers arrived from Rome ordering one consul to remain in Africa with sufficient forces and the other to bring the fleet home, it was decided that Regulus should remain with 40 ships, 15,000 foot and 500 horse, and Manlius Vulso should return to Italy (29.8–10). The latter subsequently celebrated, while still consul, a naval triumph over the Carthaginians, according to the triumphal records. Since Polybios later refers to "the first legion" in Regulus' army (30.11), his forces presumably represented two weak legions with their attached allied cohorts, and the small number of cavalry is particularly striking, bearing out what was said above about the likelihood that there were not many horse-transports in the original fleet at Ecnomus.

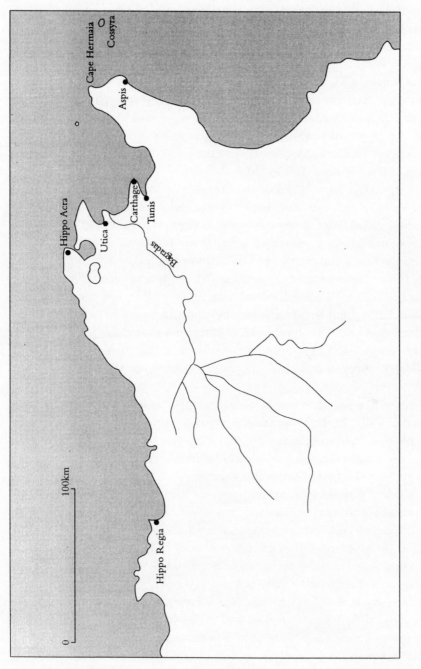

Figure 7.1 North Africa.

The Carthaginians now elected as generals Hasdrubal, son of Hanno, and Bostar, and sent for Hamilcar from Sicily (30.1).[4] This Hasdrubal was to play an important part until his death in 251, but Bostar is never mentioned again, unless he is the Bostar who was in command of mercenaries on Sardinia when they mutinied after the war (79.2), or the "Vodostor" or "Bodostor" who, according to Diodoros (24.9.1 and 12), fought under Hamilcar Barca in Sicily and died of ill treatment in captivity. When the other Hamilcar arrived, with reinforcements of 500 horse and 5,000 foot, he was appointed as a third general, and after a consultation between him and Hasdrubal it was decided to lead the army out in an attempt to put a stop to Roman depredations (30.2–3).

A few days later, Regulus also began to advance, pillaging unwalled towns in his path and besieging those that had walls. Eventually he reached a town called Adys, a place of some importance, according to Polybios (30.5), though its whereabouts is unknown. It is possibly to be identified with the later Roman town of Uthina (now Oudna), about 15 miles south of Tunis.[5] Some of the later sources (Dio *ap.* John of Damascus, *On Dragons* 1, p. 472, cf. Zon. 8.13; Oros. 4.8.10), have Regulus encamp on the Bagradas (the modern Medjerda), but this can probably be ignored. It is mixed up with a splendidly absurd story of a monstrous snake, 120 feet long, which killed a large number of Roman soldiers drinking at the river, before Regulus dealt with it with catapults (Livy, *Per.* 18; Zon. 8.13; Oros. 4.8.10 ff).

At Adys, wherever it was, Regulus encamped and set about raising siege-works, while the Carthaginians, anxious to relieve the place, occupied a nearby hill. Polybios, perhaps following Philinos (cf. DS 23.11), is critical of this decision, on the grounds that it nullified their strength in cavalry and elephants (30.8). But Carthaginian commanders were already aware of the strength of Roman infantry in a set-piece battle on level ground, and may have sought to make this a campaign of manoeuvre in which their more "professional" soldiers might win some advantage. As it was, however, the Romans, evidently full of confidence, launched a dawn assault on their position from two sides, according to Polybios (30.10) – Zonaras (8.13) says it was at night, which is improbable.

Here it was that the "first legion" was flung back by the mercenaries, but the latter then advanced too far and evidently allowed the other Roman troops to get between them and the hill: according to Polybios (30.12), they were surrounded and put to flight. The Carthaginians fled their camp, the elephants and cavalry getting away in safety, but the infantry being

100

pursued for some distance. The Romans then plundered the camp and advanced on Tunis, which they seized, spreading devastation far and wide. Polybios gives no figures for the Carthaginian losses in the battle, but those given by the later sources are absurdly inflated. Thus Orosius (4.8.16) and Eutropius (2.21.3) have 17,000 and 18,000 killed, respectively, and 5,000 and 18 elephants captured. The former adds that 82 towns surrendered to the Romans, the latter 74.

There is a divergence in the sources as to what happened next. According to Polybios (31.1ff), Regulus realized that the Carthaginians were despondent at their two defeats, and threatened by a Numidian revolt. But although he thought that he might shortly take the city, he was apprehensive in case his successor might arrive and reap the credit. So he invited the enemy to enter into negotiations. But when they responded by sending envoys – led by Hanno, son of Hamilcar, according to Diodoros (23.12) – his demands were so harsh that they decided that they had nothing to lose by continuing the struggle. The other sources, however – Diodoros (23.12), Livy (*Per.* 18), Eutropius (2.21.4), Orosius (4.9.1) and Zonaras (8.13) – are unanimous that it was the Carthaginians who took the initiative, and in Livy (*ibid.*), Frontinus (*Strat.* 4.3.3) and Valerius Maximus (4.4.6) Regulus' command is prolonged against his wishes.

Certainty is, as usual, not possible, but the story that Regulus was reluctant to continue in command is probably part of the legend that grew up around him – unless he was ill, it would have been most unusual for a Roman to want to give up his command. However, if it was Regulus who made the first move, it is odd that he ruined it by pitching his demands too high, whereas, if it was the Carthaginians, this might have convinced him that they were at the end of their tether. Moreover, since this version is in Diodoros, it may come from Philinos.

On the other hand, Polybios' version also makes sense. It was not uncommon for Roman generals to take rash action in case they were superseded before they could achieve success – one thinks of Sempronius Longus before the Trebbia, for example (3.70.7–8). Regulus may have felt that his victory at Adys was enough to secure a triumph, and that no one would expect him to take Carthage – a peace on favourable terms was all that was required. Thus he could well have taken the first step in starting negotiations, and, when this seemed to elicit a favourable response, have overreached himself. This is partly borne out by Cassius Dio, who alone of our sources says what the terms were, and seems to imply that they were set out in two stages (11, fr. 43.22–3). First, he says, the Carthaginians were required to evacuate Sicily and Sardinia, release Roman prisoners without ransom, but ransom their own, and pay the expenses Rome had incurred, followed by a yearly tribute. But then he goes on to say that the Carthaginians were angered by further demands that they should not make peace or war without Roman consent, and retain only one warship, but furnish Rome with 50 triremes whenever so required.

It is not easy to see how Dio alone could have got hold of authentic details of the terms, and some of them are dubious, for example the requirement to evacuate Sardinia, which was later not even demanded by the treaty at the end of the war. Indeed, the terms as a whole are, if anything, harsher even than those imposed upon Carthage at the end of the Hannibalic War, let alone our war. But it is just possible that Dio's version contains a glimmering of the truth. The first terms he gives, even without the evacuation of Sardinia, would have secured what Rome had been fighting for since 260. But if the Carthaginian negotiators had showed any inclination to accept these terms, it is not inconceivable that Regulus was then carried away into making further demands.[6]

Hitherto Regulus had been brilliantly successful. With an army of less than 16,000 men, he had brought the Carthaginians to the brink of defeat, whether it was he or they who had opened negotiations. He has been criticized for apparently making no attempt to win the indigenous population to his side, as Agathokles is said to have done, and in particular for not doing more to secure Numidian support, since they were already up in arms and would have provided him with much-needed cavalry.[7] But the Numidians were probably too far away, and he possibly did not have enough time to convince the Libyans that his was the winning side. Agathokles, after all, was in Africa for some four years (310–307), and even he had trouble with his Libyan allies (DS 20.18.3), who deserted him at the crucial moment (DS 20.64.2 ff). As for the Numidians, they also proved fickle allies (cf. DS 20.38.1 ff, 55.3). If, then, Regulus is to be faulted, it is for his arrogance in negotiation, not for his strategy.

So the war went on, and now took a new and dramatic turn. The Carthaginians had sent a number of recruiting officers to Greece, and at this point one of these arrived with a considerable number of soldiers, and in particular a Spartan named Xanthippos (32.1). Although termed a "Spartiate" by Diodoros (23.14.1), Polybios' remark that he was "a man who had taken part in the Spartan training-system" (ἄνδρα τῆς Λακωνικῆς ἀγωγῆς μετεσχηκότα: 32.1) may indicate that he was what the Spartans called a "mothax", i.e. a man of poor family who had been patronized by someone wealthier and brought up with his sons. Despite the statements by Appian (*Lib.* 3) and Eutropius (2.21.4) that he was an ally sent officially by Sparta – Orosius (4.9.2) even calls him "King of the Spartans" – he was clearly a mercenary, as Polybios implies and Diodoros confirms (23.15.7).

From what Polybios says about him (32.2–8), he was clearly a professional to whom Carthage's mercenaries were able to relate. For example, he is said (32.7) to have been able correctly to deploy and manoeuvre sections of the army and to give commands in the proper way. He also succeeded in persuading his masters that their strength in cavalry and elephants would give them the advantage on level ground, which hitherto they had avoided, and it is possible that he passed on a knowledge of the proper use of elephants, in particular.[8] We have already seen that they had been ineptly used at Agrigentum, and Polybios himself criticizes the way they were used, or rather not used, at Adys (30.8 ff). But they were to be handled with conspicuous success under Xanthippos' direction, as we shall see. Perhaps he had just learned about them as a result of the "considerable practice" Polybios says he had had in military matters (32.1). More particularly, he may have witnessed Pyrrhus' use of elephants against Sparta herself, in the late 270s (Plut., *Pyrrh.* 26 ff). At one point (32.5) Polybios implies that the Carthaginian generals handed over command of their forces to him, and Zonaras talks of his having assumed "complete authority" (8.13). But it is clear that the generals continued to exercise at least nominal command until it seemed certain that there would be a battle, as one would expect, and then gave him the power to deploy the army as he saw fit (33.5).

In any case, it was a rejuvenated Carthaginian army that took the field probably early in May 255.[9] It consisted of 12,000 foot, 4,000 horse and very nearly 100 elephants, according to Polybios (32.9), but some commentators have argued that these numbers are too small for a Carthaginian army in Africa: they suggest that Carthaginian tradition, reflected in Philinos, and so in Polybios, reduced the numbers to enhance Xanthippos' victory.[10] But this is far-fetched, and although Appian (*Lib.* 3), Eutropius (2.21.4) and Orosius (4.9.3) give Regulus over 30,000 men, it can hardly be true that his numbers had doubled since he had been left in Africa, even if he had, after all, received the adherence of some of the native peoples. In fact, even if Regulus had virtually every man of his forces with him – and one would assume that he left some to guard his base at Aspis – he can hardly have had more than a few more infantry than the Carthaginians, since he had presumably suffered some loss at Adys, and he was heavily outnumbered in cavalry, to say nothing of elephants.

It is unfortunately not possible to be certain where the decisive battle took place, since all Polybios says (33.1) is that it was when the Romans saw the enemy "marching through flat country" that they decided to fight. Indeed, since the last location he gives for the Romans is Tunis (30.15), it is not easy to see how the Carthaginian army managed to get out into the "flat country" in the first place, unless this just means the isthmus that separated Carthage from Tunis,[11] and this is hardly consistent with his statement that it pitched more than one camp before the battle (cf. στρατοπεδείας: 33.1). In those days Carthage was almost entirely surrounded by water, the bay to the north being now represented by the Sebkhet el Ariana, that to the south by the Lake of Tunis, and the isthmus connecting the city to the mainland was only some three miles wide by ten miles long. Thus the Roman army at Tunis should have blocked all egress. Are we, then, to understand that Regulus had withdrawn to Aspis for the winter? This would make sense, and, if so, the battle probably took place somewhere in the "flat country" southwest of Tunis.

It was now, according to Polybios (33.3–5), that the Carthaginian generals, in response to demands from their men, entrusted the disposition of their forces to Xanthippos. He is said (33.6) to have drawn the elephants up in a single line in front of the whole force, placing the Carthaginian citizen phalanx some way behind them, with some of the mercenaries on its right. But from what is said later (34.4) about the attack of the Roman left on these mercenaries, it appears that most of the elephants, if not all, were in front of the phalanx. The most mobile mercenaries were apparently placed with the cavalry in front of both wings of the infantry line (33.7). The Romans responded by placing their light infantry in front, with the heavy infantry, many maniples deep, behind them, and the cavalry divided between the two wings (33.9).

It is not certain what is meant by "many maniples deep" (πολλὰς ἐπ' ἀλλήλαις . . . σημείας: 33.9). The legions normally drew up in three lines, the ten maniples of each side by side, but with gaps between them corresponding to the width of a maniple. The maniples of the second line covered the gaps between those of the first, and those of the third the gaps between those of the second. But whether or not a legion actually fought in this formation is uncertain. Possibly, at a given moment, the maniples of each line extended formation to fill the gaps, or, alternatively, if the two centuries of each maniple originally formed up one behind the other, the rear century in each case deployed to the left and came up alongside the one in front.[12] But it is not impossible that battle was actually joined in the original formation, for although it has been argued that this would have allowed the enemy to penetrate each line, and even get behind it, in practice this would have been very dangerous. Any enemy who tried it could very soon find himself trapped and under attack from three sides.

In the present battle it is possible that each of Regulus' legions deployed in six lines, instead of the usual three, and presumably, even if gaps were normally left between the maniples of each line, this was not the case here, since the object was clearly to produce as deep and compact a formation as possible in order to withstand the elephants. Polybios comments that in making the whole line shorter but deeper "they had hit the mark as regards fighting the elephants, but as regards fighting the cavalry, which was many times as numerous as theirs, they had completely missed it" (33.10). However, in saying this, he seems completely to have forgotten that Scipio Africanus, when faced with 80 elephants at Zama, adopted a quite different plan. Far from packing his army more closely than usual, he formed it up with the maniples of each line immediately behind those in front, thus leaving corridors down which the elephants could be ushered (15.9.7–10).

The battle opened with Xanthippos ordering the elephant-drivers to advance and the cavalry on either wing to circle outwards and charge, and at the same moment, the Roman army, clashing their spears on their shields and shouting their war-cry, also advanced. The Roman cavalry was soon swept from the field by the overwhelming numbers of the enemy – we can ignore Zonaras' statement (8.13) that it was routed by the elephants; but of the infantry, those on the left wing, partly to avoid the elephants, partly because they despised the mercenaries, attacked those on the Carthaginian right wing, and having routed them, drove them back to their camp (34.1–4). Diodoros (23.14.2) says that Xanthippos rode up and down trying to rally them, but the story that when someone shouted that it was easy enough for someone on a horse to urge others into battle, he dismounted and carried on with his exhortations on foot, is suspicious. Xenophon tells a very similar story of himself, in the retreat of the Ten Thousand (*An.* 3.4.46 ff).

Meanwhile, the Romans opposite the elephants were pushed back and trampled underfoot, though for some time, because of its depth, their whole formation held firm. But in the end, those in the rear found themselves attacked in flank and rear by the cavalry, while those in front who did manage to fight their way through the elephants found themselves faced with the fresh Carthaginian citizen-phalanx, and were cut to pieces. Of the rest, most were trampled to death by the elephants, the rest shot down by the missiles of the cavalry as they stood in their ranks.

Only very few attempted to flee, and of these, since the only line of retreat was over flat ground, some were killed by the elephants and cavalry, and about 500, who initially got away with Regulus, were shortly afterwards rounded up and taken prisoner, including the proconsul himself. Only about 2,000 of the left wing, who had pursued the mercenaries, got away to Aspis. All the rest were killed, except for those taken with the proconsul. The Carthaginians lost about 800 of the mercenaries, but apparently none worth counting from their cavalry or citizen phalanx.

Polybios follows his account of the battle with a moralizing chapter (35) on the vicissitudes of fortune, but he apparently knows nothing of the legend that Regulus was later sent to Rome on a peace mission, under oath to return if he failed, and of how, having done so, he returned to be tortured to death (cf. DS 23.16; Livy, *Per.* 18; Flo. 1.18.23–6; Eutr. 2.25; Oros. 4.10.1; Horace, *Odes* 3.5). It has been suggested that the story was invented by the Romans to exonerate Regulus' widow from the charge of having had two Carthaginian prisoners tortured to death, while in the custody of her husband's family, after his death in captivity (DS 24.12).[13] It is unlikely that even the peace mission is authentic.

But Polybios clearly had heard the almost equally implausible story about Xanthippos. He himself thought that the Spartan returned home soon after the victory rather than incur the jealousy that, as a foreigner, was always likely to come his way (36.2–3). But he adds that there was another story about Xanthippos' departure that he would "try to set out at a more suitable occasion than the present" (36.4). The "other story" was presumably the improbable one told by many of the other sources – that the Carthaginians either tried to drown, or succeeded in drowning, Xanthippos, on his way home (DS 23.16; Zon. 8.13; Val. Max. 9.6, ext.1; Sil. It. 6.682; App., *Lib.* 4). Ptolemy III of Egypt is said (Hieron. *in Daniel.* 11,7–9) to have appointed a "Xanthippos" as governor of a newly won province, in 245, and if this is the same man, Polybios may have told the "other story" in a lost part of his work, in the context of something to do with Egypt.

After their victory, the Carthaginians laid siege to Aspis, but were foiled by the spirited resistance of the Roman survivors (36.6). A fragment of Naevius (fr.50 Buechner) has been thought to indicate that the Carthaginians offered to allow the defenders to depart, but that they refused; and the following fragment (51 Buechner), that there was even opposition in Rome to sending a fleet to recover them.[14] But Polybios merely says that when news reached Rome of the disaster, preparations were immediately made to despatch a relief expedition. Indeed, it is likely that a fleet would in any case have been sent to carry supplies and reinforcements to Regulus, so preparations may already have been well advanced. Meanwhile the Carthaginians, getting wind of them, also set about repairing their existing ships and building new ones. Eventually they were able to man a fleet of 200, which put to sea to guard the approaches to Carthage (36.5–9).

As we have already seen, there is considerable controversy about the number of ships in the Roman fleet. Polybios states unequivocally that there were 350 (36.10), and the first thing to be clear about is that this is consistent with what he says about the number of their ships at the battle of Ecnomus (330: 25.7) and the number they captured there (64: 28.14). Even allowing for the 24 sunk at Ecnomus (*ibid.*), and the 40 left with Regulus in Africa, they should have had 330 left at the end of the year 256, and they could easily have scraped together a further 20 for the relief expedition. The difficulty with accepting the number 350 for this is that 114 Carthaginian ships were allegedly captured off Cape Hermaia (36.11), and presumably afterwards the 40 that had been left at Aspis were safely collected. Thus there should have been 504 ships on the return to Italy. However, in the storm off Camarina, Polybios says (37.2), there were only 364. If true, what had happened to the other 140 ships in the meantime?

The solution often adopted is arbitrarily to reduce Polybios' figures for the relief expedition to 250, or to 210, if the former figure is held to include the 40 left at Aspis. An alternative is to reject Polybios' figure for the number of Carthaginian ships captured off Cape Hermaia, and instead accept Diodoros' 24 (23.18.1), which, if Orosius' statement that nine Roman ships were lost (4.9.6) is also accepted, would mean that the fleet now numbered 365.[15] This has the merit of explaining why more is not known about the battle, which Polybios dismisses in 22 words, but which, if the Romans really captured 114 Carthaginian ships, was their greatest victory of the war.

But this would still leave the problem of the 40 ships at Aspis, and would make it difficult to explain how the consuls came to be awarded a naval triumph in January 253, as we know that they were from the triumphal records, though admittedly the triumph was over the people of Cossyra (Pantelleria), as well as over the Carthaginians. Moreover, Eutropius (2.22.1) and Orosius (4.9.5–8), although they give the Carthaginian losses as 104 sunk and only 30 captured, at least, for what it is worth, confirm that the losses were very much higher than Diodoros says.

If one is going to attempt a solution by juggling with the numbers, the simplest would be to emend Polybios' figure of 364 for the number of ships, before the storm, to 464, and to assume that he forgot the 40 ships at Aspis. Numbers are notoriously susceptible to corruption in the manuscript tradition, and here Eutropius actually does give the number of ships caught by the storm as 464 (2.22.3), which could be said to "confirm" the emendation.

Perhaps, however, we should not even try to play games like this, but attempt to account for Polybios' figures in a different way. If the Romans did launch 350 ships at the beginning of the campaign, capture 114 with their crews in the battle and recover all 40 from Aspis, do we have to assume that they would now have had 504 serviceable vessels and would have tried to get them all back to Italy? Some of their original ships, for example, may have been left at Cossyra, some may have been damaged beyond repair in the battle, even if we do not resort to Orosius' report that nine were sunk; some of the captured ones may similarly have been damaged, and even if the majority were still seaworthy, could the Romans have forced their crews to row them back to Italy? Were there still 40 at Aspis – at least one had presumably been sent to Rome with the news of the disaster – and if there were, were they all still seaworthy after a winter of neglect? In short, is it not possible that the Romans simply took the 364 most seaworthy of the 504 ships they had and burned the rest?

We should also, perhaps, take a similar line with the alleged problem of the size of the Carthaginian fleet. As we have seen, Polybios says that after repairing the ships they had and building new ones, they still only manned 200 (36.8–9), and this has been held to prove that they did not have 350 at Ecnomus, since after losing about 94 there, they should still have had some 250 available. But, again, we do not have to assume that no ships were left in Sicily, or that all that returned to Carthage after Ecnomus were serviceable. There was also the problem of manning. By now the Carthaginians should have realized that any battle they fought with the Romans was likely to turn into a boarding fight, and that to stand any chance they needed at least to match the legionaries in numbers. Even if they had 250 ships available, could they have found 30,000 soldiers, after the losses at Adys and elsewhere, and while still, presumably, at least maintaining some sort of a presence at Aspis? Moreover, if the crews of their warships came from their maritime allies and colonies, would all these have still been available? Perhaps, in the circumstances, 200 ships was all they could manage.

Returning to the campaign itself, all that Polybios says is that 350 ships were launched and placed under the command of Marcus Aemilius Paullus and Servius Fulvius Paetinus, the consuls of 255/4; that they sailed along the coast of Sicily and, encountering the Carthaginian fleet off Cape Hermaia, captured 114 ships with their crews, and that having taken on board at Aspis those who had been left in Africa, they sailed back to Sicily (36.10–12).

Zonaras (8.14) says that they were overtaken by a storm on the way to Africa, and were carried to "Corsoura", by which he clearly means Cossura or Cossyra, the modern Pantelleria, and which, he says, they ravaged and garrisoned – this, as we have seen, is borne out by the triumphal records. Zonaras then claims that in the subsequent naval battle, the Carthaginians were taken in the rear by "the Romans at Aspis", which is not impossible, though Polybios says nothing about it.[16] It might help to explain the over-whelming nature of the Roman victory, assuming that over 100 Car-thaginian ships were eliminated in one way or another. But this could just as easily be explained by the overwhelming numerical superiority the Romans enjoyed in the battle – 350 to 200, if Polybios is to be believed.

Zonaras also says that after the naval battle the Romans won a battle on land, taking many prisoners, and that they then made several raids before returning to Sicily. This is partly confirmed by Orosius (4.9.7), who claims that an army commanded by two Hannos was defeated near Clupea (Aspis), with the loss of 9,000 men, and by Livy (*Per.* 18) who talks of the "all the Roman generals" being successful "by land and sea"; Eutropius (2.22.2) even claims that the whole of Africa would then have been conquered, had not lack of supplies prevented the army remaining any longer. The last at least has the merit of making a certain sense, since if the Romans had really arrived with 350 ships, and if they were as fully manned as those that had fought at Ecnomus, there would have been something like 162,000 Romans and Italians at Aspis, to say nothing of more than 30,000 prisoners! However, although it is not impossible that there were some raids to gather supplies, and even perhaps some minor skirmishes, it is unlikely that any substantial victories were won.

At all events, eventually the Romans abandoned their beachhead and set sail for home, possibly taking 364 of the warships with them, and abandon-ing the rest. Even if there was some fighting on land, it is fairly clear that it was never the intention to try to recover the situation in Africa. The fleet, though the largest ever gathered by Rome, if Polybios is right, was intended only to rescue the remnants of Regulus' forces, not to launch a new invasion. In this respect the Roman attitude contrasts with that of their descendants in the Second Punic War. The latter, for example, refused to abandon the war in Spain after the disasters of 211, but sent first Claudius Nero and then the future Scipio Africanus, to carry on the fight. One even suspects that if they had invaded Africa in 218, as they had intended to do, and if Sempronius Longus had met with a similar disaster to Regulus', as his rash conduct at the Trebbia suggests he might well have done, the Romans then would have reinforced his army, assuming any survived, despite Hannibal's invasion of Italy. After all, they backed up the elder Scipio's decision to send his army on to Spain, and subsequently reinforced it, even after Hannibal's three great victories.

Nevertheless, the abortive invasion of Africa in 256/5 was not an unmitigated disaster for Rome. Her army had been all but annihilated, and it is clear that no further serious attention was ever given in this war to invading the Carthaginian homeland. But although the Carthaginians could congratulate themselves – or Xanthippos! – on having beaten off the invasion, there is reason to believe that it had serious repercussions in Africa. Polybios (31.2) says that after Adys, the Numidians attacked the Carthaginians and did even more damage to their territory than did the Romans; and after describing the storm that struck the Roman fleet on its way home, Orosius (4.9.9) claims that the Carthaginian general, Hamilcar, had to conduct a ruthless campaign against Numidia and Mauretania, exacting 1,000 talents of silver and 20,000 head of cattle, and crucifying the tribal chiefs. Moreover, the Carthaginian navy had been shattered, if it is true that it had lost 114 ships off Cape Hermaia, and it was to be at least five years before we hear of any further Carthaginian naval operations.

CHAPTER 8

Of elements and elephants

Apart from Scipio Asina's minor *débâcle* in 260, the Roman navy had hitherto enjoyed nothing but unbroken success, so much so that sea warfare had probably begun to seem easy to this nation of alleged landlubbers. But now the "cruel sea" itself took a hand. Off Camarina, on its way back from rescuing the remnants of the "Army of Africa", the fleet was overtaken by a storm, and, according to Polybios (37.2), of its 364 ships only 80 survived. The disaster would, of course, have been even worse if there were really 464, or even 504, ships in the fleet, for there is some agreement among the sources that however many ships there were, only 80 were saved. Thus Eutropius, as we have seen, says there were 464, but only 80 survived (22.3), and Orosius (4.9.8) that out of 300, 220 went down. Diodoros does not say how many ships there were altogether, but claims (23.18.1) that 340 warships and 300 transports were lost. According to him, too, it was King Hiero of Syracuse who looked after the survivors, providing them with food, clothing and other essentials, and eventually bringing them safely to Messana.

Polybios remarks (37.3) that "a greater disaster than this has never been recorded as happening at sea at one time", and if it is true that over 100,000 Romans and Italians perished in this single catastrophe, it is still difficult to think of a greater maritime disaster – by contrast, for example, the Spanish Armada lost something like 50 ships of all sizes and from all causes, and perhaps 20,000 men.[1] One modern historian has estimated that 15% of Italy's able-bodied men may have gone down in the storm off Camarina.[2]

Polybios says (37.4) that the commanders of the Roman fleet were to blame. The steersmen had repeatedly warned them not to sail along the south coast of Sicily, because it was rugged and had few good anchorages, and that this was a particularly dangerous time of year, being "between the rising of Orion and that of Sirius" – in our terms, between about 4 and 28 July;[3] the commanders, however, were hoping to overawe some of the coastal cities, and so paid no heed to the warnings. But Polybios' criticism may not be entirely justified. Since the western, and part of the north-western coast of Sicily was in Carthaginian hands, the consuls may have felt that it was too dangerous to adopt the alternative route,[4] and whatever we may think about their responsibility for what happened, contemporaries evidently did not hold them to blame. Both, as we have seen, went on to celebrate a naval triumph "over the people of Cossyra and the Cartha-ginians".

Polybios' more general criticism of Roman attitudes here, is more inter-esting. He says (37.7–10) that they tended always to rely on force, and thought that they had to finish anything they began, nothing they had once decided to do being impossible. As he says, this spirit often carried them through to success, but sometimes led to disaster, particularly at sea, since there they were up against not just man and his works, but the forces of nature. One is reminded here of the criticisms sometimes voiced about Napoleon's attitude to naval warfare.[5]

Folly apart, it has been suggested that there were two other reasons for the disaster – undermanning, and the *corvi*.[6] But the view that the ships were undermanned depends on assumptions about the number of captured warships being taken back to Italy, and whether or not their original Carthaginian crews could have been forced to row them, none of which can be substantiated; and as for the *corvi*, Polybios, curiously enough, only mentions them again once after their introduction at Mylae, and that is in his account of Ecnomus (27.12, 28.11). There is certainly no mention of them in his account of the battle off Cape Hermaia, though, as we have seen, this is very short. If, however, it is true that the Romans captured 114 ships there, this suggests that the battle resolved itself into a boarding fight, and that the *corvi* were still being used.[7] If so, they may well have made the warships even more than usually unseaworthy.

Polybios says (38.1–5) that the Carthaginians were encouraged by news of the disaster to think that they could now match the enemy on both land and sea. Accordingly, they sent Hasdrubal, one of the two generals elected to counter Regulus, to Sicily, "giving him the pre-existing troops, those from Heraclea who had joined them, and 140 elephants". The troops from Heraclea are presumably the 5,000 foot and 500 horse Hamilcar had brought from Sicily in 256 (30.2), but it is not easy to decide whether the "pre-existing troops" (τοὺς ... προϋπάρχοντας) are those already in Sicily, or those that had been gathered in Africa to resist Regulus – probably Polybios means the former, in view of the serious situation developing in Africa.

He also clearly implies that Hasdrubal went to Sicily in 255 or 254, but his arrival is dated by Orosius (4.9.14) and Eutropius (2.24) to 251, and the fact that he apparently did nothing to stop the Roman capture of Panormus in 254 (see below) suggests that he was not then in Sicily. The only recorded Carthaginian activities on land before 251 are the capture of Agrigentum by Carthalo, at the end of 255 or early in 254, and his relief of Drepana, also in 254, mentioned by Diodoros (23.18.2–3). It has thus been suggested that in saying that Hasdrubal was sent to Sicily in 255 or 254, Polybios was drawing on Philinos, and that the latter recorded his despatch after an account of a disaster at sea, which Polybios took to be the one off Camarina, but which was really that of 253.[8]

On the other hand, Polybios does say that Hasdrubal spent some time drilling his army and elephants (38.4), and it is possible that the Roman capture of Panormus took him by surprise. We cannot just assume that if he was already in Sicily he would have done something about it. Diodoros (23.21), indeed, says that he was later berated by his own people for his continual failure to fight. The later dating of his arrival by Orosius and Eutropius may simply be due to the assumption that it shortly preceded the battle of Panormus.

There is also a problem with Polybios' statement that Carthage began to prepare 200 ships as early as the year 255 or 254 (38.3), since it is not until 250 that we hear of any Carthaginian naval activity, except for the recapture of Cossyra (Zon. 8.14) and the seizure of some Roman ships, laden with the spoils of Panormus, in 254 (Dio 11.29a, cf. Zon. 8.14). It has thus been suggested that Polybios' 200 ships were merely transports, and that they were used to carry Hasdrubal's troops to Sicily, though Polybios clearly meant that they were warships.[9] He may be wrong, but he does, after all, merely say that the Carthaginians "began to prepare" (κατεσκευάζοντο: 38.3) 200 ships, and it may be that some unknown factors such as difficulties of manning or lack of funds prevented them from being fully operational until 250. It is also possible that, for some time, recovering control in Africa absorbed most of Carthage's energies. Awareness of Carthaginian naval preparations may explain the haste with which Rome strove to build up her naval strength, but, as usual, one should be wary of assuming that the Romans did know what Carthage was doing, let alone what she had decided to do.[10]

Even if there was some Carthaginian activity both in Sicily and in the dockyards of Carthage in the year 254, it was evidently the Romans who made the quicker recovery from the disastrous year 255, and this was an earnest of things to come. According to Polybios (38.5), they immediately decided to build 220 new ships, and completed the job in three months – "which," as he says (38.6), "is not easy to believe." Inevitably, some modern commentators have not believed it, and it has been suggested that Polybios' 220 ships included the 80 that had survived the disaster off Camarina, though he clearly thought that they were additional, since to the consuls of 254 he gives 300 ships for the attack on Panormus (38.7);[11] even Diodoros (23.18.3) gives them 250. There really is no compelling reason to doubt Polybios here, and what he says about the size of the Roman fleet in the following years is consistent.

Despite the ship-building programme, however, there was evidently no intention, for the time being at any rate, of renewing the strategy of attacking Africa. Instead, clearly, the intention was to use the fleet for what would now be called "combined operations" in Sicily. It may not be entirely a coincidence that one of the new consuls for 254/3 was none other than Scipio Asina, who had so disastrously led the leading elements of the fleet in its first foray, and, after being taken prisoner at Lipara, had presumably been exchanged in the meantime. Both consuls, indeed, had held the office before – the other being A. Atilius Caiatinus – and they were presumably now chosen for their experience. But although Caiatinus had performed creditably enough, one would not have thought Scipio Asina's performance would have won him much credit with the electorate. However, the Cornelii Scipiones were one of the most influential of Roman families, and very much a law unto themselves. One thinks of the way the future Scipio Africanus secured the command in Spain, after the deaths of his father and uncle in 211, despite never having held any office higher than that of aedile.

Probably as soon as the weather allowed, then, the two consuls put to sea, and having picked up the ships that had survived the storm, at Messana, descended on Panormus (Palermo) with a fleet of 300 sail (38.6–7).[12] Diodoros (23.18.3), says that the attack was preceded by the capture of Kephaloidion (Cefalu) by treachery, and an abortive attempt on Drepana (Trapani). The latter was beaten off by the enterprising Carthalo, who had previously recaptured Agrigentum, but, evidently feeling unable to hold it, had burnt it to the ground and razed its walls, while the surviving inhabitants took refuge in the temple of Olympian Zeus. A Roman attack on Kephaloidion before the assault on Panormus, is, of course, entirely

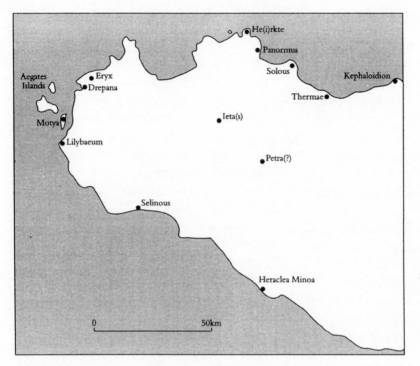

Figure 8.1   Western Sicily.

plausible, since Kephaloidion was on the way to Panormus, but an attack on Drepana, beyond Panormus, seems less likely, unless it was a feint designed to distract the Carthaginians from the real target. Since Scipio Asina alone eventually celebrated a triumph – as proconsul on 21 March 252 – the consuls possibly divided their forces, with Atilius Caiatinus being unsuccessful at Drepana.

Polybios says (38.8–9) that at Panormus the Romans constructed siege-works in two places, and having brought up their siege-engines, easily knocked down "the tower by the sea". This gave them access to the "new town", which was taken by force, whereupon the inhabitants of the "old town" surrendered. Diodoros (23.18.4) says the Romans anchored in the harbour, and entirely surrounded the city with a palisade and trench. They then breached the wall with siege-engines. He also says (23.18.5) that 14,000 of the inhabitants were released on payment of 2 minae each, the remaining 13,000 and other booty being sold. Changes since antiquity, and particularly the silting up of the harbour, have made it difficult to be certain of the topography. The area of the modern town known as "Cassaro", which derives from the Arabic "Al Qasr" meaning "fortress", is probably the "old town", and the "new town" probably lay south of the Fiume di Mal Tempo, perhaps including the area now known as "Kalsa".[13]

Diodoros (23.18.5) adds that before the consuls withdrew, the people of Ieta (Ietas, Iaitas; now San Giuseppe), in the hills about 15 miles southwest of Panormus, expelled their Carthaginian garrison and defected to Rome, and that they were followed by those of Solous, Petra (Petrina, about 25 miles south of Panormus on the route to Agrigentum?), Enattaros (whereabouts unknown) and Tyndaris. If all this is true – and there is no reason to doubt it – the only places in Sicily of any importance left to Carthage were now Thermae, Drepana, Lilybaeum, Selinous and Heraclea Minoa.

Despite what both Polybios and Diodoros say, it is probable that only one consul, Atilius Caiatinus, returned to Rome, taking the fleet with him, and that Scipio Asina remained in Sicily, with perhaps at least two legions. Diodoros (23.18.5) says that both withdrew to Messana, so possibly Scipio accompanied his colleague as far as that. Cassius Dio (11.29a, cf. Zon. 8.14), as we have seen, says that some Roman ships, laden with booty, were captured by the Carthaginians on their way home. If true, these may have been transports, though not necessarily so – evident superiority at sea may have bred a dangerous complacency in the Romans. Nor need we necessarily suppose that the Carthaginian ships were part of the "home fleet" ranging far from Carthage: there may well still have been a few based on Sicily, Sardinia or the Lipari islands.[14]

The successes of 254 had been due partly to co-operation between fleet and army, partly to Rome's evident naval superiority in Sicilian coastal waters, and one might have expected a renewal of the strategy in 253, with determined efforts against Drepana and Lilybaeum. Instead, although there were probably again four legions in Sicily, under Scipio Asina, and one of the consuls for 253/2, Cn. Servilius Caepio (see below), we hear of only one operation there – an abortive attack on Lilybaeum – and the fleet goes off to Africa under the other consul of 253/2, Gaius Sempronius Blaesus. Possibly it was felt that stirring up renewed trouble for Carthage in Africa would prevent any reinforcements coming to Sicily, and might even lead to a quicker resumption of peace negotiations, with Rome holding the stronger hand, than the slow and laborious process of storming major strongholds.[15]

As usual, Polybios implies (39.1–6) that both consuls were involved in the raid on Africa, and is supported by Zonaras (8.14), Orosius (4.9.10) and Eutropius (2.23). But in fact, since Blaesus alone celebrated a triumph, it is almost certain that it was he alone who was in command of the fleet, and that his colleague commanded in Sicily, with the proconsul, Scipio Asina. It may, however, be true, as Zonaras alleges (*ibid.*), that the fleet first made an abortive attack on Lilybaeum, before going on to Africa. Once there, according to Polybios (39.2), it made a number of landings, but accomplished nothing worthy of note, before reaching the island of Meninx (Djerba) and almost coming to grief on the shoals of the lesser Syrtis (the Gulf of Gabes).

Diodoros (23.19) appears to imply that it was prevented from anchoring by the Carthaginians, but unless it was already in serious difficulties on the shoals,[16] it is difficult to believe that the Carthaginian navy was as yet capable of intervening. Polybios says that the whole Roman fleet was involved in the operation (39.1), which should mean at least 300 ships (see above), and even if there were only 260, as Orosius (4.9.10) and Eutropius (2.23) say, and the Carthaginians had meanwhile been building up their naval strength to 200, they would hardly have ventured to interfere with a Roman fleet with such a numerical superiority, unless they felt that they had an opportunity to catch it at a serious disadvantage.

The later sources also make much more of the raids than Polybios, alleging that the whole coastline was devastated, and even many inland towns taken and plundered. One might be inclined to put all this down to Roman exaggeration, but Blaesus must have done something to warrant a triumph, particularly in view of the disaster that was to befall him on the way home, and Diodoros does mention the "booty" (cf. λαφύρων: 23.19) lost in that disaster. The raid was obviously directed at one of the richest areas of the Carthaginian dominions, and it is more than likely that the depredations were correspondingly widespread.

But any successes the Romans may have had on land were once again offset by their ignorance of the sea, though perhaps in this case they were not so much to blame. The tide normally has a negligible effect in the Mediterranean, but in exceptional circumstances can be quite dangerous. Here, according to the Mediterranean Pilot, a spring tide can be as high as 6 feet at Bordj Djillidj at the north-west corner of Djerba, and from 3 to 5 feet elsewhere in the Gulf of Gabes, and the ebb can be correspondingly low. Thus the Roman fleet found itself stuck fast, and only managed to get off by lightening the ships of all heavy objects. Was it here, one wonders, that the *corvi* were finally jettisoned?

If so, it did not save the fleet, for worse was to come. Their departure from the Syrtis was "very like a flight", according to Polybios (39.5), but they reached Sicily safely and, rounding Lilybaeum, came to anchor at Panormus. Presumably the consul, Sempronius Blaesus, was wary of taking the south-coast route after what had happened two years before, and in any case, with Panormus now in Roman hands, the alternative route round the west end of the island was less hazardous and shorter. But instead of hugging the north coast, Blaesus now chose to take the direct route back to Italy, and ran into another storm – Orosius says off Cape Palinurus (Palinuro: 4.9.11), in Lucania. Here, according to Polybios (39.6), 150 ships – by which he clearly means warships – went down, and Diodoros gives the same figure (23.19), though he adds horse-transports; Orosius says 150 transports (*naves onerariae*) perished, but this is probably a mistake.[17] As was the case after the previous storm, Blaesus was evidently not held to blame, but duly celebrated a triumph for his African "victories".

Polybios passes straight from his account of this second naval disaster to the sending of Lucius Caecilius Metellus and Gaius Furius Pacilus, the consuls of 251/0, to Sicily (39.7–8), thus omitting all mention of the intervening consulship of Gaius Aurelius Cotta and Publius Servilius Geminus in 252/1. However, he does remark (39.12) that "for the two following years", the Romans avoided battle, and these are plainly the years 252 and 251.[18] The reason he gives for the Roman reluctance to fight is that they were afraid of the Carthaginian elephants, and, as we have seen (above, p. 113), there is some reason to believe that it was in 252, after the second disaster, that Hasdrubal was sent to Sicily with his elephants, though Polybios dates this to 255 or 254, after the first disaster. He also implies that Rome abandoned naval operations after the second disaster, only manning 60 ships in 251/0 (39.7–8), and Orosius (4.9.12) and Eutropius (2.23) confirm this as the size of the fleet in 252.

However, Polybios does mention two Roman operations that took place in this period of inactivity, the capture of Therma and Lipara, both now very isolated after the Roman capture of Panormus in 254. From other sources we can date these operations to 252. Both consuls of that year evidently served in Sicily, and we know from the triumphal records that one of them, Aurelius Cotta, celebrated a triumph "over the Sicilians". Orosius (4.9.13) talks in terms of a rampage through the length and breadth of Sicily, in which Cotta allegedly won many a battle on both land and sea against both Carthaginians and Sicilians, and left unburied heaps of corpses belonging to the enemy and to his own allies. More soberly, Zonaras (8.14) says the consuls captured Himera, among other places, and by this he almost certainly means what Polybios calls Therma, which was sometimes known as "Therma of Himera" (Thermae Himeraeae).

Diodoros (23.19–20) talks of two occasions on which the Romans attacked Therma. On the first, he says, the gate-keeper, who had gone outside to relieve himself, was captured by them, but offered to open the gate at night if he was released. The Romans agreed and, having fixed a time, sent 1,000 men. At this point, unfortunately, the surviving fragment becomes somewhat obscure, but it appears to say that the Roman assault-party ordered the gate-keeper to close the gate and not allow anyone else in, hoping to seize all the plunder for themselves, whereupon they were all killed by the townspeople. Though improbable, this is partly borne out by Zonaras' claim (*ibid.*) that although the Romans took "Himera", they failed to capture any of its inhabitants because the Carthaginians had managed to evacuate them. If there was a first attack that failed, for whatever reason, the Carthaginians might have been able to get the inhabitants away, leaving an empty town for the Romans to capture at the second attempt.

The second, successful operation belonging to the year 252 was the capture, at last, of Lipara, which the Romans had already attacked three times without success, in 260, 258 and 257. This last attack on the place is mentioned by Polybios, as we have seen, and by Diodoros (23.20), and credited specifically to Aurelius Cotta by Zonaras (8.14). He says that he secured some ships from Hiero,[19] and, after landing his troops on the island, left a tribune, Quintus Cassius, to continue the siege, ordering him to avoid battle. The tribune, inevitably, disobeyed orders and assaulted the town, suffering heavy losses in the process. However, the consul subsequently took the place, massacred its inhabitants, and stripped Cassius of his command. Valerius Maximus (2.7.4) has a similar story, but says that the disobedient tribune was a relative of the consul's, one Publius Aurelius Pecuniola, and that he was flogged, though this is improbable in the case of a high-ranking Roman citizen. Aurelius celebrated a triumph as consul on 13 April 251, and it has been suggested that the coins imitating those of Lipara struck nearly 200 years later by his descendant, the consul of 65, were to commemorate his ancestor's success.[20] Less successful, if we are to believe Diodoros (23.20), was an assault on He(i)rkte (Monte Castellachio? see below, p. 147) by 40,000 men, i.e. both consular armies.

Apart from these operations, the lull in Sicily seems to have extended at least into 251, and probably into 250. The date of the campaign that ended it and culminated in Metellus' victory at Panormus is uncertain, but it probably belongs to the latter year. Polybios leaves the year unclear, but talks of the campaign's taking place "at the height of the harvest" (40.1), i.e. in June, and the fact that he also says that Metellus had been left at

Panormus when his fellow-consul departed (*ibid.*) suggests 250, since it was quite common for one or both consuls to return to Italy at the end of the campaigning season in their year of office, in this case 251. It is true that the later sources (DS 23.21; Flo. 1.18.27; Eutr. 2.24; Oros. 4.9.14; Front., *Strat.* 2.5.4) all describe Metellus as "consul" at the time of his victory, but this may derive from Livy, who sometimes seems to have confused consuls and proconsuls at this time. In any case, if the battle was fought in June 250, it is not impossible that Metellus was still consul, since the date at which consuls took office at this time is uncertain. The other argument that has been advanced for putting the battle in 251 is that there is a tradition of peace negotiations after it, and that it would be difficult to fit them into 250, since Metellus triumphed in early September. However, these alleged negotiations are part of the Regulus legend, and are probably unhistorical (see below).[21]

At all events, the lull was eventually broken by the Carthaginians. According to Polybios (40.1–2), their commander, Hasdrubal, had duly noted the wariness the Romans had shown when near his forces, and when he learnt that one of the consuls had returned to Italy with half the army, leaving the other, Caecilius Metellus, at Panormus to protect the allies during the harvest, he marched on the city from Lilybaeum, taking up a position on the frontier. Caecilius, playing upon the aggressive spirit the enemy was showing, refused to be drawn, and thus provoked Hasdrubal into a further advance "through the pass leading into the territory of Panormus (40.4)", which probably means the route via the ancient Iaetas or Ietas (modern San Giuseppe) into the valley of the Orethus (modern Oreto). Zonaras (8.14) adds that Hasdrubal sent spies into the city, but that Metellus was able to detect them by assembling its people and telling them to take hold of those they recognized. However, since he tells the same story of Mummius at the destruction of Corinth (9.31), it is difficult to know which, if either, story to believe.

Metellus, meanwhile, stuck to his plan, allowing the enemy to ravage right up to the walls, until they had been induced to cross "the river that runs in front of the town" (probably the Oreto: 40.5). But once the elephants and other forces had crossed, he kept sending his light troops out to harass them, until Hasdrubal was compelled to deploy his whole army. Metellus then ordered his light troops to take up a position in front of the ditch outside the wall and to continue firing at the enemy, paying particular attention to any elephants that charged them. If they were driven back, they were to take refuge in the trench, and then re-emerge when the opportunity came; a constant supply of missiles was to be provided by the poorer people of the town, who were ordered to pile them at the foot of the wall. Metellus himself, with his heavy infantry, took up a position inside the gate that faced the enemy left wing, feeding reinforcements out to the light troops when necessary.

As a more general engagement began to develop, the elephant-drivers, anxious to demonstrate their prowess to Hasdrubal, charged the foremost Roman troops and drove them back to the ditch. But there the elephants came under increasingly heavy fire from the wall and from the fresh forces in front of the ditch, and the wounded beasts rapidly became confused. Wheeling round, they blundered back into their own troops, trampling them down and spreading confusion in their ranks. At this moment, Metellus, seeing what was happening, made a vigorous sortie, and, falling on the flank of the disorganized enemy with his fresh forces under complete control, utterly routed them. Of their losses, Polybios merely records the taking of ten elephants with their drivers, and the subsequent capture of all the rest after they had thrown their drivers (40.15): the secondary sources report the numbers as between 60 (DS 23.21) and 140 or 142 (Pliny, NH 8.16). Eutropius (2.24) and Orosius (4.9.15) give the Carthaginian losses in men as 20,000, out of a total of 30,000 according to the latter, who also says that Hasdrubal was later condemned to death (cf. Zon. 8.14).

On the battle, Diodoros (23.21) says that Hasdrubal's Celtic mercenaries were drunk on wine supplied to them by merchants, and were yelling in complete disorder when Metellus fell upon them. Zonaras has the Carthaginian fleet play a part in the operations, though he says it only added to the rout by causing a stampede in its direction by fugitives desperate to be taken off by sea, of whom some were drowned, others trampled to death by the elephants, and others again slaughtered by the Romans.[22] More believable, perhaps, is Zonaras' story that Metellus offered freedom to any of the prisoners who could control the elephants, and thereby secured their capture, but whether we can believe that the elephants were then ferried across the straits of Messana on rafts constructed of floating jars held together by planks and made to look like a courtyard, is another question, though the elder Pliny (NH 8.16) and Frontinus (Strat. 1.7.1) have the same story. Hannibal transported his elephants across the Rhône on rafts made of tree trunks made to look like the track leading down to the river (3.46). But to transport elephants across a river on rafts is one thing; to transport them across 10 miles of sea quite another. Metellus' elephants were later slaughtered in the circus, and coins of his family subsequently often depict them.[23]

It is after Metellus' victory that many of the secondary sources place the sending of Regulus to Rome from Carthage, in an attempt to bring about a peace, or at the very least to discuss an exchange of prisoners (Livy, *Per.* 18; Oros. 4.10.1; Eutr. 2.25; Flo. 1.18.23–6; Dio 11.26; Zon. 8.15). The peace mission itself is not unbelievable, but it really stands or falls with the story of Regulus' heroic advice to his fellow-countrymen not to make peace, and of his noble return and death at the hands of his captors, and it is difficult to believe in the latter. Apart from anything else, it was not normally Carthaginian practice to use prisoners as negotiators in this kind of way. After Cannae, there are similar stories of some of Hannibal's prisoners being sent to discuss ransoming, but the negotiation of peace was entrusted to a Carthaginian. In this case, one or more of the prisoners are said to have remained or tried to remain in Rome after the failure of their mission (Livy 21.58 ff).

The battle of Panormus was the last set-piece battle fought in Sicily during the war, and it looks as though the Carthaginians now believed that they could not face the Roman army in such circumstances. Though the land-war was to last another eight years, under Hamilcar Barca it was to become very much one of guerrilla operations, in which, although he held his own, he did not venture any kind of decisive engagement. Indeed, from now on, the Carthaginian strategy on land was, to all intents and purposes, entirely defensive.

CHAPTER 9

Carthage resurgent

Polybios implies that the Romans had begun to build 50 new ships even before Metellus' victory at Panormus (39.15), and there is some reason to believe that the men responsible were the consuls of 250/49, Gaius Atilius Regulus and Lucius Manlius Vulso. Both men had been consul before – in 257/6 and 256/5 respectively – and both had had some experience of naval warfare, for Atilius Regulus had commanded against Malta and at Tyndaris, and Manlius Vulso at Ecnomus. The target this time was clearly to be Lilybaeum, and this represents a reversion to the strategy of 254, which had been interrupted by Blaesus' raid on Africa and resumed on a smaller scale in 252 only because of the disaster suffered by Blaesus' fleet on its return. Polybios later says (41.3) that the fleet with which Atilius and Manlius eventually put to sea numbered 200 ships, and this is consistent with what he says earlier about numbers. The attack on Panormus in 254 had involved 300 ships (38.7), the raid on Africa in 253 "the whole fleet" (cf. 39.1), and "more than 150" of these ships had been destroyed in the storm on their way back to Italy (39.6).

The only contrary evidence is that at the battle of Drepana, in 249, the Romans only had about 123 ships (51.11–12: see below), but these were not necessarily all that had originally been taken to Lilybaeum. A winter had intervened and it is not at all impossible that some of the ships there had been withdrawn in the meantime. This could well have happened at the end of 250, when winter drew near. It was quite usual in this war for one consul to return home at the end of the year, as we have seen, and Zonaras in fact says that it happened this year (8.15). He claims that it was because of disease and lack of food, and feeding nearly 70,000 sailors and marines in addition to the land forces would have greatly added to the difficulties.

Further evidence that the besieging forces were reduced at some point is, first, that Polybios, in his account of the mercenary officers' plot (see below), says they spoke to "the Roman consul", in the singular (43.1), and, similarly, it is "the consul" who later supervises the first attempt to capture Hannibal the Rhodian (46.8). Secondly, Polybios implies that after the arrival of the relieving forces, the besieged numbered "not less than 20,000" and the besiegers "even more than this" (ἔτι πλείους τούτων: 45.8): although vague, this can hardly mean that the latter still numbered over 100,000 men, as they once had done.

Later in 249, moreover, the consul, Iunius Pullus, having been sent to sea with 60 ships, picked up at Messana "those of the ships that had assembled there from the army and the rest of Sicily" (τὰ συνηντηκότα τῶν πλοίων ἀπό τε τοῦ στρατοπέδου καὶ τῆς ἄλλης Σικελίας: 52.6), and then went on his way to Syracuse with 120 ships. It is difficult enough to account for these numbers without presupposing that Rome had only had about 120 before the battle of Drepana, whereas if some or all of Iunius' original 60 were new, which is not impossible, those he picked up at Messana could easily have come from the fleet sent to Lilybaeum in 250.[1]

Finally, for what it is worth, Diodoros (24.1.1) gives 240 as the number of ships in that fleet, and if this was really the total available in 250, it would almost exactly account for the c.123 of Claudius Pulcher's fleet at Drepana and Iunius Pullus' fleet of 120, in the year 249. However, if there had really been 240 ships at the start of the siege of Lilybaeum, the total number of besiegers should have been nearly 122,000 men. Since both consuls were present, the army, presumably, consisted of four legions, as indeed Orosius says (4.10.2), or about 40,000 men, and 240 ships would have contained a further 81,600 (240 × 340). In fact, however, Diodoros gives the total as 110,000 (ibid.), which could represent a double consular army and the crews and marines of only 200 ships (108,000 men).[2] Thus it seems best, as usual, to accept Polybios' figure of 200 ships for the year 250.

The attack on Lilybaeum, though it never succeeded, marks another turning-point in the war, for this was the most important Carthaginian base in Sicily, and it is safe to say that its loss would have effectively put an end to their presence there. In short, the Romans were now striking at the heart of the Carthaginian enclave in Sicily instead of nibbling at its edges. Polybios, indeed, says that it was the last base left to the Carthaginians in Sicily, apart from Drepana (41.6), and Diodoros records (24.1.1) that before

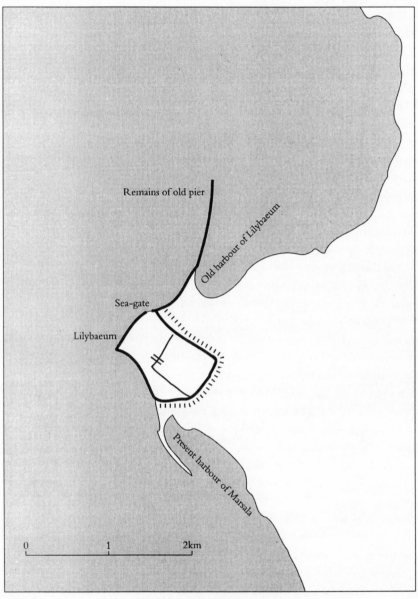

Figure 9.1 Lilybaeum.

it was laid under siege, Selinous had been razed and its population transferred thither. Possibly Heraclea Minoa had also suffered the same fate, for
although it is mentioned in Polybios' account of the naval operations in
249 (53.7), what he says does not necessarily imply that it was still inhabited, and it is never mentioned again in the course of the war.

125

The original garrison of Lilybaeum perhaps numbered 7,000 foot and 700 cavalry, as Diodoros says (24.1.1), for although Polybios (42.11) gives the number as "about 10,000", it is possible that 4,000 more troops were brought in early on in the siege, by Adherbal, as Diodoros again says (24.1.2), though Polybios does not mention this. Zonaras also mentions a relief operation commanded by Adherbal (8.15), but does not say that any troops were brought, only food and money. The alternative is that the relief force mentioned by Diodoros and Zonaras is the one Polybios says was brought in by Hannibal, the son of Hamilcar, which numbered 10,000 men (44.2), for this is not mentioned by the former two sources. The discrepancy in the names of the commanders could be explained by assuming that Adherbal was in overall charge of the expedition, but that he left his friend, Hannibal, actually to take the reinforcements in to the beleaguered city, while he went on to Drepana, as Polybios may seem to hint (44.1).

But this is certainly not what Polybios says, and does not explain the discrepancies between the numbers either for the original garrison, or for the relieving force. So probably there were two relief expeditions, the first commanded by Adherbal, who then proceeded to Drepana, the second by Hannibal, who joined him there. If so, it is interesting that Adherbal, like Hannibal (see below), possibly waited for a high wind before the run-in to Lilybaeum – Zonaras' word is *cheimôn* (χειμών – 8.15, but see above, p. 77). Whether there was one relief-expedition or two, the garrison in the end seems to have consisted largely of Celtic and Greek mercenaries (43.4; 48.3), and, presumably, included the remnants of the army defeated outside Panormus. Their commander was now Himilco (42.12).

Lilybaeum, the modern Marsala, lay at the extreme western tip of Sicily. It had been founded in 396 to replace Motya (Mozia), just to the north, after the latter had been destroyed by Dionysios I of Syracuse. It was defended by strong walls and towers, and a ditch said by Diodoros (24.1.2) to be 90 feet wide and 60 deep.[3] The modern harbour lies to the south of the town, but the ancient one was to the north, and approach to it was made dangerous by shoals for any who did not know the waters – the "pitiless shoals of Lilybaeum, with their hidden rocks" (*vada dura . . . saxis Lilybeia caecis*) of Vergil's *Aeneid* (3.706, cf. Plb. 1.42.7).

The Roman besiegers set up two camps, one on either side of the city, as was their wont when two consuls were in the field (cf. at Agrigentum: 18.2), and both Polybios and Diodoros say they linked them with continuous lines consisting of a ditch, palisade and wall (42.8, cf. DS 24.1.1). However, Polybios later again says that they did this after they had given up any attempt to assault the city (48.10), so he is possibly anticipating in the earlier passage. Diodoros also says (*ibid.*) that they constructed catapults, rams, and various types of sheds to protect their workers, and blocked the entrance to the harbour with 15 light vessels, loaded with stones and presumably sunk. The assault began, according to Polybios (42.8), at "the tower lying nearest the sea towards the Libyan Sea", by which he presumably means the tower at the south-west corner of the perimeter. After this had been demolished, the attacks were then extended eastwards until a further six towers had been demolished, and the rest damaged (42.9). The defenders replied with counter-building and counter-mining, and with sorties to try to burn the siege-works, the fighting becoming so desperate, according to Polybios (42.13), that at times more men fell than in a pitched battle.

At this point there occurred one of the rare examples of treachery among Carthage's mercenaries. According to Polybios (43), some of their highest-ranking officers, having talked things over, and convinced that their men would follow them, slipped out of the city at night to parley with the consul. A Greek from Achaia, however, by name Alexon, got wind of their treachery and informed Himilco. Polybios says (43.2 and 8) that on a previous occasion Alexon had been instrumental in saving Agrigentum from a similar plot by Syracusan mercenaries, but it is uncertain when this incident occurred.[4] On this occasion, Himilco assembled the remaining officers, and by means of lavish promises induced them to remain loyal. He then sent them to persuade their men, accompanied, in the case of the Celts, by the son of the Hannibal executed in Sardinia, also called Hannibal, and in that of the Greeks by Alexon himself. The men, too, were thus won over, and when the treacherous officers came up openly to the walls and attempted to persuade them to hand the city over, they were driven off with showers of stones and missiles.

Meanwhile, the Carthaginian government, knowing nothing of all this, but calculating that reinforcements would be required, had assembled a relieving force of 10,000 men (44.2). These were apparently crammed onto 50 warships, since nothing is said of transports: presumably, for so desperate an enterprise, warships would have been faster and handier than transports.[5] The man placed in command was Hannibal, son of the Hamilcar who had been one of the generals in the victory over Regulus, and who had subsequently been sent to subdue the Numidians and Moors. Polybios describes the son as a trierarch (i.e. captain of a ship) and "most intimate friend" (φίλος πρῶτος: 44.1) of Adherbal, who, it later appears (46.1), was in command at Drepana. Either the latter had already brought reinforcements over to Lilybaeum and had then gone to Drepana, or now he was in overall charge of this operation, and went on to Drepana while Hannibal took the relief force in to Lilybaeum (see above).

Hannibal took his fleet first to the Aegusae islands (Aegates, Egadi), where he waited for a favourable wind – he would, ideally, have wanted one from west-northwest. When it came, he hoisted sails and running before it, headed straight for the mouth of the harbour of Lilybaeum, his men drawn up on deck, ready for action (44.2–3). Recent sea-trials with the reconstructed trireme have shown that such a ship can be sailed before the wind faster than it can be rowed, and almost certainly the same was true of quinqueremes. The Roman fleet, meanwhile, partly taken by surprise, partly worried that it would be carried into the harbour with the enemy by the force of the wind, stood out to sea (44.4), presumably with its ships under oar.

Nothing is said here about the 15 block-ships that Diodoros says (24.1.1) had been sunk in the mouth of the harbour, so either what he says is untrue, or the block-ships had been ineffective, or the Carthaginians had somehow removed them. He also says that after the arrival of his relief-force of 4,000 men, which may, as we have seen, have been an earlier episode, the Romans had again blocked the entrance to the harbour with stones, jetties and anchored booms, but that this had all been destroyed in a storm (24.1.2). However, this looks more like a version of the similar action Polybios records as having been taken in response to the exploits of Hannibal the Rhodian (47.3–4: see below). The present Hannibal's exploit once again shows the inability of ancient warships to maintain a permanent and effective blockade.

Taking advantage of the renewal of confidence among his original troops, and while the morale of the relief force was still high, Himilco now decided to make a determined dawn sortie at a number of points, with his whole force, in an attempt to destroy the siege-works. However, the besiegers had foreseen this and were not taken by surprise. The result was a confused and desperate fight all round the walls, in which the besieged came very near to success. But, in the end, since they had not gained the advantage of surprise, sheer numbers probably began to tell, and Himilco, worried at his losses and seeing that success was eluding him, ordered his trumpeters to sound the retreat (45). That night Hannibal took his ships out of the harbour and proceeded to Drepana to meet his friend, Adherbal (46.1–3). It is also possible that it was he who took the garrison's 700 horse, who would be useless in a siege, to Drepana, for although Diodoros apparently dates this to after the firing of the Roman siege-works (24.1.3: see below), no further relief-expeditions are reported.[6]

But this was by no means the end either of the siege or of the Carthaginian navy's exploits, for it was now that Hannibal "the Rhodian" ('Ρόδιος: 46.4 ff) came on the scene. Such nicknames were not uncommon among the Carthaginians, who, as we have seen, seem to have had a very limited stock of personal names, at any rate as far as those mentioned in literature – i.e. leading men – are concerned. Thus we hear later, for example, of Mago "the Samnite" and Mago "the Bruttian" (9.25.4, 36.5.1). It has even been suggested that the nicknames became hereditary in certain families like similar Roman *cognomina*. In this case, there is mention of a Carthaginian envoy to Alexander named Hamilcar, and nicknamed "Rhodanus" or "Rodinus" (Oros. 4.6.21; Just. 21.6.1; Front., *Strat.*, 1.2.3), who may have been an ancestor of our Hannibal.[7] Whether or not the nickname was hereditary, it may originally have been given in recognition of outstanding seamanship, for the Rhodians at this time were regarded as being among the finest sailors in the Mediterranean. It was certainly appropriate for our "Rhodian".

According to Polybios (46.4 ff), he volunteered to sail into Lilybaeum to get news of the siege, and having fitted out his own ship, crossed to "one of the islands lying before Lilybaeum" – presumably one of the Egadi – just as the previous Hannibal had done, and after waiting for a favourable wind, sailed into Lilybaeum at about 10 o'clock in the morning, in full view of the enemy. What is more, next day he slipped out even though the Roman consul had personally seen to the preparation of ten of his fastest ships to watch the harbour entrance, and he and – it is said – his whole army were at the harbour to see what would happen. Having swept past the enemy ships "as though they were standing still", Hannibal stopped, with oars feathered, as though challenging them to fight, and when none moved, proceeded on his way.

He continued to perform the feat on a number of occasions, thereby bringing invaluable information back to Carthage, and at the same time raising the spirits of the defenders, and encouraging other captains to emulate him. Polybios says (47.1–2) that he was able to manage it because, from experience, he had exactly noted the course through the shoals. Coming in "from the parts towards Italy" (τῶν κατὰ τὴν Ἰταλίαν μερῶν: 47.2 – i.e. the north), he would get "the tower on the sea" (τὸν ἐπὶ θαλάττης πύργον – i.e., apparently one at the north-west corner of the *enceinte*, near the old sea gate) on his bow, "so that it was in front of all the towers of the city turned towards Africa" (οὕτως ὥστε τοῖς πρὸς τὴν Λιβύην τετραμμένοις πύργοις τῆς πόλεως ἐπιπροσθεῖν ἅπασι). This last phrase should mean the towers on the south wall, but this makes nonsense of the navigation, and we must remember that according to Polybios' own orientation, Lilybaeum itself was at the corner of Sicily facing towards Africa (cf. τέτραπται ... εἰς αὐτὴν Λιβύην: 42.6). Thus the towers on its west wall would for him be the ones facing Africa. In other words, Hannibal lined up the tower by the sea so that it covered the towers on the west wall, and then sailed straight in to the harbour.[8]

But his luck could not last, and eventually he was captured. Polybios says that most of the Roman attempts to block the harbour mouth failed because of the depth of water and shifting currents, but that eventually they were able to build up a bank on which an enemy quadrireme, coming out at night, ran aground and was captured. It happened to be a particularly fast vessel, and the Romans manned it with a select crew. Hannibal had sailed in the night it was captured, and when he put to sea again, he was alarmed to see the quadrireme that he thought had already gone putting out at the same time. He tried to out-run it, but finding himself being overhauled, turned to engage, and was overwhelmed by the numerous, picked boarders the Romans had crammed on board. The Romans then also fitted his ship out for stopping the blockade-runners (47.4 ff), and eventually used it as a model for the fleet that won the final battle of the war.

Meanwhile the siege of Lilybaeum went on, and it is probably here that some of the incidents Diodoros describes belong (24.1.2–3). Polybios merely says (48.1) that the besieged were still energetically building counter-works, and had given up the attempt to destroy the enemy's, but Diodoros first says that the Romans constructed a stone-throwing catapult, which the defenders countered by building an inner wall. Then the Romans filled the ditch, and by drawing off the defenders by a feint-assault on the seaward side, were able to spring a surprise attack on a different section of the wall with concealed troops, and so managed to capture the outer wall. However, Himilco was somehow able to turn the tables on these troops and annihilate them, perhaps by contriving to trap them between the inner and outer walls.

Next Polybios describes how the rise of a "steady wind" (τις ἀνέμου στάσις: 48.8)[9] blew away the sheds used for moving the siege-engines up into position and the towers in front of them, and says that this gave some of the mercenaries the idea that here was a splendid opportunity to fire the works. They were able to do so at three separate points, and with the timbers being old and dry, the steady wind did the rest. Sparks and flames were blown into the faces of the Romans as they tried to put the fires out, and since the smoke was naturally blown in the same direction, the besiegers could also see where to aim their missiles, which were given added force by the gale. The result was that the bases of the towers and the beams of the rams were made useless, and the Romans abandoned the attempt to take the city by assault. Instead they dug a trench, protected by a stockade, right round it, and settled down "to leave the matter to time", as Polybios says (48.10), while the gallant defenders rebuilt the fallen sections of the wall, and also confidently waited for the siege to run its course.

Diodoros also mentions the difficulties the Romans had in supplying their forces, and the sickness from which they began to suffer through eating infected meat. It was only through the efforts of Hiero of Syracuse in supplying them with grain that they were able to continue the siege (24.1.4). Zonaras (8.15) says much the same, and adds, as we have seen, that one of the consuls was forced to return home with his forces. He also says that the supply situation was rendered more difficult by the raiding of the cavalry based on Drepana, and that Adherbal was able to ravage the shores not only of Sicily, but of Italy. Since his base lay athwart the north-coast route, it was presumably virtually impossible for supplies to be carried to Lilybaeum by sea.

When the news of what was going on there reached Rome, it was thus evidently decided that the first thing to do was to try to recover command at sea. Presumably it was known that there was now a powerful Carthaginian fleet at Drepana, possibly as a result of its raids on Italy, because no attempt was apparently made to supply Lilybaeum by sea. Presumably it was also known roughly how many ships Adherbal had there (see below). In all, during this year, if we accept Polybios' figures, Rome seems to have been able to find something like 240 ships – about 123 at Lilybaeum (51.11–12), and about 120 that eventually made up the fleet of Iunius Pullus (52.5–6). But the problem was that Adherbal's fleet lay between the two, except by the long and dangerous south-coast route, and that neither Roman fleet probably outnumbered it by what was thought to be a sufficient margin.

In any case, it is possible that not all the ships Iunius Pullus eventually commanded were ready for sea, and, according to Polybios (49.1), it was also known that what he calls "the greatest part" (τὸ πλεῖστον μέρος) of the ships' crews at Lilybaeum had died. This is clearly an exaggeration, for he

131

later talks of "the existing crews" (τὰ προϋπάρχοντα ... πληρώματα: 49.5) being used to man the ships in addition to those brought in later. But it was obviously reckoned that there were not enough sailors left at Lilybaeum to man the ships there. So the first task was to reinforce these, and accordingly 10,000 sailors were enlisted and ferried across the straits of Messina, whence they made their way on foot to Lilybaeum. The reason why they were not carried by sea was again, presumably, the presence of Adherbal's fleet at Drepana, the alternative route via the south coast of Sicily being deemed too long.

At some point, too, presumably soon after taking office, one of the new consuls of 249/8, Publius Claudius Pulcher, also made his way to Lilybaeum to take command there, and as soon as the reinforcements for his crews arrived, he summoned a meeting of his military tribunes. History has not dealt kindly with Claudius Pulcher, who, as Polybios himself records, was held personally to blame for the disaster that ensued (52.2–3). Diodoros (24.3) describes him as a man of choleric temperament and mental instability, who denounced his predecessors as drunken incompetents, insisted on punishing his soldiers with traditional rigidity, and looked down on everyone with patrician disdain. For once, too, we probably have contemporary evidence to back this up, because a fragment of Naevius (fr. 42 Buechner) talks of someone – almost certainly Claudius – who "with pride and contempt ground down the legions".

The Romans, however, were fond of blaming defeat on the shortcomings of their commanders – one thinks of the cases of Sempronius Longus, Flaminius and Terentius Varro in the Hannibalic War – and to some extent it looks as though Claudius was trying, albeit perhaps too hard, to restore discipline and morale. In his case, too, as with the later ones, it was not his strategy that was at fault, but his tactical handling of the battle that ensued. Polybios makes it clear that the decision to fight Adherbal was taken with the support of the tribunes, the senior officers present, and there was everything to be said for doing so before more ships arrived to join the Carthaginian fleet. Whether or not it was known that another fleet under Carthalo was being got ready is questionable, but the recent activities of the Carthaginian navy at Lilybaeum had given every reason to believe the enemy was now becoming more active at sea.[10]

There is really no good reason to doubt that with the new arrivals, the Roman ships at Lilybaeum could now be fully manned, despite Polybios' earlier statement that "the greatest part" of the original crews had perished, and it is not necessary to resort to speculation about "pressing" crews from the army, with resulting loss of morale and efficiency.[11] We have Polybios' word for it that the marines for the ships were hand-picked from soldiers who volunteered, "because the voyage was short and the prospect of booty certain" (49.5), so their morale was high, and there is no reason why the crews should not have felt the same. Since nothing is said about the use of *corvi* in the battle, we can only assume that they were not used, but presumably the Romans were still relying on boarding-tactics, so one would guess that each ship had its full complement of 120 marines, as at Ecnomus.

How many ships there were is somewhat uncertain, but Polybios says that after the battle about 30 escaped with the consul, and that 93 were captured (51.11–12), which should mean that the fleet originally numbered about 123. Admittedly he also says earlier (51.7) that many were sunk, but since the Romans were caught close inshore, these may well be included in the 93 that were captured: Polybios says that the latter were taken "with their crews", except those who ran their ships ashore and so escaped. Polybios' figures are confirmed by Orosius (4.10.3) who says that, of 120 ships, 30 escaped and 90 were captured or sunk, and they are almost certainly correct. It is true that Diodoros (24.1.5) gives 210 for the total and Eutropius (2.26.1) 220, but it is suspicious that the former says that 117 were lost, which would mean that 93 survived, and this looks like a garbled version of Polybios' numbers. Similarly, Eutropius says that 30 escaped and 90 were captured, but claims that the rest were sunk (2.26.1).

As for the number of ships in the Carthaginian fleet, one can only guess, since none of the sources gives any figures. It is usually thought that there were about 100,[12] but if there is any truth in Polybios' assertion (38.3) that as far back as the year 255 or 254 the Carthaginians had begun to get ready a fleet of 200 ships (see above, p. 113), even if there had been some delay, they should have been ready by now. Polybios tells us that Carthalo arrived with 70 ships to join Adherbal after the battle (53.2), so it is possible that the latter had originally had nearer 130 than 100. Polybios' statement (50.6) that at the beginning of the battle he outflanked the Roman line with five ships suggests that, if anything, he slightly outnumbered Claudius. It may also be significant that after the battle, when joined by Carthalo with his 70 ships, he gave him 30 more to attack the remaining Roman ships at Lilybaeum (53.1–2). If he had 130, this would mean that he exactly divided the fleet between himself and Carthalo.

Claudius' intention was evidently to try to surprise the enemy and so catch him at anchor. Accordingly, he put to sea about midnight, and was in sight of Drepana by daylight (49.6–7). Polybios says nothing about the famous story that he ordered the sacred chickens carried on board to be flung into the sea, because they would not eat – that was regarded as a bad omen – and so it must remain dubious, though one would like to believe it. If it is true, the incident presumably occurred as the Roman fleet approached the enemy.[13]

Adherbal, meanwhile, had at first indeed been taken by surprise. But he soon rallied, and took the crucial decision to try to get to sea rather than tamely allow himself to be blockaded. After collecting his crews and summoning the mercenaries from the city by crier, he briefly harangued his men and then sent them to their ships with orders to follow his own (49.7–12). Drepana lies on a spit of land, curving like a sickle to the north – hence the name – the harbour being a deep, eastward-pointing inlet on the south side of the spit. By keeping close to the rocks to the north of the inlet, Adherbal managed to clear the harbour before the Romans reached the entrance, and, perhaps by rounding the islands off the spit, to get to seaward of the enemy (49.12).[14]

Claudius, for his part, had made the mistake of taking station in the rear of his fleet, perhaps to make sure that there were no stragglers, and now, when he realized that the enemy intended to fight, was in the worst possible position to take control of a rapidly deteriorating situation. He himself simply turned to port so that his prow pointed out to sea, from where the enemy attack could now be expected, and presumably the ships in front of him did the same, one by one, forming a line to his right. But some of his leading ships had already entered the harbour, and others were about to do so when the countermanding orders reached them. For some time all was confusion, with some ships even colliding and shearing away each other's oars, but eventually order was restored as each ship cleared the harbour and came into line on the right of those already outside, sterns to shore and rams pointing out to sea (50.1–5). At the same time, Adherbal formed his ships into line opposite them, with five of his ships beyond the consul's left, presumably to try to prevent escape (50.6 ff).

When battle was joined, it was at first fairly evenly balanced, since in marines at least the Romans were the equal of the enemy. But here, for the first time, the Carthaginians had nothing to fear from *corvi*, and had more sea-room than their opponents – sea-room in which they could show what they could do with their superior speed and manoeuvrability, the result of the better build of their ships and better training of their crews. If they found themselves hard-pressed, it was easy for them to turn about and make for the open water, then turn again and ram their pursuers in side

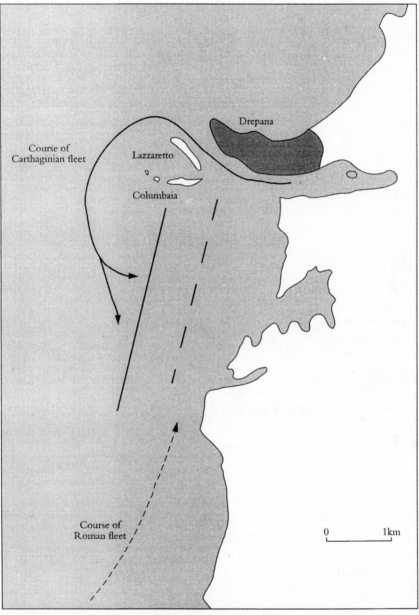

Figure 9.2 Drepana.

or stern as they desperately tried to turn themselves. Similarly, by using the open water to the rear of their fleet, they could row past the sterns of their own ships and render assistance to any that got into difficulties. The Romans, however, could not withdraw because they were too close

135

inshore, and did not have the speed or skill to row between opposing ships, and so take them in side or stern – the classic *diekplous*, followed by *periplous*, manoeuvre (51.1–10: see above, p. 92).

Realizing what was happening, the consul took to flight along the shore, followed by about 30 of his nearest ships. Presumably, as the struggle had developed, the five Carthaginian ships that had originally outflanked his line had been drawn out of position into the fight elsewhere, because now apparently the way was clear. Frontinus (*Strat.* 2.13.9) has a most improbable story that Claudius escaped by dressing his remaining 20 [*sic*] ships overall as though he had won. The rest of his ships, 93 in all, were captured, many with their crews (51.11–12).

Although a battle on a smaller scale than the colossal conflicts off Ecnomus and Cape Hermaia, proportionally Drepana was the greatest victory won by either side in the war. If it is true that Rome lost 93 ships out of about 123, her losses were over 75 per cent, as against, for example, Carthage's losses of 57 per cent off Cape Hermaia. It was also, astonishingly, the only victory Carthage won at sea, and no doubt all the more devastating for Rome for being so unexpected. No wonder a people that had been prepared to forgive and forget the two naval disasters caused by storm, in 255 and 253, was not prepared to condone this defeat, which was – possibly somewhat unfairly, as we have seen – blamed on the commander himself. But Claudius had not endeared himself to his predecessors, if what Diodoros says is true, and perhaps, after all, those chickens had something to do with it.

At all events, according to Polybios (52.3), he was later brought to trial, and condemned to pay a heavy fine. This was a most unusual occurrence among the Romans, though there is a parallel from the Hannibalic War in the condemnation of the praetor, Cn. Fulvius Flaccus, for his defeat in the first battle of Herdonea in 212 (Livy 26.2.7 ff). Piecing together what is said by later sources, it appears that Claudius, like Fulvius Flaccus, was originally prosecuted for "treason" (*perduellio*) by two tribunes, but acquitted, perhaps on a technicality, after the trial had been stopped by a storm. The tribunes then brought him to trial again on a lesser charge and succeeded in getting him fined 120,000 asses.[15] It has been suggested that the prosecution was popularly motivated, because it was set in train by tribunes. But one of them, Fundanius, was almost certainly the consul of 243, and therefore, although a "new man", obviously enjoyed the support of a majority of nobles. The prosecution by tribunes was probably normal practice: Fulvius Flaccus was prosecuted by the tribune, C.Sempronius Blaesus.

Claudius might even have got away with it, if he had kept a low profile, but according to the Livian tradition (*Per.* 19), when recalled by the Senate and ordered to nominate a dictator, presumably to take control of the situation, he nominated a low-born subordinate – perhaps even a freedman since he bore his name – Marcus Claudius Glicia. According to the *Fasti Capitolini,* this man was a scribe, and was forced to abdicate apparently before he had nominated a Master of Horse. He was replaced by the experienced A. Atilius Caiatinus, consul in 258/7 and 254/3, with none other than L. Caecilius Metellus as Master of Horse.

Nor was Claudius' defeat the last disaster Rome suffered in 249. According to Polybios (52.5), it was one of the new consuls for 248/7, Lucius Iunius Pullus, who was sent to convoy supplies to Lilybaeum, with 60 ships, but in fact he was Claudius' colleague in 249/8. It has been suggested that the historian's mistake was due to the fact that Iunius did not go to Sicily until 248, after the consular elections, and that Polybios confused him with one of the new consuls.[16] But his decision to send half his transports on from Syracuse (52.6–7), with only a few ships as escort, suggests that he had not yet heard of Claudius' defeat, which would be inconceivable if this was in 248, and his operations on land after the catastrophe to his fleet (see below) also suggest 249. Polybios' error may rather have derived from Philinos' placing of Iunius' operations in the sixteenth year of the war, because he arrived in Sicily in the second half of 249.[17] In view of the error, there is no need to accept the implication in the order of Polybios' narrative that news of the disaster at Drepana had reached Rome before Iunius Pullus left.

Perhaps in July 249, then, Iunius sailed first to Messana, where he was joined by ships "from the army and the rest of Sicily" (52.6). We have already discussed what this probably means (see above, p. 124), and there really is no reason to doubt that most, if not all, of these ships had originally formed part of the fleet sent to Lilybaeum, and that they had been withdrawn from there at the end of 250.[18] From Messana, now with 120 warships and no fewer than 800 transports, Iunius hastened to Syracuse. There, in his anxiety to ease the supply situation at Lilybaeum as soon as possible, he decided to divide his transports, and send half on with the quaestors and a few ships as escort, himself remaining at Syracuse to round up stragglers and collect more supplies (52.6–8).

The "quaestors" here may be *quaestores classici*, since there would have been only one quaestor attached to the consul himself. If so, the "few warships" they commanded may have been allied vessels, if part of their job was to organize such squadrons, although they may also have been involved in the commandeering of transports, most of which presumably came from allied ports.[19] Although Polybios seems to imply that the news of Drepana had already reached Rome before Iunius set out, it is very difficult to believe that he would have sent the quaestors on their way like this, with only a small escort, if he knew that three-quarters of the Roman fleet at Lilybaeum had been eliminated.[20]

Meanwhile the Carthaginians had also been active. Polybios says that Adherbal sent his prisoners and the captured ships to Carthage, and one wonders why he did not keep the ships to add to his fleet. Probably, however, he could not force their crews to row for Carthage, and had to send the ships off under small prize-crews so that they could be manned in Africa. He then gave 30 additional ships to his fellow-commander, Carthalo, who had recently arrived with a fleet of 70, and sent him to attack the enemy vessels at anchor near Lilybaeum – presumably the remnants of Claudius Pulcher's fleet. Coming in at dawn, Carthalo set about burning some of the ships and towing away others, and when the Romans tried to rescue them, the ever-vigilant Himilco, commanding the defenders of Lilybaeum, ordered his mercenaries to sortie (53.1–6). Despite this, however, Carthalo was content to destroy only a few of the vessels, and to tow a few more away – Diodoros (24.1.7) says five. He was evidently after larger game, for he headed away towards Heraclea Minoa with the intention, Polybios says (53.7), of intercepting the Roman convoy on its way to Lilybaeum. Diodoros (24.1.7) says that he had heard that the Roman fleet had set sail from Syracuse, and he may have acquired this information from Carthaginian sympathizers in Syracuse or elsewhere. Diodoros gives him 120 ships, but unless he had acquired others at Lilybaeum in addition to the five Roman vessels he captured, this is contradicted by Polybios.

Before Carthalo's raid on the Roman ships near Lilybaeum, Diodoros implies, Adherbal also sent Hannibal, the man who had commanded the relief expedition to Lilybaeum, to attack Panormus with 30 ships, and they "succeeded in carrying off the Roman supply of grain to Drepana" (τὴν ἀγορὰν τῶν Ῥωμαίων τοῦ σίτου ἔφερον εἰς Δρέπανα: 24.1.6). This has been interpreted as an attack on "a fleet of Roman transports which were on their way with victuals for the Roman forces round Lilybaeum",[21] but Diodoros says nothing of this. The supplies were evidently those collected at Panormus, though they may partly have been intended for the Roman forces at Lilybaeum. As it was, according to Diodoros, these and other supplies from Drepana were conveyed to the Carthaginian forces defending Lilybaeum.

Carthalo, meanwhile, informed by his lookouts – presumably on the coastal hills southeast of Heraclea Minoa – that a large fleet of all types of vessel was approaching, put to sea eager to join battle (53.8). But the Roman quaestors were warned by their scouting-vessels that an enemy fleet was approaching, and put in at what Polybios describes (53.10) as "one of the small towns subject to them, with no harbour, but roads protected by suitable headlands projecting from the land". Diodoros (24.1.7) identifies this as Phintias, and it was in fact the town immediately east of the hill from which the battle of Ecnomus derives its name (see above, p. 84).

Here the quaestors disembarked, and, according to Polybios (53.11 ff), having set up catapults and mangonels taken from the town, prepared to receive the enemy. The Carthaginians at first thought of blockading them, assuming that the crews would retreat to the town in panic, leaving the ships to be captured at leisure. But when they saw that they were prepared to defend themselves, and realized the difficulties involved in attacking the place, they contented themselves with capturing a few provision ships and made off to the mouth of a nearby river, where they waited for the Romans to re-embark. Meanwhile Iunius Pullus rounded Pachynon not knowing what had happened, and when Carthalo's lookouts reported the consul's approach, he proceeded swiftly down the coast past the quaestors' ships in order to engage him as far away as possible from his advanced squadron. The Consul then took refuge by the shore, whereupon Carthalo anchored between the two Roman fleets. However, when those among his captains who knew these waters warned him of approaching bad weather, he rounded Pachynon, leaving the Roman fleets to be separately destroyed.

Diodoros (24.1.7–9) has a somewhat different version of these events. He implies that most of the Roman fleet went ahead of the consul, and when the two fleets sighted each other off the territory of Gela, the Romans, in panic, put into Phintias. A sharp fight then ensued in which the Carthaginians "sank" 50 of the large freighters and 17 of the warships, and disabled 13 more of the latter. They then retired to the river Halykos (the modern Platani), which flows into the sea just west of Heraclea Minoa, returning to the attack when the consul joined the advance part of his fleet with 36 warships and a number of provision-ships. Thereupon Iunius burned the 13 damaged warships and withdrew, only to be overtaken near Camarina, where he put into shore for safety. There he lost all his provision ships and all but two of his warships in the ensuing storm, while the Carthaginians managed to round Cape Pachynon and ride it out in safety.

There is no way of fully reconciling these two accounts – even the numbers for the Roman warships can be reconciled only by assuming that the 17 Diodoros says were sunk at Phintias are to be included in the 105 that were caught in the subsequent storm.[22] It is also quite arbitrary to assume that even if Polybios' version is the result of his correcting Philinos from Fabius Pictor, he was wrong to do so.[23] In particular, it is difficult to believe that after the first encounter at Phintias, Carthalo retired some 40 miles to the Halykos, when quite clearly he would have been looking for any opportunity to destroy the Roman fleet. Nor is it as easy as some commentators think to believe that Polybios omitted the alleged Roman losses in this first encounter, out of pro-Roman bias. Polybios' account is also circumstantial in having the quaestors defend their ships with shore-based artillery – a most unusual incident in ancient naval warfare – and in having Carthalo interpose himself between the two fleets. Possibly the losses to Roman warships in the first encounter reported by Diodoros were really losses in the storm, Iunius burning the 13 damaged ships as he fled westwards to Lilybaeum with his two surviving ships (cf. DS 24.1.10), after the storm. At all events, there is no reason to doubt that all the transport vessels were lost, and virtually all the warships, whether by enemy action or by the storm.

This time the disaster was almost total. Even after the first storm off Camarina, 80 Roman warships had survived, and after the second off Cape Palinurus, 150. But now there were virtually none left – perhaps just the two that had survived the storm with the consul, and a handful at Lilybaeum. There is thus every reason to believe Polybios when he says (55.2) that the Romans now abandoned the sea.

The extraordinary thing is, however, that apparently no Roman even thought of trying to negotiate an end to the war. Instead, they maintained the siege of Lilybaeum, sending supplies overland (55.4), and the unfortunate consul, Iunius, once he had arrived at Lilybaeum, far from allowing himself to be overwhelmed by despair, immediately began to think of some way of striking back at the enemy by land. In fact, when a chance offered, he surprised Eryx, capturing both temple and town. Eryx is the modern Monte San Giuliano, just east of Drepana and commanding the route from there to Panormus. Polybios says (55.7) that it is the highest mountain in Sicily after Etna, though this is manifestly untrue. On its flat summit there was an ancient temple to the goddess the Romans called Venus, supposedly founded by Aeneas himself (Verg., *Aen.* 5.759 ff). But the temple prostitution practised there suggests an eastern origin, and the Carthaginians identified the goddess as Astarte. The ancient town probably lay northwest of the modern San Giuliano, and was of Elymian origin, according to Thucydides (6.2.3). Its inhabitants had been evacuated to Drepana in 259, according to Diodoros (23.9.4), but some may have returned.

Diodoros (24.1.10–11) also says that Iunius fortified a place then called "Aigithallos", but "which they now call Akellos", and garrisoned it with 800 men. Unfortunately the whereabouts of this place is unknown. It has been located at Cape San Teodoro, about 12 miles south of Eryx, but it is more likely to be nearer Eryx, and has been more plausibly identified with a spur of Eryx itself, now called Pizzo Argentaria or Sant' Anna.[24] Allegedly Carthalo immediately recaptured the place, but, if so, from what Polybios says later (58.2), the Romans then recovered it.

According to Zonaras (8.15), Iunius Pullus was himself captured by Carthalo at Aigithallos, which is not impossible. It might explain the nomination of a dictator – though Zonaras actually places this before Iunius' capture – and, more particularly, the fact that for the first time in Roman history, the dictator, Atilius Caiatinus, led an army outside Italy (Livy, *Per.* 19). It was presumably at this time that Claudius Pulcher showed his contempt for his critics by first nominating his low-born henchman, Claudius Glicia (Livy, *ibid.*). If Iunius was captured, he may have been returned at the exchange of prisoners in 247, recorded by Livy (*ibid.*, cf. Zon. 8.16). There was a story that he, too, had disregarded the auspices, and committed suicide rather than stand trial.[25] If so, it was a tragedy, for he, too, like Terentius Varro in 216 (cf. Livy 22.61.14), had not "despaired of the Republic".

CHAPTER 10

Shadow-boxing and knock-out

After the spectacular events of 249, one might have expected the war to draw rapidly to a conclusion. Instead there were seven more years of relatively desultory conflict, followed by a final naval battle and then peace. The main reason for this is that Carthage failed to press home the advantage she had gained by the destruction of the Roman fleet, while Rome naturally needed time to recover from the disaster. At the very least one might have expected Carthage to send troops to Sicily to relieve the siege of Lilybaeum, and to begin the process of recovering the ground lost there, particularly since 254, for example by attempting to recapture Panormus. She might, further, have brought pressure to bear on Hiero, whose original agreement with Rome may have been due to run out in 248, and, above all, she might have at last made proper use of her newly recovered seapower to attack southern Italy in particular, where Rome's control was new and precarious. But in so far as she did any of these things, she did them in a half-hearted way, calculated to annoy rather than to do serious damage. She ought to have learned by now that this was no way to win a war with Rome.

Part of the reason was probably that she was distracted by events in Africa. Ever since Regulus' landing and initial success, there seems to have been simmering discontent on the fringes of Carthaginian territory, which Hamilcar's savage reprisals immediately following Regulus' defeat (Oros. 4.9.9) will probably have done little or nothing to suppress, except in the short term. But this had not prevented the sending of reinforcements to Sicily in 252, if not 254 (see above, pp. 112–13), the reinforcing of Lilybaeum with at least 10,000, if not 14,000 men, and at the same time the raising of a fleet of at least 170, if not 200, ships. Why, then, could not the same or more have been done in 248?

The answer is, possibly, that there was what amounts to a change of policy in Carthage.[1] We know that at some point, probably not earlier than 247, and certainly not later than 241, the Carthaginian general, Hanno "the Great" (cf. App., *Hisp*. 4), conquered Hekatompylos (Theveste), now Tébessa, in Algeria (DS 24.10, cf. Plb. 1.73.1). Since this place lies at probably the farthest extent of Carthaginian territory – it is some 160 miles southwest of Carthage – its subjugation was probably the culmination of some years of warfare, as Polybios hints when he describes Hanno as "accustomed to make war on Numidians and Libyans" (74.7). By 241 he was apparently the commander-in-chief in Africa (67.1), and, judging by what Polybios says about his exactions from the Libyans (72.3), had been for some years.

Possibly, then, it was felt by some Carthaginians, led perhaps by Hanno, that the war against Rome was as good as won, and that the time had come to consolidate and even extend their territory in Africa. We can only guess who the opponents of this policy may have been, but one was almost certainly Hamilcar Barca, who was appointed to the Sicilian command in 248 or 247 (see below). Everything we know about this man and his family, including his son Hannibal, and of Hanno's later opposition to them, would suggest this. It has even been argued that a fragment of the Roman poet Naevius (fr. 44 Buechner), in which someone says that "this is the seventeenth year they have been sitting there", comes from a speech by Hamilcar advocating a further effort in Sicily, though the speaker could just as easily be a Roman.[2]

But if Hamilcar did advocate an aggressive strategy in Sicily, it would appear that he lost the argument. The most striking indication of this is the way in which the strength of the Carthaginian navy operating in Sicilian waters was apparently actually reduced, until, when Lutatius Catulus arrived in 242, the whole Carthaginian fleet had evidently gone home (59.9). It is also odd that we hear nothing more of Adherbal, the victor of Drepana, after his despatch of Carthalo with 30 of his warships to attack Lilybaeum (53.1–3). Since the Carthaginians normally left successful generals and admirals in command for years, unless Adherbal died, his supersession presumably indicates that he was held to have completed his assignment. Possibly – though this is not what Polybios says (53.1) – after giving Carthalo the 30 ships, he escorted the captured Roman vessels back to Carthage with the remainder, and never returned.

Certainly it is Carthalo alone who figures in the later naval operations of the year, and more significantly, he that recaptures Aigithallos (DS 24.1.11), which was near Adherbal's old base at Drepana. But Carthalo, too, despite his continuing successes, was apparently superseded at the end of 248 or early in 247, by Hamilcar (see below). Before he left, according to Zonaras (8.16), he tried everything to deter the consuls of 248/7, Gaius Aurelius Cotta and Publius Servilius Geminus, from continuing to press Lilybaeum and Drepana. The consuls were both experienced men, having previously been consuls together in 252/1, and this is another indication of how seriously the Senate took the situation. But it is even more significant that there was apparently no let-up in Rome's determination to persist in the war in Sicily.

When his operations in Sicily had no effect, Carthalo proceeded to attack Italy in an attempt to divert the consuls' forces. But even this did not have the desired result, and he tamely withdrew at the approach of the praetor, who was presumably in command in Italy in the consuls' absence (Zon. 8.16, cf. Oros. 4.10.4). A further indication of Carthaginian negligence at this time is the mutiny of mercenaries that faced Carthalo on his return from Italy, significantly because they had not been paid. Zonaras (*ibid.*) says that he marooned a number of them on desert islands, and sent many back to Carthage, and although it is implied that the latter was also by way of punishment, it may really be because they were now required in Africa. Thus the new Carthaginian commander in Sicily, Hamilcar Barca, was probably left with a reduced army as well as a reduced fleet. Meanwhile Rome pre-empted any move to bring pressure on Syracuse by concluding a generous new agreement with Hiero, which was not limited in time and by which the remaining instalments of the war indemnity were remitted (Zon. 8.16).

Zonaras (8.16) dates Hamilcar's arrival to the consulship of Cotta and Geminus, and although Polybios says it was in the eighteenth year of the war that he commenced operations (56.2), which should mean the summer of 247, it may well be that he arrived earlier, since he apparently also had to deal with the continuing mutinous behaviour of the mercenaries. Zonaras (8.16) says that he slaughtered many of them at night and had others thrown into the sea. Since his famous son, Hannibal, was nine years old when Hamilcar took him to Spain in 237 (3.11.5), he was presumably born at about the time of his father's departure for Sicily.

Hamilcar was clearly a charismatic commander, who fully lived up to his family name, which probably means "lightning" or "sword-flash" (Semitic

Bârâq). Polybios says (56.1) that the naval command was entrusted to him, but it is clear that he was at least in effect commander-in-chief in Sicily from his arrival. His first operation, though not mentioned by Polybios, may have been one recorded only by Zonaras (8.16). The latter says that while one of the consuls of 247/6, L.Caecilius Metellus, the victor of Panormus in his previous consulship, was near Lilybaeum, the other, Numerius Fabius Buteo, was investing Drepana. Under cover of darkness, the latter succeeded in capturing an island called Pelias that had previously been occupied by the Carthaginians, and when next day Hamilcar attacked it, Buteo successfully diverted him by launching an assault on Drepana itself. He then filled in the channel between Pelias and the mainland, and made good use of it in his investment of the city.

This story has been doubted, on the grounds that Hamilcar's superior fleet should either have prevented the operation or enabled him rapidly to recapture the island, and that the details about the latter do not fit.[3] The former objections are not serious because although Hamilcar may have had more ships than the Romans, this had not deterred them in the past – one thinks of Ap. Claudius' crossing of the straits of Messina – and Hamilcar may not have thought it worthwhile trying too hard to recapture the island. The problem lies in identifying the island. There are, or were, two – now Lazzaretto and Columbaia (or Columbia) – of which Lazzaretto is the nearest to the mainland and is now joined to it. Obviously the detail about the Romans' filling in the channel points to Lazzaretto, but the ancient name, "Pelias", is almost certainly connected with the Greek word for "dove" (πέλεια/πελειάς), which clearly points to Columbaia. But perhaps the name was originally applied to the nearer of the two islands and was transferred to the other when the nearer ceased to be an island.

The first operation ascribed to Hamilcar by Polybios was an attack on Italy in which he ravaged the territory of Locri and Bruttium (56.3). It was probably in reply to these and subsequent raids that Rome founded citizen colonies at Alsium (Ladispoli) and Fregenae (Fregene) just up the coast from Ostia, in 247 and 244, and, possibly, the Latin colony at Brundisium (Brindisi) in 244. Another response may have been a series of raids on Africa organized by private individuals, who borrowed ships from the Roman navy on condition of returning them, but keeping any booty they might acquire. The evidence for this comes from Zonaras (8.16), who says that amongst other places they attacked "Hippo" (probably Hippo(u) Acra, now Bizerta), burning the ships in the harbour and some of the buildings on shore.

Zonaras also says that when the inhabitants stretched chains across the mouth of the harbour, the Romans escaped by rowing at speed towards the chains, and at the last minute, getting the crew – i.e., presumably, the marines and any sailors on deck – to rush to the stern, thus lifting the bows clear of the chains, and then to rush to the bows to lift the sterns. This may seem far-fetched, but there is a modern parallel involving a ship of the Royal Navy.[4] Frontinus (*Strat.* 1.5.6) tells the same story of the consul, "Duellius", "in the harbour of Syracuse" (*in portu Syracusano*), where it has been suggested that the word *Syracusano* should be emended to *Hippacritano* (i.e. "of Hippo(u) Acra").[5] It would be nice to think that the victor of Mylae was still going strong 13 years later, but it must obviously remain dubious, and Zonaras does not help by claiming a Roman naval victory off Panormus on the way home. He later seems to imply (8.16–end) that the privateers' activities continued right down to the renewal of official Roman naval activity in 242.

Hamilcar, for his part, after returning from his raid on Italy, descended on the coast north of Panormus with his whole fleet, and seized what Polybios terms "the so-called place at Heirkte" (56.3). This curious circumlocution is generally taken to mean that Heirkte was actually the name for a fort or strongpoint below the hill on which Hamilcar now established himself. The hill is described (56.3 ff) as being "between Eryx and Panormus near the sea", and as steep-sided with a flat top about 12 miles in circumference. This was suitable for cultivation, as well as providing good pasturage, was well protected against winds from the sea and without any dangerous animals. It was also defended by steep cliffs on the sides facing the sea and the land, and even the other sides needed very little additional strengthening. Upon it was a knoll, serving both as an acropolis and as an observation post over the surrounding countryside, and it also commanded a good harbour with an excellent water supply. There was a difficult approach to the hill from this harbour, and two others, equally difficult, from the landward side.

It used to be thought that the hill in question was what is now called Monte Pellegrino, just north of Panormus,[6] but it is more likely to be Monte Castellachio about six miles to the north. Heirkte will then, strictly speaking, be a fort guarding the pass between Monte Castellachio and Monte Gallo, just above and to the south of the modern village of Sferracavallo. Apart from anything else, the top of Monte Pellegrino is really too small to fit what Polybios says about the circumference of the top of his hill, whereas that of Monte Castellachio is just about right, and in the former case it is also difficult to identify the harbour, whereas in the latter it will be the one at Isola delle Femmine.[7]

Of the next three years' warfare we can say very little since even Polybios contents himself with a mere summary, in which he likens the two sides to equally matched boxers (56.9–57). The only two details he gives are that Hamilcar made a number of forays from his base by sea during which he ravaged the coast of Italy as far as Cumae (56.10), and that the Romans took up a position between Panormus and his base and less than a mile from it (56.11), though they did not necessarily stay there for the whole three years.

The only other incidents that may have occurred in these years are an attack by Hamilcar on a fort called Italion, near Longon in the territory of Catana (Catania), recorded by Diodoros (24.6); and a Roman victory at sea off Aegimurus (now Zembra or Djeziret Djamur) recorded by Florus (1.18.30–2). In the former case, unfortunately, neither Italion nor Longon can be identified, but if Hamilcar was really operating near Catana, it shows how far-ranging his raids were, while he enjoyed command at sea, and perhaps that he did toy with the idea of bringing pressure to bear on Hiero. Although Catana was not in the latter's kingdom, it was only some 30 miles north of Syracuse. The latter incident is much more dubious. Florus attributes the victory to Marcus Fabius Buteo, one of the consuls of 245/4, claiming that it was over a Carthaginian fleet sailing for Italy. But his description of the storm that spoiled the victory makes it almost certain that he has transferred to this point the battle off Cape Hermaia, which he omits.

After maintaining the struggle for some three years from his base at Heirkte, in 244 Hamilcar suddenly shifted to Eryx, which, as we have seen (above, p. 140), was the modern Monte San Giuliano, a mile or two north-east of Drepana (58.1). Presumably he had realized that he was now very unlikely to succeed in recapturing Panormus, which was, presumably, at least one of the reasons why he had chosen his base at Heirkte, and was beginning to feel his isolation from the other Carthaginian forces still holding out in Drepana and Lilybaeum. By basing himself at Eryx, he could threaten any Roman forces operating against Drepana, and would still be athwart the communications between it and Panormus.

If Diodoros is right (24.8), he moved to Eryx at night and by sea. The Romans had troops both on the summit at the temple of Venus, and at the foot of the hill facing towards Drepana, but Hamilcar, landing perhaps at the modern Tonnara di Bonagia to the north, managed to seize the town between the two (58.2).[8] Diodoros (*ibid.*) says that he killed the Roman troops holding the town, and removed its inhabitants to Drepana, and since he says earlier (23.9.4) that the inhabitants had already been moved in 259, we must presume that some or all of them had returned in the meantime.

Here again Hamilcar contrived to maintain himself for another two years, despite being between two Roman forces, and although he held only a single road down to the sea, up which all his supplies had to come (58.3). But we hear no more of raids by sea in these years, and it seems that either Hamilcar abandoned such operations or that his ships were actually withdrawn, as Polybios certainly implies they had been by 242 (59.9). If he had any strategy other than just to fight on as best he could, he presumably still hoped that the Romans would grow weary of the struggle and come to reasonable terms. But it was a futile hope, as events were to show.

Details are once more sparse. Diodoros (24.9.1–3) tells of only two incidents. In the first, a Carthaginian officer named "Vodostar", who may be the "Bostar" appointed as one of two generals in 256 (see above, p. 100), disobeyed Hamilcar's orders and engaged in plundering. As a result, he not only lost many of his men, but wrecked one of his commander's plans, the situation being saved only by the sterling performance of a small force of only 200 cavalry. In the second, the Roman consul, Fundanius (243/2), refused a request from Hamilcar for a truce to recover the dead, saying that he would be better advised to ask for a truce to recover the living. However, later, when he himself suffered severe losses and asked Hamilcar for a truce, the Carthaginian replied that he was at war with the living, but had come to terms with the dead, and granted the request.

A more interesting episode is the attempted betrayal of Eryx to the Romans by some of Hamilcar's Celtic mercenaries. We happen to know about this because Polybios chose to tell us something about the infamous career of this particular band (2.7.6–11; cf. also Zon. 8.16). After being driven out of their own country, he says, they had first been employed by the Carthaginians as part of the garrison of Agrigentum, being then about 3,000-strong. This place they had pillaged as a result of a dispute over pay, perhaps early in the war, but presumably they had managed to break out with the rest of the mercenaries in 261 (19.12). Now apparently about 1,000 of them tried to betray Eryx, and when this plan failed, deserted to the enemy, by whom they were put to guard the temple of Venus on the summit of the hill. Inevitably, they also plundered that, and as soon as the war with Carthage was over, the Romans expelled them from Italy. Still numbering about 800 (2.5.4), they were then hired by the people of

Phoinike in Epirus, and naturally betrayed them, too, to the Illyrians. The remaining 2,000, under their commander, Autaritos, returned to Africa and joined in the great mutiny of the mercenaries (77.4). Most of them were probably killed there in battle against their old commander, Hamilcar himself (78.12), though Autaritos escaped to be finally crucified (86.4).

But to return to our war, the stalemate was broken by the Roman decision, probably taken late in 243, to build another fleet. Presumably, all this time, the surviving Carthaginian outposts at Drepana and Lilybaeum were being supplied by sea, as Polybios implies Hamilcar himself was at Eryx (58.3). Thus, if the Romans had thought that they could finish the war by land operations alone, after the disasters of 249, it will have become apparent to them that this was impossible.[9] Polybios' story (59.7) is that leading citizens, either singly, or in groups of two or three, offered to pay for the building and equipping of a quinquereme on condition that they were reimbursed if all went well. Modern commentators are inclined to be more cynical, even to the extent of wondering whether the loan was as voluntary as Polybios makes out, and whether it was repaid with interest.[10] But this is to go too far in the opposite direction. There is, after all, no evidence that the loan was not voluntary, or that it was repaid with interest, and any repayment did depend on victory, which was far from certain. Did the leaders of Carthage, one wonders, ever behave like this?

Polybios also says that the ships were built on the model of the captured vessel of Hannibal the Rhodian, and that eventually 200 such ships were built (59.8). As to the number, there is no reason to doubt him, though Diodoros (24.11.1) gives 300 warships and 700 transports, and is followed as to the warships by some of the later sources (Eutr. 2.27.1; Oros. 4.10.5; de vir. ill. 41). Nor is there any reason to believe that any vessels that had survived the disasters of 249 were added to the fleet, since these would have been built on the old model and would have hampered the movement of the new ships.[11] But Diodoros may be right about the transports: one of the tasks entrusted to Iunius Pullus in 249 had been the escorting of 800 transports for the reprovisioning of the forces at Lilybaeum and elsewhere (52.5–6), and this may similarly have been part of the plan in 242. Indeed, the first operations of the commander of the new fleet, C. Lutatius Catulus, one of the consuls of 242/1, were the seizure of the harbour at Drepana and the anchorages at Lilybaeum, and the construction of siege-works round the former (59.9–10).

But Polybios emphasizes (59.11–12) that Lutatius also foresaw that Carthage was bound to dispute command of the sea, and presumably the reason for building the new ships on the model of the Rhodian's was to create a fleet that could stand up to the Carthaginian in a fleet action. Rome's victories hitherto, certainly at Mylae and Ecnomus, and probably in the other sea battles down to and including the one off Cape Hermaia, had been won with the use of *corvi*. But these had evidently been discarded before Drepana, possibly, as we have seen, because they made the warships too unseaworthy. However, Drepana had demonstrated that without the *corvi* the poorly constructed Roman ships, with their badly trained crews, stood no chance in a sea fight against faster and more manoeuvrable Carthaginian vessels. Hence the new-model fleet.

The command of the new fleet was oddly entrusted not to both consuls of 242/1, but to Lutatius Catulus and the *praetor urbanus*, Quintus Valerius Falto. The ancient explanation for this was that Lutatius' colleague, Aulus Postumius Albinus, was forbidden by the *Pontifex Maximus* to leave the city, on the ground that he was the *flamen Martialis* (Priest of Mars: Livy, *Per.* 19, and 37.51.1–2; Val. Max. 1.1.2; Tac., *Ann.* 3.71). Inevitably, modern scholars have seen some kind of intrigue behind this, but we should not be so cavalier with such reports of religious taboos. It is certainly going too far to suppose that Postumius was deliberately kept from the command because he was incompetent, whereas Lutatius and Falto were regarded as able admirals,[12] since we have no evidence that any of the three had ever before seen action. It is possible that Lutatius was the man principally responsible for having the new fleet built and for its new design, and that this was expressly to use the kind of tactics which had brought Adherbal victory at Drepana, but even this is uncertain.

There was a rather similar incident in 205/4, when the then *Pontifex Maximus*, who was also consul in that year, agreed that his colleague, Scipio, should have Sicily and himself Bruttium as consular provinces, without resorting to the drawing of lots, on the ground that as *Pontifex Maximus* he could not leave Italy in any case (Livy 28.38.12). But in this instance Scipio had just returned from a victorious command in Spain, and most people expected and wanted him to have Sicily as a springboard for the invasion of Africa. Something like this may lie behind what happened in 242, but there is no proof.

It may also be significant that it was possibly in this year that a second praetor, the *praetor peregrinus*, was elected for the first time: the Livian tradition (*Per.* 19), records this immediately before the notice of the ban on Postumius Albinus' leaving the city. The existence of another praetor would have made it easier for what was now the *praetor urbanus* to command

outside Italy, though if Zonaras is to be believed, there was already a precedent for this in 260 (8.11). The intention in 242 may have been to give
Lutatius a lieutenant, who could not interfere. But there is no evidence that
there had been any friction between the consuls who had jointly commanded on many previous occasions during this war, and, if we are to believe Valerius Maximus (2.8.2), Falto's lesser authority did not prevent his
quarrelling with Lutatius when the question of a triumph for the victory
arose. Incidentally, Polybios never mentions Falto, and our information
about his role comes entirely from Valerius Maximus (2.8.2) and Zonaras
(8.17), who are not the most trustworthy authorities. However, we know
from the triumphal records that he celebrated a naval triumph, as
propraetor, so he clearly did play a significant part.

At all events, it was at the beginning of summer 242, according to
Polybios (59.8), that Lutatius, presumably accompanied by Falto, was sent
to Sicily with his fleet. After seizing the harbour at Drepana and the
Lilybaeum anchorages, which were now bare of Carthaginian ships, he
settled down to the siege of the former. But anticipating the arrival of a
Carthaginian fleet, he did not neglect his own, practising its rowers every
day, and paying particular attention to their food and drink to get them into
tip-top condition (59.9–12). Diodoros says that he anchored at "the trad-
ing-station of the Erycinians" (τὸ Ἐρυκίνων ἐμπόριον: 24.11.1), which
might mean the harbour near Eryx which Hamilcar had been using to
supply his army (cf. 58.3). If so, this would have cut Hamilcar's supply route
and in time would have rendered his position untenable. But there is no
reason to doubt that Drepana was at this stage the consul's main concern.
Orosius (4.10.5) says that he was wounded in the thigh there, and this is
confirmed by Zonaras (8.17), Eutropius (2.27.1) and Valerius Maximus
(2.8.2).

Meanwhile, when the news reached them that the Roman fleet had
sailed, the Carthaginians, Polybios says (60.1–2), immediately began to
prepare ships, and having loaded them with supplies for the troops at Eryx,
sent them to sea. In fact, however, if Lutatius arrived in Sicily in the early
summer of 242, and if the decisive battle was fought on 10 March 241, as
Roman tradition held (Eutr. 2.27.2), the Carthaginians took something
like eight or nine months to get their fleet ready.[13] Some scholars talk of
their having to build ships,[14] but this should not have been necessary. They
had had at least 170, if not 200, of their own, in the year 249, and had captured 93 Roman ships at Drepana and a few more later. Thus, even allowing for losses in the intervening years, they should still have had well over

200 available, and before Lutatius' arrival, according to Polybios (59.9), all their ships had left Sicily for home.

A more probable explanation for the delay is that they found it difficult to find enough men to man the ships. Whether or not there were transports as well as warships is uncertain (see below), but if, as seems likely, there were eventually at least 250 of the latter, 75,000 sailors would have been needed for a start, assuming that there were as many on each ship as at Ecnomus. If Philinos' statement (*ap.* DS 24.11.1), that 6,000 Carthaginian prisoners were later taken, is to be pressed, it is possible that they had to rely far more than was normal on the citizen population of Carthage itself, and this may have created difficulties and delays.[15] But even if most of the crews were drawn from towns and cities allied to Carthage, as was probably usual, there might still have been problems about raising such a number, after years of neglect of the navy.

There may also have been a problem in finding marines. If Polybios is right in saying that the intention was to take the best of Hamilcar's mercenaries on board before risking a battle (60.3), only a skeleton force may have been carried on each ship for the crossing, particularly if deck space was taken up with supplies. But even at, say, only 40 per ship, some 10,000 would have been required, and if Hanno the Great was still conducting serious operations in the interior, soldiers may have been hard to find. The timing of the departure, finally, may have been partly deliberate. The weather was still likely to be stormy and possibly it was hoped that the Roman fleet would be kept in harbour, or that a stiff breeze would aid the run in to Eryx, as it had aided Hannibal's run into Lilybaeum in 250.

It is possible, indeed, that even after eight or nine months, Carthage could still not find enough men, and that the ships were undermanned when they finally sailed.[16] This is suggested, first, by Polybios' statements (61.6 and 8) that the Romans captured 70 ships and 10,000 men. Although some allowance could be made for losses among the crews of captured ships, these figures, as they stand, would mean that only about 140 men were captured for each ship taken, and even then we would have to assume that there were no prisoners from the ships that were sunk, though this is unlikely; Diodoros actually says that some were captured in this way (24.11.3). As we have seen, we would normally expect a quinquereme to be manned by a crew of 300 and a minimum of about 40 marines.

In tackling this kind of problem, it is difficult to know how seriously to take the evidence of such later sources as Eutropius and Orosius, but, for what it is worth, both give the number of Carthaginian prisoners as 32,000, with 13,000 and 14,000 killed, respectively, for 63 ships captured and 125 sunk (Eutr. 2.27.2; Oros. 4.10.7). If one adds the number of prisoners to the number of those killed, even taking Eutropius' figure for the latter, this would still mean that each ship had carried only about 245 men. It might be argued that what is meant is that the prisoners were those taken with the captured ships, in which case they were, if anything, overmanned at over 500 men per ship. But this would mean that the ships sunk carried only just over 100 men each, which is absurd. In either case, we may perhaps legitimately ignore what these authors say, but it is obviously a different matter with Polybios, and if the implication of what he says is to be accepted, the Carthaginian ships were, on this occasion, grossly undermanned.

Diodoros, however, who seems to be reliable on the size of the Carthaginian fleet (see below), has different figures for its losses. He says that in all they amounted to 117 ships – which is near enough Polybios' total of 50 sunk and 70 captured (61.6) – but that only 20 were captured, and the number of prisoners, he says, for once explicitly on the authority of Philinos, was 6,000 Carthaginians, though he adds that others said 4,040.[17] We can, thus, probably assume that his figure for the number of ships captured also comes from Philinos, and if, despite Polybios, these figures are to be accepted, the number of men taken for each ship would be 300, which is much nearer what one would expect.

One is, naturally, reluctant to part company with Polybios on such a matter, and, it could be argued that the figure given by Eutropius and Orosius for the number of captured ships is at least nearer his than Diodorus', even if their figure for those sunk is larger than that given by either. But, in addition to the problem created by Polybios' figures, there is the point that if the Romans had built their ships to a particular design with the specific intention of employing ramming tactics for the first time, we might have expected them for once to have sunk more ships than they captured, whereas Polybios says only 50 were sunk for 70 captured.

Certainty is not possible. The alternatives are, first, that Polybios' figures are right, and that either the Carthaginian ships were grossly undermanned, or that many more of their crews were killed or drowned than one would think; or, secondly, that Diodoros is right and no question of undermanning arises. But even if the ships were fully manned, there is all the more reason to believe Polybios when he says (61.4) that the crews were untrained and the marines hastily raised levies.

The problem would be even more complicated if there were transports with the Carthaginian fleet in addition to the warships, unless we assume that no transports were captured. Polybios says nothing about transports, and implies that the supplies were all carried on warships, and although Diodoros (24.11.1) mentions transports, one wonders whether he is right. They would inevitably have slowed the warships, and in a similar situation in 250, Hannibal and, possibly, Adherbal had run reinforcements and supplies into Lilybaeum on warships alone (44.1, Zon. 8.15: see above, p. 127). On the other hand, if a fragment of Naevius (fr. 48 Buechner) that talks of "laden transports wallowing in the swells" (*onerariae onustae stabant in flustris*) refers to this battle, we perhaps have contemporary evidence that transports were present.[18]

It is also uncertain how many warships there were, but although Polybios does not say, Diodoros says that there were 250 (24.11.1), and there is no compelling reason to doubt him. As we have seen, Carthage should have had at least that number available. Orosius (4.10.6) and Eutropius (2.27.1) say there were 400 "ships", probably meaning warships, though their figure could conceivably be reconciled with Diodoros' on the assumption that 150 of the "ships" were transports. The same could even be true of the 600 ships "hampered by supplies and other cargoes" of the treatise "*On famous men*" (*de vir. ill.* 41.1). But we can probably discount this evidence.[19]

Undermanned or not, it was probably a scratch Carthaginian fleet that finally put to sea early in 241. Its commander was yet another Hanno, possibly the same man who had been defeated at Agrigentum and Ecnomus, but in view of the usual Carthaginian response to one defeat, let alone two, possibly someone else. He made first for "the so-called Holy isle" (now Marettimo, the westernmost of the Egadi), his intention being, according to Polybios (60.3), to try to reach Eryx without being spotted by the enemy. Only then, after unloading his supplies and taking Hamilcar and his mercenaries on board, did he intend to engage the enemy.

But Lutatius, even if he was wounded, was not to be caught napping. Hearing of Hanno's arrival and guessing what he intended to do, he took on board picked men from the army and crossed to Aegusa, the modern Favignana (60.4), the easternmost island in the Aegates group and about ten miles from the Holy Isle. There he addressed his men and told his steersmen that the battle would take place next day. In the morning, however, a fresh wind was blowing from the west, favourable to the enemy, but making it difficult for the Romans to row against it through a rough and heavy swell. At first Lutatius hesitated, but then he decided to fight. He calculated that if he fought now, it would be just against Hanno and the forces he had with

155

him, and against heavily laden ships, whereas, if he waited for a calmer sea, he might let the enemy slip by and would then have to fight him with Hamilcar and his soldiers on board, and with lighter and more manageable ships (60.6–9). So, seeing the enemy approaching under sail, he got under way. According to Valerius Maximus (2.8.2), Valerius Falto later claimed to have exercised operational command in the battle, while Lutatius lay lame on a litter, but even if this is true, there is no reason to doubt that it was Lutatius who took the crucial decision to fight, and one suspects that Valerius Maximus may have been biased in favour of his namesake. But whoever gave the order, it was one of the decisive moments in history.

The highly trained Roman crews found that they could in fact quite easily master the swell, and formed for battle in single line abeam, for over 160 years the formation adopted by the superior fleet.[20] The Carthaginians had come out under sail for the crossing to Eryx, but now that they knew they had to fight, they lowered their masts and closed with the enemy. Thus, as Polybios says (61.2), the situation at Drepana was reversed. The Roman ships were of superior design, their rowers highly trained, their marines the pick of the army, while their opponents' vessels were heavily laden with stores, possibly undermanned, and probably manned by poorly trained crews and hastily raised levies.

The result, if we are to believe Polybios, was a foregone conclusion. The Carthaginian ships almost immediately found themselves in difficulties, and it would have been far worse if the wind had not gone round unexpectedly to the east so that those that managed to disengage could hoist sails and make a run for it (61.7). As it was, 50 of their ships were sunk, 70 captured with their crews, with apparently no Roman losses. Diodoros, however, though his figure for the overall losses – 117 ships – is very similar (24.11.1), claims, as we have seen, that only 20 were captured, and gives the Roman losses as 80 ships, 30 completely and 50 partially disabled. If this is true, the battle was harder fought than Polybios implies, though assuming that the 50 ships only partially disabled were still more or less seaworthy, it was still a crushing victory. Eutropius (2.27.2) and Orosius (4.10.7), again as we have seen, are nearer to Polybios' figure for the number of Carthaginian ships captured, each giving 63, but say that 125 were sunk, for only 12 Roman ships sunk, which looks like considerable exaggeration on both sides.

Certainty is thus not possible, but it would appear that the Carthaginian fleet was at least approximately halved in strength, and it was obviously in no state to renew the fight. Polybios implies, and Diodoros says, that it returned to Carthage, but Orosius (*ibid.*) claims that some ships fled to Lilybaeum, which seems unlikely since the Roman fleet was in the way, and in any case, according to Polybios (61.8), it was there that Lutatius went. The unfortunate Hanno got away to Carthage only to be crucified (Zon. 8.17). After the battle, Lutatius put back not to Drepana, but to Lilybaeum, to dispose of his prisoners (61.8), and though Orosius claims (4.10.8) that he then proceeded to attack Eryx, where he killed 2,000 men, this can probably be ignored.

All the sources are agreed that as soon as the news reached Carthage, its leaders decided to sue for peace. The main reason, Polybios says (62.2), was that they could no longer supply their forces in Sicily since the Romans now commanded the sea, and if they were to abandon these forces, they would have no others and no commanders with whom to carry on the war. This is largely accepted by modern scholars,[21] but one wonders why the collapse should now have been so sudden. Admittedly there are signs that even before the battle, the morale of Hamilcar's forces was beginning to crack – for example the desertion of the Celts mentioned above – and one can only guess at how the garrisons of Lilybaeum and Drepana were faring. Perhaps, despite the almost total silence of the sources, all three forces depended more upon supplies from Carthage than appears, though this is rather belied by the time that elapsed before the relief fleet set sail. In the end, it may have been the psychological blow resulting from their having made a supreme effort and seen it fail, rather than any rational calculation, that finally tipped the balance in favour of peace, though this is actually almost the opposite of what Polybios says (62.1).

At all events, according to Polybios (62.3–6), the Carthaginian govern-ment swiftly sent a message to Hamilcar giving him full powers, and he it was who in turn sent to Lutatius. It has been suggested that in doing this the leaders of Carthage were trying to avoid taking the responsibility for ending the war, and this may be the case. If so, however, Hamilcar, too, showed an astuteness in creating the impression that he had not really been defeated, and in using the commander of the forces at Lilybaeum, Gesco, as an intermediary (DS 24.13; Plb. 1.66.1).[22] He had one bargaining counter in that Lutatius was probably anxious to finish the war before his term of office came to an end, and it is, thus, probably true that he was able to resist Lutatius' initial demand that he surrender his arms and deserters (DS 24.13; Nepos, *Ham.* 1.5). Zonaras (8.17), however, may be right that in the end the deserters were given up, though hardly that Hamilcar was threatened with having to pass under the yoke.

The terms eventually agreed upon with Lutatius were that the Carthaginians should evacuate the whole of Sicily and not make war upon Hiero or bear arms against the Syracusans and their allies; that they should hand over all prisoners without ransom, and should pay an indemnity of 2,200 Euboic talents (nearly 56 tons) of silver in 20 annual instalments (62.8 –9). These terms were, however, subject to ratification by the Roman People, and were rejected when referred to Rome. Instead, ten commissioners were sent to examine the whole question. But their chairman was Lutatius' brother, Quintus Lutatius Cerco, who became consul in 241/0 (Val. Max. 1.2 Ext.2; 1.3.1), and not surprisingly, very little change was made to the terms. According to Polybios here (63.3), the time for paying the indemnity was halved, and a further 1,000 talents added; in addition, the evacuation of the islands between Sicily and Italy – certainly the Lipari islands and possibly the Aegates – was required.

Later, however, in connection with his discussion of the outbreak of the Second war (3.27.2–3), Polybios formulates the treaty in somewhat different terms. The evacuation of Sicily and the islands between it and Italy is the same, but in place of the clause relating to Hiero and the Syracusans, there is a general clause providing that the allies of both parties are to be immune from attack by the other. This is more favourable to Carthage, and it has been suggested that Hamilcar secured it as a concession in return for agreeing to the new, unfavourable terms.[23] In addition, both sides were forbidden to impose any tribute on each other's dominions, to erect public buildings or recruit mercenaries in them, or to form alliances with each other's allies. Finally, 1,000 talents were to be paid at once, instead of by instalments.

Although nothing is said in Polybios about the return of Carthaginian prisoners, this was almost certainly also provided for in the treaty. Eutropius (2.27.4) says that the Senate decreed that those held in public custody should be returned free of ransom, and that although those held privately should be paid for, the money should come from the Roman treasury, not from the Carthaginians. Zonaras, finally, says that the Carthaginians were also forbidden to sail with warships along the shores of Italy or of Rome's allies abroad (8.17), though it is a little difficult to see what this means, unless the reference is to Marseille, or to Sicily, since at this date Rome had no other allies abroad. Zonaras also applies the ban on recruiting mercenaries only to Carthage, but although this at least makes sense, it cannot stand against Polybios' considered formulation.

Once the terms had finally been agreed and ratified, Hamilcar took his troops from Eryx to Lilybaeum, and handed over his command to Gesco, and it was the latter who arranged for their despatch to Africa. Nothing is said about the garrison at Drepana, but it was probably also first taken to Lilybaeum. Nor is anything said about Heraclea Minoa, but it may never have had a garrison, or may have been evacuated before the siege of Lilybaeum began (see above, p. 125). Lutatius and Falto returned to Rome to celebrate triumphs, on 4 and 6 October 241, respectively, the one as proconsul, the other as propraetor. The longest war in ancient history was at an end.

CHAPTER 11

Conclusions

To Polybios the question why Rome won the war and Carthage lost seems primarily to have been a moral one. Thus, towards the beginning of his account, he says that the two states were, among other things, "still uncorrupted in morals" (13.12), and at the end he declares that they were a match for each other in "enterprise, loftiness of spirit and, above all, ambition for supremacy" (64.5). But then he adds that "as men the Romans were not a little, but far superior, on the whole", though he rates Hamilcar as the best general. Here he was presumably thinking of the difference between citizen soldiers and mercenaries (cf. 6.52), and one wonders whether he was right (see below).

In any case, it was surely not just the quality of her men that gave Rome victory, but their quantity. In another, famous passage (2.24), Polybios lists the forces available to her in 225, and although there are difficulties with the figures,[1] the totals the historian records – 700,000 foot and 70,000 horse – give some idea of her huge reserves of manpower. Forty years before, when our war began, the Veneti and Cenomani, later accounting for 20,000 men, were not yet allies, but there may have been even more men available in the area already controlled by Rome. According to the census-figures covering Roman citizens themselves, there were 292,234 in 265/4 and 297,797 in 252/1 (Livy, *Per.* 16 and 18), but possibly only 270,713, if the text is right, in 234/3 (Livy, *Per.* 20).

In the Hannibalic War these reserves enabled Rome to survive disasters on land, such as the Trebbia, Trasimene and, above all, Cannae, and to build her forces up to a total of 25 legions in 212. With attached allied contingents, this would have meant well over 200,000 men, and at about the same time there would have been presumably nearly 63,000, at least, manning the 185 warships operating in Sicilian and Greek waters. In our war, although we lack Livy's year-by-year record of dispositions, there were probably never more than four legions in service in any one year, and at most six, but some of the fleets were much larger, and the loss of life in the storm off Camarina was more than twice as high as that at Cannae.

If, as has been argued in this book, Polybios' figures for the number of ships in the fleets of the years 256 and 255 – 330 and 350, respectively – are to be accepted, and if there were 420 men aboard each ship at both Ecnomus (26.7) and Cape Hermaia, there were just under 139,000 men in the fleet at Ecnomus, and 147,000 off Cape Hermaia. The loss of life off Camarina in 255, again assuming Polybios' ship-numbers to be correct, would have been 119,280: at Cannae, in possibly the worst disaster ever suffered on a single day by a European army, only 48,200 Romans and allies were killed.

This, in itself, is not conclusive, since if we are to believe Polybios, there were actually more Carthaginian ships at Ecnomus (350: 25.9), each manned by as many men as the Roman warships. But whereas the Carthaginians could apparently make only one such effort, Rome could do so over and over again. Thus after the loss of about 94 ships at Ecnomus (28.14), Carthage could man only 200 ships to fight off Cape Hermaia (36.9). But after the loss of perhaps 284 ships and their crews in the storm off Camarina (37.2), Rome could still find the men for 300 ships the very next year, according to Polybios (38.7), whereas it took Carthage perhaps five years before they could again bring their fleet up to 200 ships. By this time Rome had lost another 150 in the second great storm (39.6), but could still find enough men for a fleet of similar size (41.3).

Even Rome could evidently not cope with the loss of over 200 ships in the black year of 249, and for six years we hear hardly anything of official Roman naval activity – only the dubious tales of privateers raiding Africa. But in these years Carthaginian naval activity also apparently dwindled away, until in 242 there was not a ship left in Sicilian waters (59.9). When the final test came, both sides rose magnificently to the call, but whereas Carthage evidently had extreme difficulty in manning the ships she had, Rome not only built a new fleet virtually from scratch, but apparently found the men to man it. In any case, this was apparently the last effort Carthage could make.

Although the fighting on land was on an altogether smaller scale than in the Hannibalic War, the story there is similar. Whereas Rome was able to find the men for at least four legions and their accompanying allied contingents year in and year out, Carthage's efforts to send troops to Sicily were sporadic. We have no means of knowing how many men she originally had there, but it seems unlikely that there were more than about 25,000, of whom some would have been required for garrison duty. Thus Hanno's army at Messana, for example, is unlikely to have been as large as Appius Claudius', on its own. In 262, according to Philinos (*ap.* DS 23.8.1), Hanno the Elder brought a further 50,000 infantry and 6,000 cavalry to Sicily, but thereafter we hear of no further troops being sent there, until the despatch of Hasdrubal, probably in 252, and before that 5,000 infantry and 500 horse had actually been withdrawn from the island to confront Regulus (30.2). These were apparently sent back with Hasdrubal (38.2), possibly with some additional forces (see above), but at Panormus, in 250, according to Orosius (4.9.14), he only had 30,000 men. Possibly 14,000 in all were then sent to reinforce Lilybaeum (see above, p. 126), but that is all. Hamilcar Barca, for example, is not said to have brought any fresh troops with him in 247, and, as we saw, the Hanno who was defeated at the Aegates Islands had been intending to take on board Hamilcar's mercenaries before he engaged.

Unfortunately, as we have seen (above, pp. 65–6), it is not certain who exactly manned the Roman warships, but it was probably a mixture of the Roman proletariat and "naval allies" (*socii navales*). Even if the proportion of the latter was only about half – and it was probably more, as was also probably the case in the land forces – it is nevertheless evident that Rome relied heavily on the loyalty of her allies, and this was clearly a second factor in her success. We only once hear of any trouble, and this from a late source – Zonaras' report of a near-mutiny among Samnite recruits for the navy (8.11), apparently in 259 – and coming as it does, right at the start of the naval war, this may be due to resentment at being required to serve at sea at all rather than to any real strain on allied manpower.

Possibly, as modern commentators have argued, the temporary reduction in fleet numbers in 251, and the much more lengthy one from 248 to 242, were due to difficulties in recruiting fresh sailors. But though plausible, this is only guesswork. We never hear, for example, of allied communities refusing to supply their quotas of men as we do in the Second war (cf. Livy 27.9–10). Even the revolt of Falerii in 241, which might have had something to do with allied dissatisfaction with Roman exactions during the war, may equally have had quite different causes, and in any case, is the exception that proves the rule.[2] The quarrel between Roman troops and those of the "allies" in Sicily in 259 (24.3) almost certainly involved Sicilian, not Italian, allies.

By contrast Carthage certainly had trouble with her allies from 255, as is proved by Polybios' reference to attacks by the Numidians in that year (31.2), by Hanno the Great's war with both the Numidians and the Libyans from 247 onwards (DS 24.10; Plb. 73.1, 74.7), and above all by the revolt of the Libyans and Numidians after the war (65.3, 70.8 ff, 77.6, etc.). In the end, indeed, even Hippo(u) Acra and Utica, Phoenician colonies like Carthage herself, joined the mutineers (82.8).

Nor should we forget the sacrifices made by Rome's own citizens during the war. Even if the allies provided well over half her soldiers and sailors, nevertheless, year after year, the four legions in service would have required 16,800 men, assuming that legions at this date had the same normal paper strength as in Polybios' day (2.24.13). In addition, each warship appears to have had a normal complement of 40 marines, drawn from the poorest section of the citizen population, so that, on Polybios' figures, the huge fleets of 256/3 would have required between 12,000 and 14,000 such men.

Although it is not quite certain who were included in the census figures,[3] they may give us at least some idea of the losses amongst citizens. Just before the war 292,234 adult males were registered (Livy, *Per.* 16), and in 252/1 297,797 (Livy, *Per.* 18), but in 247/6 there were only 241,212. This represents a drop of over 17 per cent since 265/4 and 19 per cent in the last five years, which cannot be accounted for simply on the hypothesis that citizens serving in Sicily were not included. We have no census-returns from Carthage, of course, but since, as far as we know, officers apart, Carthaginian citizens saw service only in 256/5 in Africa, and, possibly, in 241 at the battle of the Aegates islands, their losses cannot have been high. Indeed, none are reported in the battle near Tunis in 255, and only 6,000 at the Aegates islands, if that is the correct interpretation of Diodoros' text (see above, p. 153).

One might be tempted to think that another reason for Rome's victory was precisely that she relied on her own citizens and those of her allies, whereas Carthage relied on mercenaries, apart from when Regulus invaded Africa (cf. 33.6 and 34.6), and this seems to have been Polybios' view, as we have seen. But it is not borne out by the evidence. On the whole, Carthage's mercenary soldiers were worth their salt until the war was over, and we hear of only five occasions during the war when there was trouble among troops actually in service, four of them involving exclusively Celtic troops, and two, indeed, the same men.

The first was the occasion when Celtic soldiers forming part of the garrison of Agrigentum pillaged the city as a result of a dispute over pay (2.7.7). It was some of this same band who attempted to betray Eryx towards the end of the war and deserted to the enemy when their plot failed (2.7.8–9). In addition, Frontinus tells two anecdotes in which Carthaginian generals dealt with treacherous Celts (*Strat.* 3.16.2 and 3), the second of which is confirmed by Diodoros (23.8.3) and Zonaras (8.10). For good measure, Diodoros also attributes the defeat at Panormus partly to the drunken behaviour of Hasdrubal's Celtic soldiers (23.21). The only incident not just involving Celts was the one at Lilybaeum in 250 (43.1–8), and there the moving spirits were some of the officers, not the rank and file.

There is thus no reason to believe that Carthage was let down by her mercenaries, though whether they were as good soldiers as the Roman legionaries is another question. On the whole they seem to have fared badly in the set-piece battles, for example the one outside Agrigentum in 261 (19.8 ff), and at Panormus in 250 (40.4 ff), though in the latter the Roman forces were brilliantly handled. At Adys the mercenaries displayed great dash in routing one of Regulus' legions (30.11), but then let their success go to their heads and were surrounded and cut to pieces. Even in the subsequent battle near Tunis in which Regulus was defeated and taken prisoner, it was the mercenaries who came off worst on the Carthaginian side (34.4 and 9). In the day-to-day fighting, however, the mercenaries held their own, particularly in the long-drawn-out siege of Lilybaeum and under Hamilcar in the later stages of the war.

Mention of Hamilcar leads naturally to an assessment of the various commanders in the war, and it is immediately obvious that none measures up to the standards of a Scipio, let alone a Hannibal. Hamilcar himself, as we saw, was rated the best general of the war by Polybios (64.6), and was clearly a highly competent soldier. But this was perhaps at a tactical rather than at a strategic level. For all his ability to maintain himself in an increasingly isolated situation and to avoid defeat, there is no hint that he had any better idea than other Carthaginians at this time how to defeat Rome.

It is interesting and significant that two of the finest soldiers of antiquity, Alexander and Hannibal, were both the sons of good soldiers, and one would very much like to know what they learnt from their fathers. Alexander certainly inherited his father's highly integrated fighting machine, including its engineers, but judging from what very little we know of Philip's battles, Alexander devised his tactics for himself, and he was, if anything, not his father's equal as a strategist.

Hannibal, one suspects, learnt his supreme competence and confidence as a fighting soldier from his father, and there is more than a hint of Hamilcar, though on a grander scale, in his son's ability to maintain himself in a foreign land for so many years, particularly when things started to go wrong. But there is no hint that Hannibal learned his battle tactics from his father, let alone from that other Hamilcar's tactics at Ecnomus, and as a strategist he was in a class all his own.

Of other Carthaginian officers during the first war we can say little. Like Hamilcar, they often displayed tactical competence, if not brilliance – one thinks of Hanno's ruse of enticing the Roman cavalry to pursue his Numidians at Agrigentum (19.2–4), for example, or of the later break-out from the same city by Hannibal, son of Gisgo (19.12–13). But it does not say much for their abilities in general that they had to be taught by a Spartan how to defeat Regulus, and, as was said in Hamilcar's case, none of them seems to have had any idea of how to defeat Rome other than by simply keeping going. The one strategic stroke of any significance was the seizure of Agrigentum by Hanno, son of Hannibal, in 264 (DS 23.1.2), and its subsequent occupation by a powerful force in 263/2 (17.4–5). If, at the same time, they had maintained a second front in the north of the island, they could have divided Rome's forces, and might have been able to defeat them piecemeal. But, after the fall of Agrigentum, they seem to have contented themselves with responding to Rome's thrusts, except for Hasdrubal's march on Panormus in 250, and that led to his defeat.

At sea, again, they had some competent officers – Hamilcar, at least, at Ecnomus, certainly Adherbal at Drepana, and possibly Carthalo later in the same year. But they also had some incompetent ones, for example the Hannibal who commanded in the fight off Cape Vaticano and later at Mylae (21.10–11 and 23.3 ff), and by sea, too, they seem to have lacked any real purpose other than to respond to Roman initiatives. For all the raiding of Italy that went on, as far as we know no substantial body of Carthaginian troops was ever landed on Italian soil, and yet Hannibal was to show – though ultimately he, too, failed – that the only way to defeat Rome was to do so in Italy, and so induce her allies to desert.

One has only to imagine what he might have made of the almost total command of the sea Carthage enjoyed in the early years of the war, to realize how much more she could have done. Apart from anything else, he would not have had to undertake the long and exhausting march to Italy, emerging from the Alps, still over 300 miles from Rome, with only 26,000 men and between 30 and 40 elephants. He could have come ashore somewhere in southern Italy with 50,000 foot, 6,000 cavalry and 60 elephants, like Hanno in Sicily in 262 (DS 23.8.1), assured of an endless flow of re-inforcements, and the support of Samnites, Lucanians, Bruttians and Italiot Greeks even more likely in the 260s than after Cannae.

On the Roman side, one has a similar impression of a mixture of com-petence and incompetence at the tactical level, on land, with here and there the odd suggestion of something more − one thinks of Regulus' envelop-ment of the Carthaginian army at Adys, for example (30.12), and, still more, of Metellus' masterly handling of the battle at Panormus (40.5 ff). At sea, one can perhaps allow Scipio Asina the blunder that got him his name, but Atilius' handling of Tyndaris was hardly a model for aspiring sea-officers (25.1–4), and although Claudius Pulcher perhaps did not deserve the odium heaped upon him for Drepana, he certainly deserved little credit. But although some of the others have come in for too extravagant praise, Duilius was evidently at least competent, and Lutatius and Valerius Falto not only made the correct decision to fight on that fateful, windy, March morning off the Aegates, but clearly made the best of the advantages they had.

In addition, there were two occasions when, most unusually in ancient warfare, technology played a part, and it is remarkable that it was the Romans who both times made use of it. The first was, of course, the inven-tion of the *corvus*. Even if the suggestion came from elsewhere, it was pre-sumably Duilius who saw its potential and gave the go-ahead for its use. The second occasion was off Phintias in 249, when the quaestors used cata-pults and mangonels (53.11) to protect their anchored ships. Why did not the Carthaginians devise some such method for dealing with the *corvus*, for example? Catapults and *ballistae* had been carried on ships in the east since at least 307 (DS 20.49.4). Instead, they even apparently had to wait for Xanthippos to teach them how to use elephants (32.2 ff).

But it is at the higher levels of strategy that there was a crucial difference between the two sides. As we have seen, no Carthaginian seems to have had the slightest inkling how to defeat Rome, except in the short term, whereas the Romans made a series of decisions that show that some of them at least knew how to fight a war like this. Even if some of the guesses about indi-vidual responsibility for various decisions are right, ultimate credit for the strategy adopted must presumably go to the Senate. But one wonders why, if Carthage had a "senate" too, to say nothing of its inner "Council of Thirty", her strategy was so weak. Too much has, perhaps, sometimes been made of the differences between Rome as a nation of "farmers" and

Carthage as one of "businessmen",[4] but it is arguable that Rome fought for "victory" in a far more real sense than Carthage. To Rome, wars ended when the Republic dictated its terms to a defeated enemy: to Carthage, wars ended with a negotiated settlement – even Hannibal was later to think in much the same terms.

This may explain why it is that at every stage in our war it seems to be Rome that takes the initiative and Carthage that just responds. Thus Rome shipped an army across to Messana with only very limited interference from the enemy – and if some sources are to be believed, the Carthaginians even apologized for the limited interference they offered. Then, when the Roman army advanced on Syracuse, Carthage did nothing to help her ally, beyond sending a fleet, which apparently arrived too late (DS 23.4.1). As we have seen, the one aggressive move made by Carthage at this stage was the occupation of Agrigentum, but even then she made nothing of it, and although she tried to respond to the Roman investment of the city, that is all it was – dancing to Rome's tune.

Rome again seized the initiative when she decided to build a fleet. Polybios suggests that this was for two reasons, to counter the threat of the Carthaginian navy to Sicilian coastal cities so that they could the more easily be induced to side with Rome, and to carry the war to Africa (20.6–7). In reality, as we saw, the move may have been more defensive, in other words, to protect Italy from Carthaginian raids, and it was certainly not until four years later that the second objective was attempted, unless it is true that Sulpicius Paterculus had plans to attack Africa in 258 (Zon. 8.12). But the fleet was sent to Sicilian waters as soon as it was ready, even if it does not appear to have ventured further than Mylae in the first instance, and it was used aggressively against the Lipari islands, albeit unsuccessfully, and against Corsica and Sardinia.

But it is the decision to invade Africa that shows that some Romans knew exactly how to defeat Carthage, whereas, as far as we know, no Carthaginian even dreamt, in this war, of invading Italy. Perhaps if Regulus had not been quite so arrogant, the war would have been brought to a successful conclusion in 255, for it is by no means certain that the Carthaginians would not have agreed to evacuate Sicily and to pay an indemnity. The situation was comparable to the one facing Carthage in 203, when, after Scipio's victory at the Great Plains, he occupied Tunis, just as Regulus did after Adys. In the end, in 203, the Carthaginians decided to fight on, until they learned of the final overthrow of their ally, Syphax. But before this, according to Polybios, they had already given some consideration to the sort of terms they would be prepared to accept (14.9.5–11).

Regulus' defeat apparently convinced Rome's leaders that it was, in fact, too difficult to secure victory by invading Africa. But even after the appalling disaster that befell their relief mission in 255, we find them, in the very next year, adopting the slower, but perhaps surer, strategy of using their fleet to attack Carthaginian bases in Sicily, when they captured Kephaloidion and Panormus. In 253 they even carried the war to Africa again when Blaesus raided the Gulf of Gabes, while the year 252 saw the capture of Himera and Lipara.

Meanwhile, Carthage continued just to respond to these threats, and it was not until late 251 or early 250 that she made her first aggressive move since the occupation of Agrigentum in 264, when Hasdrubal attacked Panormus, only to be defeated by Metellus. Typically it was Rome that immediately followed up this victory by investing Lilybaeum, the most important Carthaginian base in Sicily. Again, it failed, but that is not the point: the strategy was correct, even if its implementation was too difficult.

The same is also true of Claudius Pulcher's disastrous attack on Adherbal at Drepana. Even if he did not know that Carthalo was on his way with a further 70 ships, he was using his fleet as a fleet should be used, to "seek out and destroy" the enemy – something that the Carthaginians had never done, or at least not since Hannibal blundered into the Roman fleet off Cape Vaticano in 260. Indeed, throughout the war, the Carthaginian navy hardly made an aggressive move unless prompted by some move of the Romans.

The year 249, when the Roman navy was reduced to a handful of ships by Adherbal's victory off Drepana and the disaster to Iunius Pullus off Camarina, was surely the moment, if ever, for Carthage at last to "go for the jugular", at least in Sicily, if not in Italy. But she made nothing of it. Even Drepana and Lilybaeum were not relieved, let alone any serious attempt made to recover Panormus; and Agrigentum, which had at least been briefly reoccupied in 254, if only to be razed, this time was not even approached. It was somehow typical of Carthage's weak-kneed approach to the whole war that Carthalo should abandon a raid on Italy, undertaken, it is alleged (Zon. 8.16), with the purpose of drawing the Roman armies away from Sicily, at the approach of the *praetor urbanus*: did he really imagine, after 16 years of fighting, that there were no Roman troops left to defend Italy? Even Hamilcar, for all the brilliance of his guerrilla tactics, in five years achieved nothing of any importance even in Sicily, let alone by his raids on Italy.

So it was left to Rome to make the last effort, and to Carthage, as usual, merely to respond. There can be no doubt that, militarily speaking, Rome deserved to win.

CHAPTER 12

Epilogue

Looking back on the First Punic War with the benefit of hindsight, as we do, we can see that it was just the first in a series of struggles that ended in the total destruction of Carthage in 146, and there is a certain inevitability about the outcome. In reality, of course, nothing is inevitable in history, and Rome and Carthage could have gone their separate ways in peace. After all, the treaty that brought the First war to an end was a reasonable one, which did not impose too heavy a burden on a wealthy state like Carthage or interfere with her control of her African empire or even her expansion into other areas. There was no Masinissa this time.

Nevertheless, Polybios believed that the seeds of the second conflict lay in the first, and he was undoubtedly right. He thought that there were three causes of the Second war (3.9.6ff) – the "wrath" (θυμός) of Hamilcar Barca, which was passed on to his son, Hannibal, the "anger" (ὀργή) of their fellow-citizens, and the "success" (εὔροια) of their activities in Spain. The first he explains as due to Hamilcar's feeling that he himself had never been defeated, but had been forced to make peace because of the naval defeat at the Aegates. Livy even claims (21.1.5) that Hamilcar felt that Sicily had been given up too soon. It has been argued that the view that Hamilcar was planning revenge from the moment the First war ended is belied by his subsequent behaviour,[1] and it is not certain that it rests on anything more than guesswork on the part of Polybios or his source. But it is not impossible that Hamilcar, like many a German soldier in 1918, including a certain Corporal Hitler, believed that he had been "stabbed in the back".[2]

But Polybios' second cause – the "anger" of the Carthaginians in general – is obviously a more serious matter, and requires a brief consideration of

171

what happened after the First war ended. According to Polybios (1.66 ff), after Hamilcar had handed over command of his mercenaries to Gesco at Lilybaeum, the latter took the precaution of sending them to Carthage in batches, in the hope that they would be paid off and dispersed before any serious trouble could arise. This indicates that trouble was already brewing, but the Carthaginian authorities, with typical shortsightedness, not only failed to pay the soldiers, but when they began to get out of hand, moved them in a body to Sicca (El Kef), and even allowed them to take their baggage, including their families, with them.

At Sicca, with nothing to do and with discipline relaxed, the soldiers began to tot up what was due to them, and when told by Hanno the Great, the commander-in-chief in Africa, that Carthage could not pay, to talk of taking matters into their own hands. Polybios (67.4 ff) makes the shrewd observation that the Carthaginian practice of hiring troops of various nationalities – in this case there were Spaniards, Celts, Ligurians, Balearic islanders, Greeks and Libyans – though it made it difficult for them to combine, also had disadvantages. Since no Carthaginian could know all their languages and it was too laborious to address each group through a different interpreter, the only way to explain matters was through their own officers, and these frequently told them something quite different. It also did not help that they had not served under Hanno.

Eventually, all 20,000 of them marched on Carthage, camping at Tunis, and, in a panic, the Carthaginians now began to concede everything demanded, with the inevitable result that the demands increased – payment for lost horses, for example, and in lieu of rations never received. The mutineers agreed, however, to refer their grievances to one of the generals under whom they had served in Sicily, and since Hamilcar was unacceptable, Gesco was sent to Tunis. He began to pay off the arrears nationality by nationality, but at this stage two leaders emerged who had their own personal reasons for not wanting negotiations to succeed. One, Spendius, was an ex-slave from Campania who feared that he might be surrendered to his former master; the other, Mathos, a Libyan, who was afraid that when all was over, he might be singled out to bear the brunt of Carthage's wrath. The latter, in particular, was able to play upon similar fears amongst his fellow-countrymen, the largest single contingent among the mutineers. By the use of terror tactics the two men were able to cow any opposition, and were eventually chosen as "generals" by the troops.

Gesco did his best, but when directly confronted by a crowd of Libyans who had not yet received their pay, foolishly told them to ask their "general", Mathos, for it. At this the fury of the Libyans overflowed, and not only did they commandeer the rest of the cash Gesco had brought, but they also seized him and the other Carthaginians with him. From this point on, Polybios says (70.6), they were at open war with Carthage.

Such was the origin of the "War against the Mercenaries" which Polybios says was called the "Libyan War", clearly because, as he goes on to explain, nearly all the Libyans soon joined the mutineers (70.7–9). It was marked by a savagery and vicious cruelty on both sides that clearly appalled even contemporaries (cf. 81.5 ff, 88.7), and though Carthage won in the end, it was not before she had been brought to the brink of destruction. The chronology of the war is uncertain, but it probably broke out in the autumn of 241 and lasted at least until the end of 238, if not into 237.[3]

The details do not concern us, but the wider repercussions do, and chiefly the effects on Carthaginian relations with Rome. At first there was some friction when Carthage began to intern merchants from Italy who had been caught trading with the enemy (83.7), especially when it was rumoured that some Roman citizens had actually been thrown overboard (App., *Lib.* 5). But when, on sending an embassy, Rome managed to recover all the prisoners by diplomatic means, her leaders were so gratified that they in turn handed back all the prisoners still in their hands from the late war – precisely 2,743 of them according to Valerius Maximus (5.1.1a). They also lent a ready and benevolent ear to various Carthaginian requests, for example permitting Italian traders to traffic with Carthage but forbidding them to do so with the mutineers (83.8–10, cf. 3.28.3), and evidently put no difficulties in Hiero's way of doing the same. According to Appian (*Sic.* 2.3) and Zonaras (8.17), they even permitted Carthage to hire mercenaries from their own allies, though this is somewhat improbable, and tried to broker a peace between her and the mutineers.

A potentially more serious issue arose, however, when first Carthage's mercenary troops on Sardinia mutinied (cf. 79.1–4) and invited Rome to take over the island, and then the people of Utica offered to place themselves under the Republic's protection (83.11). But on both occasions Rome refused, in the latter case scrupulously adhering to her treaty with Carthage, which expressly forbade either party to accept into alliance the allies of the other (3.27.4). Although we should not too readily assume that Roman notions of "honour" had no bearing on these decisions, it is, nevertheless, probably not too cynical to suppose that Rome's leaders also reflected that it was not in the interest of one "imperial" power to poach the allies of another, when two could play at that game.

But the situation in Sardinia later took a turn for the worse. Having killed their officers, the mutineers there had been joined by another force sent over to deal with them, and had proceeded systematically to murder all the Carthaginians on the island. But after their appeal to Rome had been rejected, the native Sardinians had grown tired of their high-handed ways, and they had been forced to flee to Italy (79.1–5). At about the time the Mercenary War came to an end, they made a second appeal to Rome, and this time the Romans began to prepare an expedition to take over the island.

Presumably when the Carthaginians heard of this, they sent an embassy to Rome to protest that Sardinia belonged to them, and began themselves to make preparations to recover the island. But the Romans affected to believe that these preparations were against themselves, and declared war. Carthage was in no state to fight, and was forced not only to give up Sardinia, but to agree to an additional indemnity of 1,200 talents (88.8–12). The precise dating of this is as uncertain as the chronology of the Mercenary War as a whole, but a plausible explanation of the divergent traditions is that the appeal to Rome from the mutineers and the resulting expedition belong to the consular year 238/7, but that the Roman ultimatum and the Carthaginian climb-down occurred in 237/6, and probably in the summer of 237.[4]

Why the Romans behaved like this is a mystery. Later they evidently tried to claim either that the annexation of Sardinia was in response to the Carthaginian ill-treatment of Italian merchants during the Mercenary War (cf. App., *Hisp.* 4, *Lib.* 5 and 86; Zon. 8.18), or that the island had been ceded to them by the treaty of Lutatius (cf. Livy 21.40.5, 22.54.11; Eutr. 3.2.2; Oros. 4.11.2; *de vir. ill.* 41.2). But, as Polybios points out (3.28.3), the first was belied by the friendly exchange of prisoners that then took place, and the second is clearly equally untrue. Even if Sardinia could have been regarded as one of the islands lying between Sicily and Italy that the treaty obliged Carthage to evacuate, Rome's failure to make a move against the island until some four years later shows that even she did not interpret the treaty in this light, since there would have been nothing to stop her. Indeed, her initial refusal to accept the mutineers' offer surely implies that she accepted that the island was still at that time Carthaginian.

The only conceivable justification for Rome's behaviour would be that by expelling the mutineers, the Sardinians had asserted their independence, and that therefore Rome might legitimately step into Carthage's shoes.[5] But, in reality, the seizure of the island was "contrary to all justice", as

174

Polybios says (3.28.2), and the decision to do it was presumably taken for no other reason than that the Senate was convinced that it was in Rome's interests. Perhaps when faced with the prospect of the island's reverting to Carthage's control and being again occupied by troops loyal to her, Romans were reminded that they had gone to war in 264 ostensibly to prevent this happening in Messana: could not Sardinia also be a bridge for crossing to Italy (cf. 10.9)? Behind such arguments would, as usual, lie the ambitions of those who might hope to win glory by conquering the island, and no doubt the greed of all, from soldiers to slave-traders, who might hope to profit from its conquest.

The tragedy was that by acting like this, the Romans dissipated any friendly relations that may have started to blossom as a result of their behaviour during the dark days of the Mercenary War. Instead, as Polybios saw (cf. 3.10.1–5, 13.1, 28.1–3, 30–4), they exacerbated the bitterness left by the first war – he, indeed, regarded this as the "greatest cause" of the Second war (3.10.4). Nor were relations improved by the trouble Rome had in subduing Sardinia, trouble that was suspected, rightly or wrongly, of being fomented by Carthage (Zon. 8.18): in 233, the consul, Quintus Fabius Maximus, who was later to be one of Hannibal's stubbornest opponents, is even alleged to have threatened Carthage with war (Gellius, *NA* 10.27.3–5; Zon. *ibid.*).

But the Roman occupation of Sardinia cast an even longer shadow. The prolonged resistance of the islanders required an almost continuous military presence, and this meant also the presence of a Roman magistrate with *imperium* – one or both consuls in 238 and from 235 to 231. As a result, it has been suggested,[6] in 227 the number of praetors was raised from two to four, one, in future, being assigned to Sardinia and one to Sicily. Thus, in a sense, was born the Roman Empire, for, from now on, the "*provincia*" of these two praetors became not merely a "sphere of duty", but a "province" in the modern sense. The first "provincial governor" of Sicily was none other than Gaius Flaminius, who, ten years later, was to meet his death at Hannibal's hands at Lake Trasimene.

But what of Polybios' "third cause" of the Second war – the success of Carthaginian operations in Spain? Again the details lie outside the scope of this book, but here the links between the First and Second wars come full circle, for the man chosen by Carthage to command her forces in Spain, in the first instance, was Hamilcar Barca, whose "wrath", as we saw, was Polybios' first cause of the Second war. Before he left for Spain, probably towards the end of 237, he performed a no doubt customary sacrifice to the god Polybios calls Zeus (3.11.5), but whom the Carthaginians probably knew as Ba'al Shamim. After he had completed the rites, he told the others who were present to leave him alone with his nine-year-old son, and asked the boy whether he wanted to come to Spain. On his gladly accepting, and, as Polybios delightfully says (3.11.7), "even somewhat overdoing his begging, in a childish way", Hamilcar took him to the altar and bade him swear, with his hand on the victim, "never to show goodwill to the Romans". The boy's name, of course, was Hannibal.

Notes

Chapter 1

1. All dates in this book are BC unless otherwise specified. Unfortunately, there are two problems in translating Roman dates into our terms. First, consuls did not take office on 1 January until 153 (Broughton i. 452 *sub anno*), so before this any "consular year" has to be expressed in the form, e.g., "264/3". It is sometimes said – e.g. Thiel, 170 *n*332; Caven, pp. 17, 31, etc. – that at the time of the First Punic War consuls entered office on 1 May, but in fact they appear to have entered office on a variety of different dates – recorded examples vary from 15 May (Livy 3.36.3) to 13 December (Livy 4.37.3): see O. Leuze, *Die römische Jahrzählung* (Tübingen, 1909), pp. 335 ff; Broughton, ii pp. 637 ff; A. K. Michels, *The calendar of the Roman republic* (Princeton, 1967), pp. 97 ff

   Secondly, the Roman calendar, being lunar, was often out of step with our own. For example, in 190, the eclipse of the sun dated by Livy (37.4.4) to 11 July actually occurred on 14 March. M. G. Morgan, *Chiron* 7 (1977), pp. 89 ff, argues that the Roman calendar was regularly a month or two ahead of ours, in the early years of the war, but that it was brought into rough agreement between spring 258, and spring 255, and thereafter remained so until the end of the war.

   References to Polybios Book 1 are given by chapter and verse, references to other books by book, chapter and verse. If it seems likely that some confusion might result, the abbreviation "Plb." is used. For the abbreviations used for other works see pp. 193 ff.

2. This distinction is often claimed for the battle of Leyte Gulf, in October, AD 1944, particularly by American naval historians. But at that battle fewer than 200,000 men took part, compared with over 285,000 at Ecnomus, according to Polybios, and only 282 American, Japanese and Australian ships, as compared with 680 Carthaginian and Roman at Ecnomus: see now Thomas J. Cutler, *The battle of Leyte Gulf* (New York, 1994), xiii, and compare Polybios 1. 25. 7–26. 8.

3. For the date of Polybios' birth see Walbank, p. 1, *n*1.

4. For surveys see E. Mioni, *Polybio* (Padua, 1949), pp. 119 ff, and *RE*.

5. F. Jacoby, *FGH* iiD, p. 598; A. Klotz, *Hermes* 80 (1952), p. 326. See also refs. in Walbank, p. 65.
6. Walbank, p. 65, and *CQ* 39 (1945), pp. 5 ff
7. What this kind of thing consisted of can best be seen by the modern reader in T. S. R. Broughton's monumental *Magistrates of the Roman Republic* (New York, 1951), of which vol. i. pp. 202–20 covers the First Punic War. On Fabius Pictor's work see refs. in Walbank, p. 65.
8. For a full discussion of these treaties see the Ph. D. thesis of Dr Rhoda Lee (Newcastle upon Tyne, 1993).
9. On what follows see Walbank's excellent introduction (pp. 6 ff) and refs. there.
10. Although a story about Stalky and his friends, it appeared first in the collection of short stories entitled *A diversity of creatures*.
11. Cf. Walbank's comment, p. 26: "The vast literature which exists on Polybius' sources is perhaps disproportionate to the results it has achieved." See also the pertinent remarks of B. D. Hoyos, *Antichthon* 23 (1989), pp. 54 ff.
12. For example, the suggestion of E. Lo Cascio, *Annali del'Istituto Italiano di Numismatica*, 1980–1, pp. 345–8, that the "Prow" series of Roman cast-bronze coinage belongs to the First Punic War, is rejected outright by M. H. Crawford, *Coinage and money under the Roman Republic* (London, 1985), p. 52, *n*1.

Chapter 2

1. On what follows see, e.g., Scullard, *Hist.*, pp. 126 ff ; E. S. Staveley, CAH^2, pp. 428 ff.
2. See A. N. Sherwin White, *The Roman citizenship*[2] (Oxford, 1973), pp. 38 ff. On Caere see now T. J. Cornell, CAH^2, pp. 313 ff.
3. See, e.g., Sherwin White, pp. 119 ff.
4. E. Badian, *Foreign clientelae (264–70 BC)* (Oxford, 1958), pp. 25 ff.
5. T. Mommsen, *Römisches Staatsrecht* (Leipzig, 1887–8), iii. pp. 676 f; *contra:* H. Horn, *Foederati* (Frankfurt, 1930), pp. 83 ff.
6. Cf. P. A. Brunt, *Italian manpower 225 BC–AD 14* (Oxford, 1971), pp. 545–8.
7. Lawrence Keppie, *The making of the Roman army* (London, 1984), p. 22.
8. There is some doubt about whether the term *velites* was already in use. The earlier term was *rorarii* and it appears to have continued in use until the end of the second century (cf. Lucilius 7. 290, 10. 393). Livy asserts that *velites* were instituted in 211 (26. 4. 9), but the passage is self-contradictory. He says that the javelins of the supposedly newly instituted *velites* were "tipped with iron such as on the spears of the velites" (*praefixa ferro, quale hastis velitaribus inest*: 26. 4. 4), and the statement that the new *velites* came into action on the cavalry horses, mounted behind the riders, also does not make sense. Apart from anything else, there would not have been enough cavalry horses to carry 1,200 extra men. For what it is worth, too, Livy refers to *velites* in accounts of fighting before 211 (21. 55. 11, 23. 29. 3, 24. 34. 5).
9. On the *gladius* see P. Coussin, *Les Armes romaines* (Paris, 1926), pp. 139 ff, 220 ff; J. Kromayer & G. Veith, *Heerwesen und Kriegführung der Griechen und Römer* (Munich,

1928), p. 325 and fig. 18. On the *pilum* see A. Schulten, *RhM* 66 (1911), pp. 373 ff;
RE, cols 1336 ff.

10. For the form of his *cognomen* see Broughton, i. p. 207, *n*1.

11. See Broughton, i. p. 215, *n*1 and *n*2.

12. See, e.g., T. J. Cornell, *CAH²*, pp. 400 ff, and E. S. Staveley, *ibid.*, p. 447. The latter finds A. Lippold's attempt – *Consules: Untersuchungen zur Geschichte des römischen Konsulates von 264 bis 201 v. Chr.* (Bonn, 1963), pp. 104 ff – to reconstruct the composition of rival factions in the Senate by examining the role that was played by successive generals, "totally unconvincing" (pp. 450–51).

13. On all this see, e.g., Warmington, pp. 143 ff, and, more recently, Scullard, *CAH²*, pp. 486 ff.

14. For what follows see Warmington, pp. 63 ff.

15. The Carthaginian operations in Sicily during the war were probably paid for by the large electrum and silver issues of Carthaginian coins that form the later part of G. K. Jenkins's Series 6 (see G. K. Jenkins & R. B. Lewis, *Carthaginian gold and electrum coins*, London, 1963), and which are found only in Carthaginian territory; the issues apparently ceased with the stalemate on land from 247 onwards: cf. M. H. Crawford, *Coinage and money under the Roman Republic* (London, 1985), p. 106.

16. On war elephants in general see H. H. Scullard, *The elephant in the Greek and Roman world* (London, 1974); on the identification of Carthage's elephants see the same author, *Numismatic Chronicle* 1949, pp. 1 ff, and with Sir William Gowers, *Numismatic Chronicle* 1950, pp. 271 ff.

17. On the pay of Roman troops see Crawford, pp. 22–3; Crawford suggests that the spread of the use of coinage, both Roman and local, to the Apennine area and elsewhere in Italy reflects the service of men from these localities in the Roman army from the Pyrrhic War onwards (pp. 36 ff).

Chapter 3

1. See, e.g., Walbank, pp. 337 ff ; and Scullard, *CAH²*, pp. 517 ff.

2. For discussions see, e.g., K. Meister, *Riv. fil.* 98 (1970), pp. 408 ff; R. E. Mitchell, *Historia* 20 (1971), pp. 648 ff; B. D. Hoyos, *CQ* 35 (1985), pp. 103 ff.

3. On the Philinos treaty see Hoyos, pp. 92 ff, and for lists of "believers" and "non-believers", pp. 92–3, *n*6. I side with the "non-believers" as does Hoyos, who, I think, has now effectively demolished the treaty.

4. P. Lévêque, *Pyrrhos* (Paris, 1957), pp. 409 ff; G. Nenci, *Historia* 7 (1958), pp. 263 ff.

5. For the suggestion that what Diodoros actually wrote was "Locri" not "Rhegion" see Thiel, p. 30, following de Sanctis ii. 407; for the alternative see Scullard, *Hist.*, p. 123. That the incident was a purely Carthaginian affair is argued by R. E. Mitchell, *Historia* 20 (1971), p. 650.

6. Cf., e.g., Beloch, iv. 1. p. 642. As Harris remarks, *War and imperialism in Republican Rome 327–70 BC* (Oxford, 1979), p. 184, *n*2, "Zonar. viii. 6 is by far the most credible source."

7. Harris, pp. 183–4.

8. See B. D. Hoyos, *Antichthon* 19 (1985), pp. 32 ff.

9. The latter is Caven's suggestion, p. 14.

10. Cf., e.g., Walbank *ad* 10. 3 ff ; Scullard, *CAH²*, pp. 540 ff; and J. W. Rich, *Declaring war in the Roman Republic in the period of transmarine expansion* (Collection Latomus 149; Brussels, 1976), pp. 120 ff, for full references.

11. For Alfius' view of the Mamertines' behaviour see Cichorius, pp. 58 ff. For the suggestion that it may echo Mamertine propaganda in 264 see Scullard, *CAH²*, pp. 541, *n*51.

12. Cf., especially, A. Heuss, *Historisches Zeitschrift* 169 (1949/50), pp. 471 ff. For an excellent account of Rome's fears see Scullard, *CAH²*, pp. 540–41.

13. Cf. Scullard, *Hist.* p. 144; Thiel, pp. 132–3.

14. Walbank, p. 61 *ad* 11. 2–3. Harris, p. 184, evidently thinks that the word στρατηγῶν refers to Ap. Claudius' "colleagues" (in the plural).

15. Cf., e.g., Thiel, pp. 139 ff; Warmington, p. 181.

16. G. C. & C. Picard, *Life and death of Carthage*, pp. 187 ff – for "Caudex" meaning "dinghy" see 191; for the meaning "blockhead" cf. Terence, *Heautontimorumenos* 5.1.4; for "popular/democratic leaders" Scullard, *Hist.*, p. 144, and *CAH²*, pp. 542. For an interesting discussion of the tradition that lies behind Florus', Cassius Dio's and Ampelius' statements about the causes of the war see B. D. Hoyos, *Antichthon* 23 (1989), pp. 51 ff.

17. See Harris, esp. pp. 182 ff.

18. Cf., e.g., Badian, *Foreign clientelae 264–70 BC* (Oxford, 1958), pp. 34–5.

19. Cf. Badian, *Foreign clientelae*, p. 35; Harris, p. 189.

20. See Barbara W. Tuchman, *August 1914*, p. 123.

Chapter 4

1. Walbank, p. 62, *ad* 1. 11. 6.

2. Thiel, pp. 150–51.

3. Among those who accept the story of C. Claudius are de Sanctis, iii. 1. pp. 104, 236; Thiel, pp. 149 ff; Scullard, *Hist.*, p. 145 and *CAH²*, p. 543; Dorey & Dudley, p. 5; Caven, pp. 18–19. The story is doubted by Beloch, iv. 1. 647, *n*2; A. Heuss, *Historische Zeitschrift* 169 (1949–50), pp. 483–4; and Walbank, pp. 61–2 *ad* 11. 4.

4. Thiel, p. 152. By rejecting various passages in the Cassius Dio/Zonaras story as the result of confusion between the two Claudii, Thiel is able to "reconstruct" an ingenious scheme whereby C. Claudius is sent ahead to seize Messana before the Carthaginians station any ships there. But this is methodologically dubious, and would the Carthaginians have left Hanno in Messana with no ships at all?

5. Caven, p. 17, does not mention the advance to Solous, and has the meeting with Hiero's envoys take place at Lilybaeum, after Hanno had won over Agrigentum; he seems to assume that it was only then that the agreement was made.

6. See, e.g., Warmington, p. 182; Thiel, p. 155; Scullard, *Hist.*, p. 146. Caven, p. 17, conjectures that Messana was to be razed, its non-Greek inhabitants sold and the Greeks incorporated into the Syracusan citizen-body.

7. Thiel, p. 159 and n298, thinks that there were three embassies, two from Ap. Claudius before and after he had occupied Messana, and one from the Carthaginians after his first, abortive attempt to cross.

8. Thiel, p. 156 and n290, but he underestimates the size of a consular army at 16,000 men. Two legions plus cavalry amounted to 9,000 men, and the allied troops will have been at least as numerous.

9. Thiel, pp. 157–8.

10. *The Mediterranean pilot* I. pp. 456 ff, cf. Thiel, p. 158 and n296.

11. Cf. Walbank, pp. 62–3 and 66–7; Scullard, *Hist.*, p. 146 and n2, and *CAH²*, p. 545; Thiel, pp. 60–62; Caven, pp. 19–20. Dorey & Dudley, p. 5, do not appear to see the problem and just accept Polybios.

12. Hülsen, *RE*, cols 1915–16.

13. Walbank, pp. 66–7; Beloch, iv. 2. pp. 533 ff; Scullard, *Hist.*, p. 146 and n2; Warmington, p. 183; Caven, p. 20.

14. Beloch, iv. 2. pp. 533 ff, suggests that Ap. Claudius' arrival in Sicily dates to early 263, and that he failed even to raise the siege of Messana; this was accomplished only by the arrival of the double consular army later in the year.

15. De Sanctis, iii. 1. pp. 114–15.

16. It is usually thought that Hiero had a treaty with Rome, but see A. M. Eckstein, *Chiron* 10 (1980), pp. 183 ff. M. H. Crawford, *Coinage and money under the Roman Republic* (London, 1985), pp. 108–9, makes the interesting suggestion that Hiero paid the indemnity in bronze coins that went directly to Roman troops – hence the hoards of his Head of Poseidon/Trident bronze coins found at Agrigentum.

17. *RE*, cols 772–3.

18. Caven, p. 22.

19. Thiel, pp. 70–3.

20. Warmington, p. 183.

21. It is Thiel, pp. 167–8, who suggests that Zonaras may wrongly have excerpted Dio. He – and Caven, p. 26 – imply that raids on the Italian coast commenced immediately, but there is no evidence that they occurred before the arrival of Hamilcar in 261 (Zon. 8. 10), except for Polybios' vague reference (20.7) to Italy's being "often ravaged by naval forces", and this might also refer to the raids of Hannibal and Hamilcar recorded in Zonaras.

22. The "Libyans" of 19. 4 must be the Numidians mentioned just before, in this instance.

23. Caven, p. 25.

24. Walbank, p. 72, *ad* 19. 2, unaccountably relates this anecdote to Hannibal's breakout from the city.

25. Walbank, pp. 72–3, *ad* 20. 1–2.

26. For the possibility that the hoards of Syracusan bronze coins with the Head of Poseidon/Trident come from the pay of Roman troops garrisoning Agrigentum between 261 and 255 see M. H. Crawford, n16 above.

Chapter 5

1. Cf., e.g., Caven, p. 26; Tenney Frank, CAH^1, 677; Warmington, p. 184; Scullard, *Hist.*, p. 147 and CAH^2, p. 547; Bagnall, pp. 57–8.

2. *Pace* Broughton, i. p. 206, under 259.

3. See Walbank, p. 345, *ad* 3. 23. 1–6. Thiel, p. 9, claims that the first two treaties "presuppose" that Rome had warships, but it is not clear why he thinks this.

4. Thiel, p. 33, appears to assume that the *quaestores classici* had something to do with the fleet, and this is also the view of Scullard, CAH^2, pp. 548–9. For different interpretations of their functions see E. S. Staveley, CAH^2, p. 438, and W. V. Harris, *CQ* (ns) 26 (1976), pp. 92 ff.

5. But cf. E. S. Staveley, CAH^2, p. 449, for a salutary warning against assuming that those who implemented Rome's policies were also those who advocated them.

6. De Sanctis, iii. 1. p. 125, *n*61; p. 185 *n*89; Scullard, p. 160. Dorey & Dudley, p. 8, claim that Polybios contradicts himself in the same chapter, but they appear to have misunderstood "pentekontors" (πεντηκοντόροι: 20. 14) as "quinqueremes" (πεντήρεις). For convincing reasons for believing Polybios' story see Thiel, pp. 172 ff. Thiel, pp. 176–7, himself raises and dismisses another possible argument against believing Polybios, namely that if the Roman ships were modelled on a Carthaginian one, why were they "poorly constructed and difficult to move" (φαύλων ταῖς κατασκευαῖς καὶ δυσκινήτων: 22. 3, cf. Florus 1. 18. 8). Thiel's own argument is that the Romans adapted the model for their boarding tactics, but a better one is that they did not build their ships as well as the more experienced Carthaginian shipwrights, and that their crews, for all their training, still could not match their opponents.

7. For the Carthaginian ship see H. Frost, A. E. Werner & W. A. Oddy, *Notizie degli Scavi di Antichita* 26 (1972), pp. 651 ff; H. Frost, *International Journal of Nautical Archaeology* 1 (1972), pp. 113 ff, and *Mariner's Mirror* 59 (1973), pp. 229–30.

8. For the view that the fleet was built at Ostia see Caven, p. 28, and R. Meiggs, *Trees and timber in the ancient Mediterranean world* (Oxford, 1982), p. 141, where it is suggested that the timber came from Etruria and Umbria. W. V. Harris, *War and imperialism in Republican Rome* (Oxford, 1979), p. 184, suggests that the reason for confiscating half the forest of Sila from the Bruttians was to have it available for shipbuilding (for which see DH 20. 15), and the point is taken up by Staveley, CAH^2, p. 422. The huge Minerva/Horse's head issue of Roman silver coins almost certainly struck at Cosa during the war, may well have had something to do with the building of the first Roman fleet, and, indeed, suggests that it may have been partly or wholly built at Cosa: see M. H. Crawford, *Coinage and money under the Roman Republic* (London, 1985), 38. The similarly huge issue of silver didrachms and bronze coins by Naples during the war – Crawford, p. 34 – bears witness to the strenuous efforts made by Rome's allies, now and later.

9. See J. S. Morrison & J. F. Coates, *The Athenian trireme* (Cambridge, 1986).

10. For five men rowing each oar see Rodgers, p. 306, though the rest of his views are eccentric; Thiel, p. 97, *n*128; Walbank, p. 74 *ad* 20. 9; G. K. Tipps, *Historia* 34 (1985), p. 435. For other arrangements see R. C. Anderson, *Oared fighting ships* (London, 1962), pp. 21–30; J. S. Morrison & R. T. Williams, *Greek oared ships*

900–322 BC (Cambridge, 1968), pp. 290–1; J. Rougé (tr. Susan Frazer), *Ships and fleets of the ancient Mediterranean* (Middletown, Connecticut, 1981), pp. 93–4; F. Meijer, *A history of seafaring in the classical world* (London and Sydney, 1986), pp. 118 ff. For the method of rowing with longer sweeps see L. Casson, *The Ancient Mariners*[2] (Princeton, 1991), p. 130: Casson, pp. 130–31 and 145, would have it both ways, arguing that although the earliest, Greek quadriremes and quinqueremes were multi-levelled, later such ships became one-levelled, and that Roman quinqueremes were of the latter type. But he seems to forget that they were modelled on a Carthaginian warship.

11. Thiel, pp. 41 ff, 73 ff.
12. Thiel, pp. 77–8.
13. Thiel, pp. 76–7, argues that Claudia was thinking of freedmen.
14. Cf. J. F. Lazenby, *Hannibal's War* (Warminster, 1978), pp. 100–101 and 291, *nn*20–21.
15. J. Kromayer, *Philologus* 56 (1897), 481 ff; S. Casson, *Ships and seamanship in the ancient world* (Princeton, 1970), p. 105, *n*1.
16. Thiel, p. 181.
17. For the theory see Beloch, iv. 1. p. 654 *n*1; Tarn, *JHS* 27 (1907), p. 51 *n*19; de Sanctis, iii. 1. p. 128–9 *n*73. *Contra* Thiel, pp. 122–7; P. Bung, *Q. Fabius Pictor, der erste römische Annalist* (Diss. Cologne, 1950): Walbank, p. 77, *ad* 21. 7. Thiel and Caven, p. 28, think that Polybios exaggerated.
18. See Thiel, pp. 187 ff, who suggests the inscriptions followed the order *"terra marique"*. However, his argument that Zonaras' story of the defeat of the tribune, C. Caecilius, also shows that Polybios' order of events is right is contorted.
19. For doubts cf. Tarn, *JHS* 27, p. 51, *n*19, and *Hellenistic military and naval developments* (Cambridge, 1930), pp. 111–12, 149–50, but for a defence of Polybios see H. T. Wallinga, *The boarding bridge of the Romans* (Groningen, 1956). Thiel, p. 183, *n*381, tentatively suggests that Archimedes was the inventor. For the possibility that the Romans modified their model to suit their boarding tactics see Thiel, p. 177.
20. For the argument that there must have been a second line of Roman ships see Thiel, pp. 114–5, 184–5. Scullard, *CAH*[2], p. 552, finds Thiel's hypothesis "attractive".
21. Cichorius, pp. 32 ff, suggests that the fragment refers to C. Caecilius.
22. I do not understand why Walbank, p. 80 *ad* 4. 3, and Caven, p. 30, say that Hamilcar captured Mazarin: Diodoros' words are "ἦν δὲ καὶ τὸ Μάζαριν φρούριον ὑπὸ Ῥωμαίων ἐξηνδραποδισμένον."
23. Thiel, p. 194 and *n*420.
24. For speculation on the size of the fleets in 259–257 see Tarn, *JHS* 27, pp. 48 ff, and Thiel, pp. 83 ff. In my view there are too many imponderables for such speculation to be worth while, and I do not propose to discuss fleet numbers at this time.
25. *RE*, col. 1662.
26. *RE*, cols 1427–8.
27. For "Laberius" see Claudius Quadrigarius, frs 42–3 Peter; for "Caedicius" Cato, fr. 83 Peter; and for "Calpurnius" Livy, *Per.* 17 and 22. 60. 11, Pliny, *NH* 22. 11, Flor. 1. 18. 13–14, *de vir. ill.* 39, Ampel. 20. 5; Oros. 4. 8. 2; Zon. 8. 12.
28. Broughton, i. p. 208, *n*2, is almost certainly right to argue that Caiatinus was praetor in this year, despite Thiel, pp. 201–2, *n*446.

29. Thiel, pp. 198 ff, though he tends to exaggerate the element of planning and foresight in all this.

30. Most scholars, however, put the attack on Malta first: Scullard, *Hist.*, p. 150 and *CAH*², pp. 553–4; Thiel, p. 203; Caven, p. 32.

31. Thiel, p. 202 and *n*447, following Tarn, *JHS* 27, p. 52, gives the Romans 155, of which 100 were quinqueremes, against 100 for the Carthaginians, but these figures are entirely speculative. Nor is it true that Polybios' account "proves clearly ... that the Romans *were* in greatly superior numbers", as Thiel argues.

Chapter 6

1. There is an admirable analysis of the strategic situation in Bagnall, pp. 63–7. Thiel, p. 206, *n*458, suggests the possibility that Hiero told the Romans about Agathokles.

2. See Tarn, *JHS* 27 (1907), pp. 51–2; Thiel, pp. 84 ff; Walbank, pp. 82–5 *ad* 25. 7–9; Scullard, 150. Polybios' figures are convincingly defended by G. K. Tipps, *Historia* 34 (1985), p. 433 ff. Dorey & Dudley, p. 10, also accept them, as does Caven, pp. 32–3, who points out that if the Carthaginians had got wind of a Roman fleet of more than 300 ships, they could easily have outbuilt it.

3. Thiel, pp. 209 ff; Walbank, p. 86 *ad* 26. 7–8.

4. As Walbank, pp. 85–6 *ad* 26. 6, admits.

5. J. Kromayer, *Philologus* 56 (1897), pp. 481 ff; S. Casson, *Ships and seamanship in the ancient world* (Princeton, 1970), p. 105, *n*1.

6. Thiel, pp. 211–12; Caven, p. 32.

7. This is one of the few points on which I differ from Tipps, who thinks – *Historia* 34, p. 436 – that Polybios was wrong to assume that the Carthaginian ships had the same number of marines as the Roman, following de Sanctis iii. 1. p. 136, *n*101.

8. Thiel, pp. 207–9.

9. This is undoubtedly what Polybios means, and I do not understand why Thiel (p. 214, *n*486) claims that "given the fact that according to Polybios (1. 26, 12) the prow of each ship in this wedge formation was directed to the open sea and not to the ship in front of it (see Paton *ad locum*), the first Roman line could not have budged without being immediately dissolved!" Cf. Tipps, *Historia* 34, p. 449.

10. The pronouncement is Tarn's – see, for his view, *Hellenistic military and naval developments* (Cambridge, 1930), pp. 149–51, and cf. de Sanctis, iii. 1. p. 141 *n*102; Thiel, p. 214. Polybios' account is accepted by Kromayer, *Schlachtenatlas*, Röm. Abt., col. 5; Tenney Frank, *CAH*¹, p. 681; Rodgers, pp. 278 ff; Dorey & Dudley, p. 10; Caven, p. 33; and Bagnall, p. 68; it is again convincingly defended by Tipps, *Historia* 34, pp. 445 ff: he cites the "vee-shaped and finger-four formations" adopted by fighter aircraft (p. 449).

11. The quotation is from Thiel, p. 117, as is the argument that the Roman formation indicates that they did expect an attack.

12. In his *n*491 on p. 215 Thiel claims that Polybios 26.15 shows that the ships of the fourth squadron – what he calls "the third line" – were more widely spaced than those of the third (his second line), but the passage refers to the inverted V forma-

tion of the first and second squadrons! Tipps, p. 447, also says the ships of the fourth squadron were "widely spaced".

13. So Rodgers, p. 280, and Tipps, p. 452 and n68. Carthalo may have used such spotters in his operations against Iunius Pullus in 249 (see Polybios 53.8).

14. The idea is Thiel's, p. 116, but cf. Tipps, p. 462 and n90.

15. So Paton in the Loeb translation – "move round the enemy's flank" – and Scott-Kilvert in Penguin – "sail round the enemy's flank". Better is Shuckburgh, *The histories of Polybius* (Bloomington, Indiana, 1962) – "they darted out from the line and rowed round the enemy", but even this does not make the situation clear. See Walbank, pp. 87–8 *ad loc.,* for the correct explanation, and cf. J. F. Lazenby, "The diekplous", *Greece & Rome* 34 (1987), pp. 169 ff, and I. M. Whitehead, "The periplous", *Greece & Rome* 34, pp. 178 ff.

16. The quotation is from Rodgers, pp. 286–7, who, without any evidence, has the horse-transports make for Ecnomus; Thiel also sees unnecessary problems with them, pp. 220–1. Tipps, p. 456 and n76, rightly sees that the *triarii* could easily have made their way through the drifting transports. For the meaning of ἐν ἐπικαμπίῳ see Walbank, p. 87 *ad* 27. 4.

17. Thiel, pp. 117–20, 218–22. As usual, Thiel is cavalier with the evidence: for example, he refers Polybios' words in 27. 3 ὡς κυκλώσοντες τοὺς ὑπεναντίους to both wings of the Carthaginian fleet, whereas in fact they refer only to its right, and he assumes that the ὑπεναντίοι in question are just the first and second Roman squadrons, whereas Polybios clearly meant the whole Roman fleet.

18. Rodgers, p. 280.

19. Tipps, pp. 452 ff.

20. Thus Tarn, *Hellenistic military and naval developments* (Cambridge, 1930), p. 150, in his magisterial way, "Ecnomus is Cannae with the result reversed" – quoted, with apparent approval, by Walbank, p. 87 *ad* 27. 6, and accepted by Thiel, pp. 120–21, n193a, and even Tipps, pp. 454 and 463–4. It is Thiel who suggests that Hannibal had studied Hamilcar's plan. In ancient warfare, one suspects, the land almost always took preference over the sea.

21. See J. F. Lazenby, *International History Review* 3 (1987), pp. 446 ff. I do not know where Rodgers, p. 275, gets the notion that the Carthaginians used Balearic slingers on board their warships, and could thus stay at missile range.

22. Tipps, p. 458.

23. Tipps, p. 460, n83, suggests that these shoals may also have deterred the Carthaginians from pressing their attacks home on the third squadron.

Chapter 7

1. Dorey & Dudley, p. 11, have the Romans refit at Ecnomus; Thiel, p. 224, while referring to Zonaras, quite arbitrarily makes the refit take place at Syracuse.

2. As Thiel suggests, p. 224, n523.

3. Thiel, p. 225, n528, rightly, as against Eliaeson's suggestion, *Beiträge zur Geschichte Sardiniens und Corsicas im ersten punischen Kriege* (diss. Uppsala, 1906), p. 86, that

Regulus' expedition was originally planned as a mere raid.

4. I do not know on what grounds Dorey & Dudley, p. 12, say that Hasdrubal and Bostar were the sufetes – this is certainly not what Polybios implies.

5. O. Meltzer, *Geschichte der Karthager* (Berlin, 1879–96), ii. pp. 569–70; de Sanctis, iii. 1. p. 147, *n*5.

6. Cf. Dorey & Dudley, p. 12; Caven, p. 37. Scullard, however, *CAH²*, p. 556, does not think that the Carthaginians would have agreed to evacuate Sicily in 256. There is a tradition (Livy, *Per.* 18; Val. Max. 4.4.6; Front., *Strat.* 4.3.3) that Regulus wanted to return home because his family was only supported by a small farm, and his slave-steward had recently died!

7. Thiel, p. 228; Scullard, p. 151; Bagnall, pp. 73–4. For what it is worth, Plutarch (*Par. Min.* 23G) does record an embassy from Regulus to the Numidians.

8. Caven, pp. 35–7.

9. For the date see Walbank, p. 91, *ad* 32. 8.

10. De Sanctis, iii. 1. pp. 150–51; Caven, p. 38.

11. Warmington, p. 191, e.g., says that the battle must have taken place "somewhere between Carthage and Tunis", and Appian (*Lib.* 3) has it fought near a lake.

12. Lawrence Keppie, *The making of the Roman army* (London, 1984), pp. 38–9.

13. See *RE*, "Atilius (51)", cols 2088–92. For a defence of the peace mission at least see Tenney Frank, *CP* 21 (1926), pp. 311 ff.

14. Cichorius, pp. 41–2.

15. See refs. in *n*2 to Chapter 6 above. Tenney Frank, *CAH¹*, p. 684, *n*1, de Sanctis, iii. 1. p. 157, *n*25, and Caven, p. 40, accept Diodoros' figures.

16. Thiel, p. 232, *n*554, goes far too far in claiming that "if the presence of these ships during the battle had not been handed down to us, we should have to presuppose it." He also argues, p. 233, that the Romans succeeded in backing the Carthaginians up against the shore, and this is accepted by Scullard, *Hist.*, p. 152, and *CAH²*, p. 557, but there is no evidence for the hypothesis.

Chapter 8

1. Michael Lewis, *The Spanish Armada* (London, 1960), pp. 228 ff.

2. Tenney Frank, *CAH¹*, p. 685.

3. Walbank, pp. 96–7, *ad* 37. 4.

4. De Sanctis, iii. 1. p. 138; cf. Meltzer, ii p. 308. Thiel, pp. 237–8, in turn tries to defend Polybios by arguing that the Romans could have crossed directly to Cape Pachynon via Cossyra, or could even have disembarked their crews in the roadstead at Phintias.

5. See, e.g., David Howarth, *Trafalgar: the Nelson touch* (London, 1970), p. 81: "Napoleon was accustomed to order his army to do what seemed impossible, and under his direct command the army often did it. But his orders to his navy sometimes overstepped the mark." An example of the Emperor's attitude was the incident on 20 July 1804, when he ordered a review of his Boulogne flotillas, despite the protests of his admirals – one of whom was dismissed the service and exiled to

Holland – and lost 2,000 men drowned as a result: see David Chandler, *The campaigns of Napoleon* (London, 1966), p. 323.

6. Thiel, pp. 235–6.

7. But Thiel, pp. 232–3, goes too far in stating outright that "the battle of Hermaeum was the last battle in which the corvus played a part".

8. De Sanctis iii. 1. p. 164 *n*46, 227; Meltzer, ii. p. 309, 374–5; Thiel, p. 243, *n*584; Scullard, *Hist.*, p. 154; Caven, p. 44. Dorey & Dudley, p. 14, accept that Hasdrubal arrived in 255 or 254.

9. Tarn, *JHS* 27 (1907), p. 56.

10. Walbank, pp. 97–8 *ad* 38. 1–4, suggests lack of funds delayed the Carthaginian naval programme, but difficulties of manning may be more likely. Caven, p. 42, suggests that the Carthaginian naval activity spurred the Romans to outbuild them, and that Carthage devoted most of her energies in 254 to recovering control in Africa.

11. Tarn, *JHS* 27, p. 55; Thiel, p. 87; and Walbank, pp. 98 *ad* 38. 5, all think that the 220 include the 80. Dorey & Dudley, p. 14, accept the building of 220 new warships by the Romans, as does Caven, 42.

12. Thiel, pp. 242 and 243, n. 582, following de Sanctis, iii. 1. p. 160, *n*32, insists that since the consuls of 255/4 celebrated their naval triumphs as proconsuls in January 253, they commanded the fleet in 254. But this is certainly not what the sources say, and it would have been unheard of for two consuls and two proconsuls all to be commanding in the same sphere of operations. Probably the *imperium* of the consuls of 255/4 was prorogued so that they might triumph for their conquest of Cossyra and their victory off Cape Hermaia, but the actual triumph was delayed until the men from the surviving 80 ships of their fleet returned to Rome at the end of 254.

13. De Sanctis, iii. 1. p. 160–61, *n*33.

14. Thiel, pp. 245–6, though he believes the tradition, makes an unnecessary mountain out of this particular mole-hill.

15. Thiel, pp. 247 ff. Thiel even raises the possibility that Blaesus simply went off to Africa on a whim, but rightly dismisses it since he not only triumphed, but was re-elected to the consulship in 244/3.

16. As Thiel, p. 249, *n*601, and p. 250, *n*604, suggests. For the dangers of these waters see *The Mediterranean pilot* i (1937), pp. 369 ff.

17. Tarn's argument, *JHS* 27, p. 55, that only 27 ships were lost is based on a series of conjectures, and such a small loss would hardly explain the reversal of Roman policy which Polybios says followed the disaster (39.7 ff). Thiel, p. 251, *n*607, rightly argues that 150 warships perished, but makes an unnecessary fuss about Diodoros' "horse-transports", arguing that "we can hardly suppose that Blaesus had dragged cavalry all the way to Africa for the sake of a mere raid". Why not? Cavalry would have been particularly useful for raiding, and, in any case, the Romans had good reason to fear Carthaginian cavalry.

18. Walbank, p. 101 *ad* 39. 12.

19. There is no need, with Thiel (p. 254, *n*618) to speculate about whether Cotta also asked for ships from Rome's south-Italian allies, or about any possible reactions from the Carthaginian fleet, which are only hinted at in Orosius' obviously sensational account of Cotta's operations.

20. H. A. Grueber, *Coins of the Roman Republic in the British Museum* (London, 1910), i.

p. 200 f; S. L. Cesano, *Studi di Numismatica* 1 (1942), p. 158.

21. See Walbank, p. 102 *ad loc.*, M. G. Morgan, *CQ* (ns) 22 (1972), pp. 121 ff, and Notes to Chapter 1, *n*1, above.

22. The story is accepted by Thiel, p. 254, *n*618, but rejected by de Sanctis iii. 1. p. 167, *n*51.

23. Grueber, *Coins of the Roman Republic in the British Museum*, i. pp. 155–6, ii. pp. 357, 570; Cesano, *Studi di Numismatica* 1, p. 160 f.

Chapter 9

1. For the contrary argument see Thiel, pp. 89–90 and 256 ff. Caven, p. 51, argues that Iunius Pullus' original 60 warships were ones withdrawn from Lilybaeum in winter 250/49, but then accounts for the 60 he picked up in Sicily by supposing that these were ones brought to Messana after Drepana, together with other scattered vessels. But it is surely impossible that Claudius could have got any ships past Adherbal at Drepana after the latter's victory.

2. Walbank's note, p. 107 *ad* 42. 8, is typical of the problems that arise once one abandons the figures given by Polybios and starts to juggle with hypothetical ones.

3. For the fragmentary remains of the Carthaginian walls at Lilybaeum see M. W. Frederiksen, *Archaeological reports for 1976–7* (Society for the Promotion of Hellenic Studies and British School at Athens Archaeological Reports 23; London, 1977), p. 74 f.

4. Cf. Walbank, p. 108.

5. Thiel, p. 269, also makes Hannibal's ships warships, though for slightly different reasons. He expresses doubts about the element of surprise in his success, arguing that "the Romans were almost certainly aware of his presence" (cf. Rodgers, pp. 294–5). As usual, such an argument assumes that the Roman navy behaved like a modern one.

6. Thiel, p. 271 and *n*688, suggests that the cavalry was got out later when most of the crews of the Roman ships had allegedly perished in the siege. But if Claudius Pulcher was later able to man *c.* 123 ships, and yet only had 10,000 fresh sailors, there were presumably some 27,000 left from the original crews, enough to man some 90 quinqueremes – surely enough to stop horse-transports leaving the harbour. Thiel, p. 266, *n*669 – "a number of horse-transports must have been present at Lilybaeum" – is a good example of the misuse of the word "must".

7. Walbank, p. 110 *ad* 46. 4–47. 10. Many more Carthaginian names than appear in the literary sources are known from inscriptions – cf. Scullard, *CAH*². p. 492.

8. Walbank's discussion of this passage – p. 110 *ad* 47. 2, cf. Thiel, p. 270 and *n*686 – is, I think, vitiated by his failure to take account of Polybios' earlier mistaken orientation of Sicily as a whole. By my reckoning, Hannibal would not even have had to have "swerved left" from his course once he was past the shoals, as Walbank claims.

9. See Walbank, p. 111 *ad loc.*

10. Tarn, *JHS* 27 (1907), p. 54, suggests that Claudius knew of the imminent arrival of Carthalo's fleet. Thiel, p. 272, typically, just asserts that he "knew that Adherbal had

some 100 warships at Drepana, [and] that he was about to receive a reinforcement of 70 new ships". For kinder assessments of Claudius see de Sanctis, iii. 1. p. 170; Scullard, *Hist.* p. 155; Dorey & Dudley, p. 19; Caven, p. 48.

11. As Thiel, pp. 273–4, does.

12. Thiel, p. 265, *n*667, and pp. 272, 275, etc., following Tarn, *JHS* 27, p. 55; Caven, p. 48 – Caven gives Claudius 150.

13. The story appears first in extant literature in Cicero (*Nat. De.* 2. 7; *de div.* 1. 29, 2. 20 and 71); see also. Livy, *Per.* 19, cf. 22. 42. 9; Val. Max. 1. 4. 3, 8. 1, ext. 4; Suet., *Tib.* 2; Flor. 1. 18. 29; Eutr. 2. 26. It is accepted by Thiel, p. 274, *n*698, rejected by de Sanctis iii. 1. p. 170, and doubted by Walbank, 113 *ad* 49. 6–51. 12; Dorey & Dudley, pp. 18–19; and – though not specifically – by Caven, p. 48.

14. The plan of Kromayer, followed by Walbank, p. 112, and Caven, p. 49, shows this manoeuvre, but Polybios actually says nothing of these islands.

15. For the evidence see Broughton i. p. 215, *sub anno* 248 BC, Tribunes of the Plebs. For the suggestion that the motivation was "popular" see Walbank, p. 114 *ad* 52. 3.

16. Beloch, iv. 2. p. 289.

17. De Sanctis, iii. 1. pp. 263–4.

18. Thiel, p. 88, argues that these ships were auxiliary ships from Sicilian and south-Italian allies, but Polybios clearly meant that they were Roman warships, and Thiel's despair – see p. 88, *n*94 – at finding a meaning for ἐκ τοῦ σπρατοπέδου is mainly due to his refusal to believe what Polybios says. Paton, in the Loeb edition of Polybios, translates "from Lilybaeum", and although this is not what the Greek actually means, it is surely what Polybios intended to imply.

19. See Thiel, p. 33, but cf. Notes to Chapter 5, *n*4 above. Curiously Thiel does not cite this passage as evidence for his contention that Iunius' fleet contained auxiliary warships. Dorey & Dudley, p. 20, translate Polybios' plural τοῖς ταμίαις as "his [Iunius'] quaestor".

20. Thiel, pp. 283 ff, who assumes without question that the news of Drepana had reached Rome before Iunius set out, then has great difficulty in explaining his decision to send the Quaestors on with so few warships. Caven, p. 51, even thinks that Iunius knew of Carthalo's arrival with his 70.

21. Thiel, p. 281. Caven, p. 51, rightly just says that Hannibal "captured the Roman supplies". Having conjured "transports" from what Diodoros says, Thiel then has to explain them – cf. p. 282, *n*722. Walbank, p. 116 *ad* 53. 2, also talks of the seizure of a Roman convoy off Panormus.

22. See Thiel, p. 287, *n*734, following de Sanctis iii. 1. p. 175, *n*72. On the face of it Diodoros gives the Romans 135 warships (105 + 17 + 13), whereas Polybios gives them 120.

23. As Thiel does, pp. 285–9 and *nn*731–4. Thiel's *n*731 is typical of this approach in claiming that "Polybius (1,53,7–13), influenced by Fabius Pictor, has evidently modified the Roman losses" – cf. also Caven, p. 52. But why should not Diodoros, influenced by Philinos, have exaggerated them?

24. Kromayer, *AS*, iii. 1. p. 35.

25. For the evidence see Cic., *Nat. De.* 2. 7, *de div.* 1. 29, 2. 20 and 71; Val. Max. 1. 4. 4; Minuc. Felix 7. 4, 26. 2.

Chapter 10

1. On what follows see Thiel, pp. 294–6; Warmington, pp. 195–6; Scullard, *Hist.*, p. 156; Caven, pp. 55–6.

2. Cichorius, p. 50, suggests that the speaker is Hamilcar, and this is accepted by Thiel, p. 295, *n*754, but the speaker is not named in the fragment, and Buechner comments that he is "a Roman speaker (hardly a Carthaginian)" (*orator Romanus (vix Carthaginiensis)*).

3. Thiel, p. 298, *n*764. His argument that if the channel between the island and the mainland was shallow enough for the Romans to fill it in, it could not have been used by Adherbal before the battle of Drepana, assumes that Adherbal did use the channel – see Notes to Chapter 9, *n*14, above. The map in *CAH²*, p. 561, confusingly shows Lazzaretto as already joined to the mainland. Caven, p. 58, places the seizure of Pelias while Hamilcar was off raiding Italy, though it must be admitted that Zonaras rather implies that it came later.

4. She was the ram HMS *Polyphemus*: Rodgers, p. 301.

5. Gsell, *Histoire ancienne de l'Afrique du nord* (Paris, 1913–29), iii. 95. 3.

6. J. Schubring, *Historische Topographie von Panormos* (Lübeck, 1870), i. p. 24 ff; A. Holm, *Geschichte Siciliens in Altertum* (Leipzig, 1870–98), i. 15. p. 334 f., iii. p. 28 f, 354; de Sanctis, iii. 1. p. 181, *n*83; K. Ziegler, *RE*. "Heirkte", col. 2645; Dorey & Dudley, p. 21.

7. J. Kromayer, *AS* iii 1. pp. 4 ff. More recently traces of a camp, with pottery of the first half of the third century, have been found on Monte Pecoraro, west of Monte Castelaccio, and it has been suggested that this is Heirkte; a ship found off Terrasina, west of Palermo, with amphorae and two swords of Roman type, may also be of mid-third-century date, and could be a merchantman or transport: V. Giustolisi, *Le nave romane di Terrasina e l'avventura di Amilcare sul Monte Heirkte* (Palermo, 1975).

8. De Sanctis, iii. 1. p. 183, following Kromayer.

9. Thiel declares, p. 302, that "the Roman senate had known from the start (i. e. from 248) that they could not decide the war by sending armies to Sicily year by year without a fleet", but produces no evidence or arguments to justify this assertion.

10. Cf. Tenney Frank, *CAH¹*, p. 691; de Sanctis iii. 1. p. 184 *n*87; Thiel, pp. 302–3; Walbank, pp. 123–4 *ad* 59. 6; but, as Caven, p. 60, rightly says, "modern cynicism should not be allowed to belittle this expression of patriotism in view of Rome's more recent performance at sea".

11. So, rightly, Thiel, pp. 93 and 305, *n*786 as against Tarn, *JHS* 27 (1907), p. 56.

12. As Thiel, pp. 305–6, does – most of his arguments amount to little more than *post hoc, ergo propter hoc*.

13. There are difficulties about both the date of Lutatius' arrival and that of the battle, but most scholars now seem to accept that the former was in summer 242, and the latter in March 241: see Walbank, pp. 124–5 *ad* 60–61, and add Dorey & Dudley, p. 24, and Caven, pp. 60–61.

14. e.g. Dorey & Dudley, p. 24.

15. Thiel, pp. 307–8, but this really depends on acceptance of de Sanctis's emendation – see *n*17 below.

16. Cf. Thiel, pp. 307–9, accepted by, e.g., Scullard, *CAH²*, p. 565.
17. Because 6,000 + 4,040 comes to very nearly Polybios' 10,000, de Sanctis, iii. 1. p. 235, proposed to emend Diodoros' text to mean not that "the others [sc. "authors"] (ὡς δὲ ἕτεροι) said 4,040", but that "of the others [sc. "prisoners"] (τῶν δὲ ἑτέρων) there were 4,040".
18. Thiel, p. 307, *n*798, accepts the transports without question, but says that there cannot have been many of them. Unfortunately, the text of Diodoros is dubious at the critical point. The MSS simply refer to "the transports" (τοῖς φορτηγοῖς), but this makes the sentence awkward, and it has been suggested that the article τοῖς has been substituted for the numeral τ´ (i.e. 300).
19. The figure of 170 argued by Tarn, *JHS* 27, pp. 56–7, and accepted, e.g., by Thiel, p. 307, *n*799, and Scullard, *CAH²*, p. 565, is really quite arbitrary. Caven, p. 61, rightly argues for 250.
20. Cf. the Spartans at Arginousai in 406: Xen., *Hell.* 1. 6. 31.
21. De Sanctis iii. 1. pp. 187 ff ; Dorey & Dudley, pp. 25–6; Warmington, p. 197; Thiel, p. 316.
22. Cf. Caven, pp. 62–3, for an excellent treatment of the subject.
23. E. Täubler, *Die Vorgeschichte des zweiten punischen Kriegs* (Berlin, 1921), pp. 64, 110.

Chapter 11

1. See Walbank, pp. 196–203.
2. E. S. Staveley, *CAH²*, p. 431.
3. For the meaning of the census figures see Brunt, *Italian manpower 225 BC–AD 14* (Oxford, 1971), pp. 15 ff.
4. Cf. , e.g., Caven, pp. 17, 22–3, 54–5.

Chapter 12

1. V. Ehrenberg, *Karthago: ein Versuch weltgeschichtlicher Einordnung* (Leipzig, 1927), p. 31; Walbank, pp. 312–3 *ad* 3. 9. 6.
2. For the origins of this phrase see the very interesting footnote on p. 49 of William L. Shirer's *Rise and fall of the Third Reich* (London, 1960).
3. See Walbank, pp. 148–9 *ad* 88. 7.
4. See Walbank, pp. 149–50 *ad* 88. 8.
5. Caven, p. 71, makes this interesting suggestion.
6. A. E. Astin, *CAH²*, pp. 571–2.

Abbreviations and bibliography

Amp. = Ampelius, *Liber memorialis* (ed. Terzaghi, Turin 1943).

Anderson, R. C., *Oared fighting ships* (London, 1962).

App., *Hisp.* = Appian, *History of Rome*, Book 6: *The Wars in Spain* (Loeb Classical Library edition, 1912).

App., *Sam.* = Appian, *History of Rome*, Book 3: *The Samnite History* (Loeb Classical Library edition, 1912).

App., *Sic.* = Appian, *History of Rome*, Book 5: *Of Sicily and other Islands* (Loeb Classical Library edition, 1912).

App., *Lib.* = Appian, *History of Rome*, Book 8: *The Punic Wars* (Loeb Classical Library edition, 1912).

Apu., *Apol.* = Apuleius, *Apologia*.

Arist., *Pol.* = Aristotle, *Politics*.

Ath. = Athenaios (Athenaeus).

Badian, E. *Foreign clientelae (264–70 BC)* (Oxford, 1958).

Bagnall = Bagnall, Nigel, *The Punic wars* (London, 1990).

Beloch = Beloch, K. J. *Griechische Geschichte* (2nd edition; Strasburg-Berlin and Leipzig, 1912–27).

Broughton, i = Broughton, T. R. S. *The magistrates of the Roman Republic*, vol. i (New York, 1951).

Broughton, ii = Broughton, T. R. S. *The magistrates of the Roman Republic*, vol. ii (New York, 1953).

Brunt, P. A. *Italian manpower 225 BC–AD 14* (Oxford, 1971).

Buechner = Buechner, C. *Fragmenta poetarum latinorum* (Leipzig, 1982).

Bung, P. Q. *Fabius Pictor, der erste römische Annalist* (Diss. Cologne, 1950).

CAH[1] = *The Cambridge Ancient History*, vol. vii (1st edition, Cambridge, 1928).

CAH[2] = *The Cambridge Ancient History*, vol. vii, Part 2 (2nd edition, Cambridge, 1989).

Cassius Dio, *Roman history* (Loeb Classical Library edition, 1914).

Casson, L. *The Ancient Mariners*[2] (2nd edition, Princeton, 1991).

Casson, S. *Ships and seamanship in the ancient world* (Princeton, 1970).

Caven = Caven, B. *The Punic wars* (London, 1980).

Cesano, S. L. I Fasti dell Repubblica Romana sulla moneta di Roma. *Studi di Numismatica* 1 (1942).

Chandler, D. *The campaigns of Napoleon* (London, 1966).

Cic. *de div.* = Cicero, *de divinatione;* Cic., *de nat. de.* = Cicero, *de natura deorum;* Cic., de off. = Cicero, *de officilis;* Cic., *Verr.* = Cicero, *in Verrem.*

Cichorius = Cichorius, C. *Römische Studien* (Leipzig-Berlin, 1922).

CIL = Corpus Inscriptionum Latinarum.

Coussin, P. *Les armes romaines* (Paris, 1926).

CP = Classical Philology.

CQ = Classical Quarterly; CQ (ns) = *Classical Quarterly* (new series).

Crawford, M. H., *Coinage and money under the Roman Republic* (London, 1985).

Cutler, Thomas J. *The battle of Leyte Gulf* (New York, 1994).

De Sanctis = de Sanctis, G. *Storia dei Romani* (Turin-Florence, 1907–23).

de vir. ill. = [Sextus Aurelius Victor], *liber de viris illustribus* (Teubner edition, 1966).

DH = Dionysios of Halikarnassos.

Dorey & Dudley = Dorey, T. A., & D. R. Dudley. *Rome against Carthage* (London, 1971).

DS = Diodorus Siculus, *Library of History* (Loeb Classical Library edition).

Eckstein, A. M. Unicum subsidium populi Romani. Hiero II and Rome, 263–215 BC. *Chiron* 10 (1980), 183 ff.

Ehrenberg, V. *Karthago: ein Versuch weltgeschichtlicher Einordnung* (Leipzig, 1927).

Ennius, Q., *Annales.*

Eutr. = Eutropius, *Breviarium ab urbe condita* (ed. Morino: Milan, 1925).

Flo. = Florus, *Epitome of Roman history* (Loeb Classical Library edition).

Frank, T. Two historical themes in Roman literature. *CP* 21 (1926), pp. 311 ff.

Frederiksen, M. W. *Archaeological Reports for 1976–7* (Society for the Promotion of Hellenic Studies and British School at Athens Archaeological Reports 23; London, 1977).

Front., *Strat.* = Frontinus, *Stratagems* (Loeb Classical Library edition).

Frost, H. The discovery of a Punic ship. *International Journal of Nautical Archaeology* 1 (1972), pp. 113 ff.

Frost, H. The Punic wreck off Sicily. *Mariner's Mirror* 59 (1973), pp. 229 ff.

Gell., *NA* = Gellius, *Noctes Atticae.*

Giustolisi, V. *Le nave romane di Terrasina e l'avventura di Amilcare sul Monte Heirkte* (Palermo, 1975).

Grueber, H. A. *Coins of the Roman Republic in the British Museum* (London, 1910).

Gsell, S., *Histoire Ancienne de l'Afrique du nord* (Paris, 1913–28).

Harris, W. V. The development of the Quaestorship, 267–81 BC. *CQ* (ns) 26 (1976), pp. 92 ff.

Harris = Harris, W. V. *War and imperialism in Republican Rome 327–70 BC* (Oxford, 1979).

Hdt. = Herodotos.

Heuss, A. Der erste punische Krieg und das Problem des römischen Imperialismus. Zur polititischen Beurteilung des Krieges. *Historische Zeitschrift* 169 (1949), pp. 457 ff.

Holm, A. *Geschichte Siciliens im Altertum* (Leipzig, 1870–98).

Horn, H. *Foederati* (Frankfurt, 1930).

Hoyos, B. D. Treaties true and false: the error of Philinos of Agrigentum. *CQ* (ns) 35 (1985), pp. 92 ff.

Hoyos, B. D. The rise of Hiero II. Chronology and Campaigns 275–264 BC. *Antichthon* 19 (1985), 32 ff

Hoyos, B. D. A forgotten Roman historian: L.Arruntius and the "true" causes of the First Punic War. *Antichthon* 23 (1989), pp. 51 ff.

Howarth, D. *Trafalgar: The Nelson touch* (London, 1970).

HRR = Peter, H. *Historicorum Romanorum reliquiae.*

Ined. Vat. = *Ineditum Vaticanum.*

Jacoby, *FGH* = Jacoby, F. *Die Fragmente der griechischen Historiker* (Berlin–Leiden, 1923–58).

Jenkins, G. K. & R. B. Lewis. *Carthaginian gold and electrum coins* (London, 1963).

JHS = *Journal of Hellenic Studies.*

Just. = Justin (us), *Historiarum ex Trogo Pompeio libri.*

Keppie, Lawrence. *The making of the Roman army* (London, 1984).

Klotz, A. Studien zu Polybios. *Hermes* 80 (1952), pp. 325 ff.

Kromayer, *AS* = Kromayer, J. & G. Veith. *Antike Schlachtfelder* (Berlin, 1903–31).

Kromayer, *Schlachtenatlas* = Kromayer, J., & Veith, G., *Schlachtenatlas zur Antiken Kriegsgeschichte* (Gotha, 1922–).

Kromayer, J., & Veith, G., *Heerwesen und Kriegführung der Griechen und Römer* (Munich, 1928).

Lazenby, J. F. *Hannibal's war* (Warminster, 1978).

Lazenby, J. F. The diekplous. *Greece & Rome* 34 (1987), pp. 169 ff.

Lazenby, J. F. Naval warfare in the ancient world: myths and realities. *International History Review* 3 (1987), pp. 438 ff.

Leuze, O. *Die römische Jahrzählung* (Tübingen, 1909).

Leveque, P. *Pyrrhos* (Paris, 1957).

Lippold, A. *Consules: Untersuchungen zur Geschichte des römischen Konsulates von 264 bis 201 v. Chr.* (Bonn, 1963).

Livy = Livius, T., *Ab urbe condita libri.*

Livy, *Per.* = Livy, *Periochae.*

Lyd., *de Mag* = Lydus, *de Magistratibus.*

Meiggs, R. *Trees and timber in the ancient Mediterranean world* (Oxford, 1982).

Meijer, F. *A history of seafaring in the classical world* (London and Sydney, 1986).

Meister, K. Der sogenannte Philinosvertrag (Schmitt, Staatsvertr ge III Nr.438). *Riv. fil.* 98 (1970), pp. 424 ff.

Meltzer = Meltzer, O., *Geschichte der Karthager* (Berlin, 1879–96).

Michels, A. K. *The calendar of the Roman Republic* (Princeton, 1967).

Minuc. Felix = Minucius Felix.

Mioni, E. *Polybio* (Padua, 1949).

Mitchell, R. E. Roman-Carthaginian treaties, 306 and 279/8 BC. *Historia* 20 (1971), pp. 633 ff.

Mommsen, T. *Römisches Staatsrecht* (Leipzig, 1887–8).

Morgan, M. G. Polybius and the date of the battle of Panormus. *CQ* (ns) 22 (1972), pp. 121 ff.

Morgan, M. G. Calendars and chronology in the First Punic War. *Chiron* 7 (1977), pp. 89 ff.

Morrison, J. S. & J. F. Coates. *The Athenian trireme* (Cambridge, 1986).

Morrison, J. S. & R. T. Williams. *Greek oared ships 900–322 BC* (Cambridge, 1968).

Nenci, G. Il trattato romano-cartaginese κατὰ τὴν Πύρρου διάβασιν , *Historia* 7 (1958), pp. 263 ff.

Nepos, *Ham.* = Nepos, *Hamilcar.*

NH = *Historia Naturalis.*

Oros. = Orosius, *Historiae adversum paganos* (Teubner edition; Leipzig, 1889).

Ovid, *Fasti* = Ovidius Naso, P., *Fasti.*

Par. Min. = Plutarch, *Parallele minore.*

Picard, G. C. & C. (trans. D. Collon). *The life and death of Carthage* (London, 1968).

Plut., *Mor.* = Plutarch, *Moralia.*

Plut., *Pyrrh.* = Plutarch, *Pyrrhus.*

Polyainos, *Strategemata* (Teubner edition, 1970).

Plb. = Polybios, *The histories* (Loeb Classical Library Edition, 1922).

RE = Pauly-Wissowa, *Real-encyclopädie der classischen Altertumswissenschaft* (Stuttgart, 1893–).

RhM = *Rheinisches Museum für Philologie.*

Rich, J. W. *Declaring war in the Roman Republic in the period of transmarine expansion* (Collection Latomus 149; Brussels, 1976).

Riv. fil. = *Rivista di filologia e d'istruzione classica.*

Rodgers = Rodgers, W. L. *Greek and Roman naval warfare* (Annapolis, 1937).

Rougé, J. (trans. S. Frazer). *Ships and fleets of the ancient Mediterranean* (Middletown, Connecticut, 1981).

Schubring, J. *Historische Topographie von Panormos* (Lübeck, 1870).

Schulten, A. Der Ursprung des Pilums. *RhM* 66 (1911), pp. 573 ff.

Scullard, H. H. *The elephant in the Greek and Roman world* (London, 1974).

Scullard, H. H. Hannibal's Elephants. *Numismatic Chronicle* 8 (1949), pp. 158 ff.

Scullard, H. H. & Sir W. Gowers. Hannibal's elephants again. *Numismatic Chronicle* 10 (1950), pp. 271 ff.

Scullard, *Hist.* = Scullard, H. H. *A history of the Roman world, 753–146 BC* (3rd edition, London, 1961).

Sherwin White, A. N. *The Roman citizenship* (2nd edition, Oxford, 1973).

Shirer, William L. *The rise and fall of the Third Reich* (London, 1960).

Shuckburgh, Evelyn S., *The Histories of Polybius,* translated from the text of F. Hultsch (Bloomington, 1952).

Silius Italicus, C., *Punica.*

Suet. = Suetonius. Suet., *Tib.* = Suetonius, *Tiberius.*

Tac., *Ann.* = Tacitus, *Annales.*

Tarn, W. W. The fleets of the First Punic War. *JHS* 27 (1907), pp. 48 ff.

Tarn, W. W. *Hellenistic military and naval developments* (Cambridge, 1930).

Täubler, E. *Die Vorgeschichte des zweiten punischen Kriegs* (Berlin, 1921).

Thiel = Thiel, J. H. *A history of Roman sea-power before the Second Punic War* (Amsterdam, 1954).

Thuc. = Thucydides.

Tipps, G. K. The Battle of Ecnomus. *Historia* 34 (1985), pp. 432 ff.

Tuchman, Barbara W. *August 1914* (London, 1962).

Val. Max. = Valerius Maximus, *Factorum et dictorum memorabilium libri* (Teubner edition; Leipzig, 1888).

Verg./Vergil = Vergilius Maro, P., *The Aeneid*.

Walbank, F. W. Polybius, Philinus and the First Punic War. *CQ* 39 (1945), pp. 1 ff.

Walbank = Walbank, F. W. *A historical commentary on Polybius*, vol.i (Oxford, 1957).

Wallinga, H.T. *The boarding bridge of the Romans* (Groningen, 1956).

Warmington = Warmington, B. H. *Carthage* (Harmondsworth, 1964).

Whitehead, I. M. The periplous. *Greece & Rome* 34 (1987), pp. 178 ff.

Xen., *Hell.* = Xenophon, *Hellenika*.

Zon. = Zonaras ap. Dio's *Roman history* (Loeb Classical Library edition 1914).

Index

Note: Romans are listed under their last names, unless these are unusual *cognomina*: e.g. Cn. Cornelius Scipio Asina appears under "Scipio (Asina), Cn. Cornelius".